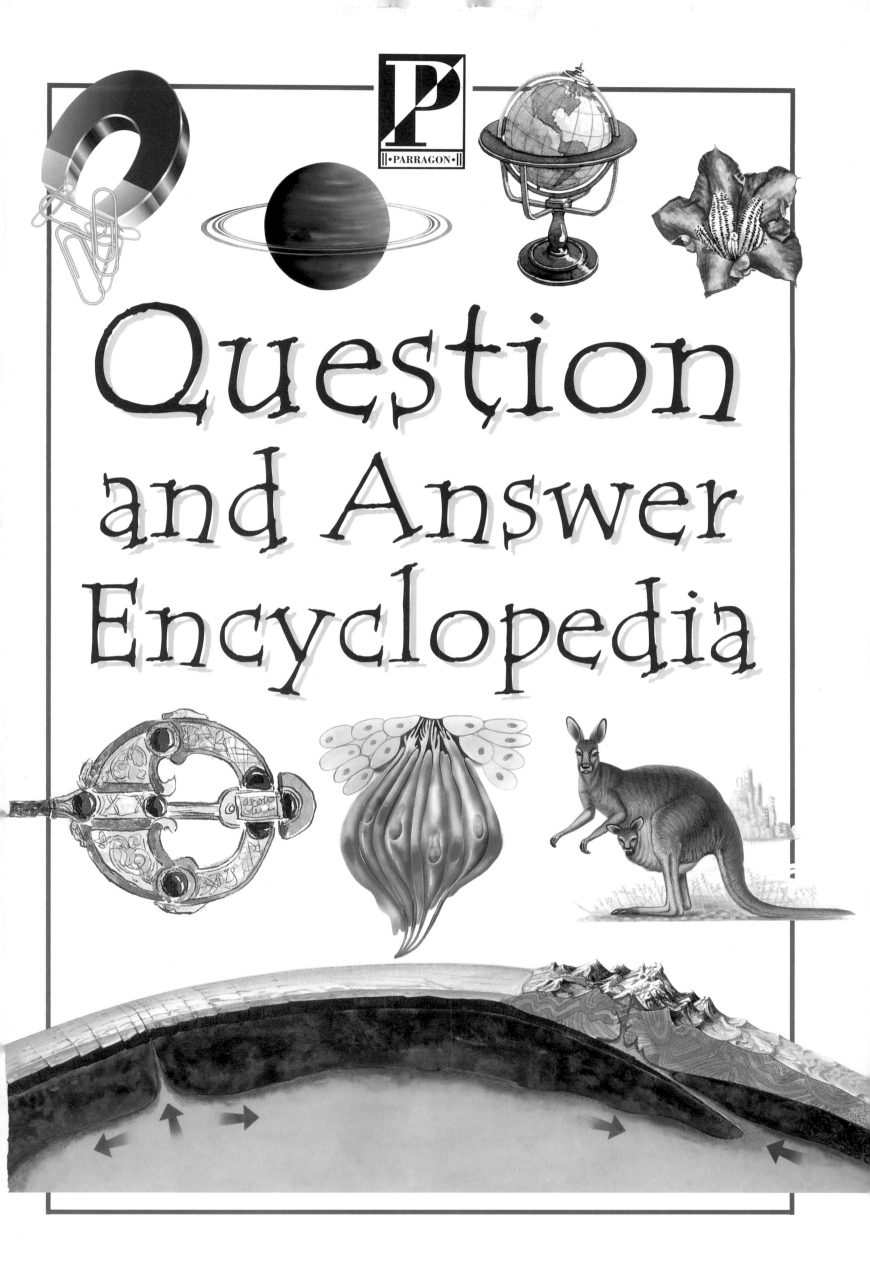

Question and Answer Encyclopedia

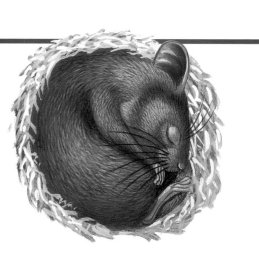

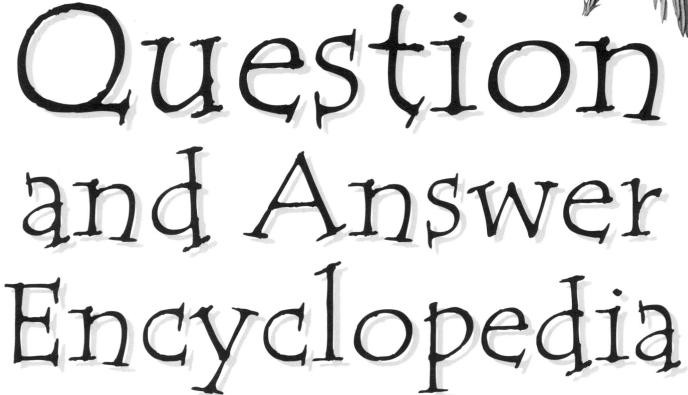

Question and Answer Encyclopedia

First published in Great Britain in 1999 by
Parragon
Queen Street House
4 Queen Street
Bath
BA1 1HE

ISBN: 0-75253-174-3

Printed in Italy

Produced by Miles Kelly Publishing Ltd
Bardfield Centre
Great Bardfield
Essex
CM7 4SL

Written by John Farndon, Ian James,
Jinny Johnson, Angela Royston,
Philip Steele and Martin Walters
Illustrated by David Ashby,
Mike Atkinson, Julian Baker, Andrew Farmer,
Rob Jakeway, John James and Roger Kent
Edited by Linda Sonntag
Designed by Diane Clouting
Artwork commissioning: Branka Surla
Project manager: Margaret Berrill
with additional help from Jenni Cozens and Pat Crisp

Contents

Universe

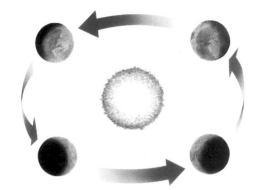

As the Earth orbits the Sun, the hemisphere of the planet that faces the Sun has its summer. The hemisphere facing away is in winter.

How long is a day?

A day is the time Earth takes to turn once. The stars come back to the same place in the sky every 23 hours 56 minutes 4.09 seconds (the sidereal day). Our day (the solar day) is 24 hours because Earth is moving round the Sun, and must turn an extra 1° for the Sun to return to the same place in the sky.

Why does the Earth spin?

The Earth spins because it is falling around the Sun. As the Earth hurtles round the Sun, the Sun's gravity keeps it spinning, just as the Earth's gravity keeps a ball rolling downhill.

How did the Earth begin?

AROUND FOUR AND A HALF BILLION YEARS AGO, NEITHER THE EARTH nor any of the other planets existed. There was just this vast dark very hot cloud of gas and dust swirling around the newly formed Sun. Gradually, the cloud cooled and the gas began to condense into billions of droplets. Slowly these droplets were pulled together into clumps by their own gravity – and they carried on clumping until all the planets, including the Earth, were formed. But it took another half a billion years before the Earth had cooled enough to form a solid crust with an atmosphere around it.

The early Earth was a fiery ball, then the surface cooled to form a hard crust.

How old is the Earth?

The Earth is about 4.6 billion years old. The oldest rock is about 3.8 billion years old. Scientists have also dated meteorites that have fallen from space, and must have formed at the same time as the Earth.

Earth began life as hot gases and dust spiralling around the newborn Sun congealed into a ball.

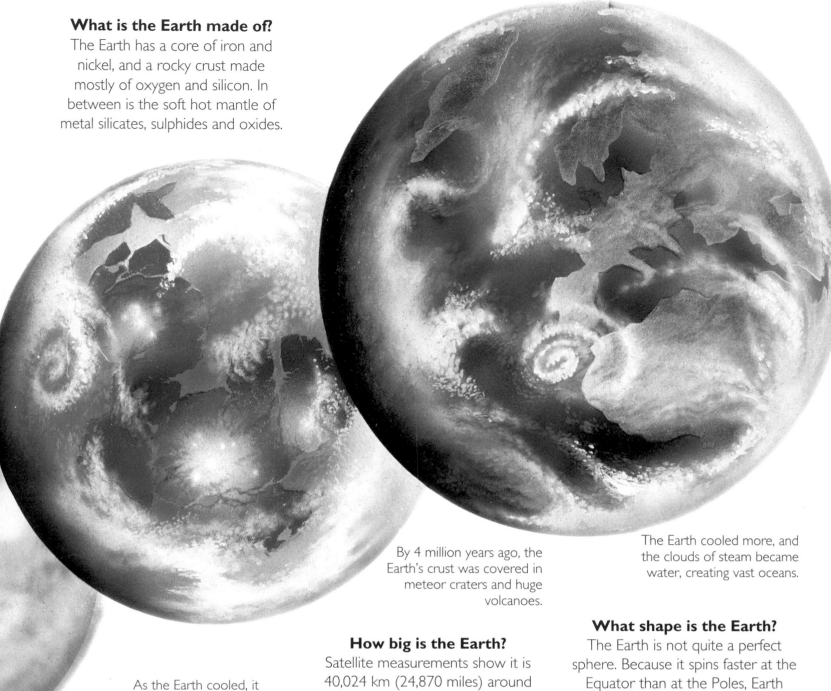

What is the Earth made of?
The Earth has a core of iron and nickel, and a rocky crust made mostly of oxygen and silicon. In between is the soft hot mantle of metal silicates, sulphides and oxides.

By 4 million years ago, the Earth's crust was covered in meteor craters and huge volcanoes.

The Earth cooled more, and the clouds of steam became water, creating vast oceans.

As the Earth cooled, it gave off gases and water vapour, which formed the atmosphere.

How big is the Earth?
Satellite measurements show it is 40,024 km (24,870 miles) around the equator and 12,578 km (7,927 miles) across. The diameter at the Poles is slightly less, by 43 km (26.7 miles).

What shape is the Earth?
The Earth is not quite a perfect sphere. Because it spins faster at the Equator than at the Poles, Earth bulges at the Equator. Scientists describe Earth's shape as 'geoid', which simply means Earth-shaped!

Who was Copernicus?
In the 1500s, most people thought the Earth was fixed in the centre of the universe, with the Sun and the stars revolving round it. Nicolaus Copernicus (1473-1543) was the Polish astronomer who first suggested the Earth was moving around the Sun.

Exactly how long is a year?

EVERY YEAR THE EARTH TRAVELS ONCE AROUND THE SUN. THIS EPIC JOURNEY measures 938,886,400 km (548,018,150 miles) and takes exactly 365.24 days, which gives us our calendar year of 365 days. To make up the extra 0.24 days, we add an extra day to our calendar at the end of February in every fourth year, which is called the leap year – and then we have to knock off a leap year every four centuries.

What's so special about the Earth?
The Earth is the only planet with temperatures at which water can exist on the surface and is the only planet with an atmosphere containing oxygen. Water and oxygen are both needed for life.

What is the Moon?

THE MOON IS THE EARTH'S NATURAL SATELLITE AND HAS CIRCLED AROUND IT for at least four billion years. It is a rocky ball about a quarter of Earth's size and is held in its orbit by mutual gravitational attraction. Scientists believe that the Moon formed when early in Earth's history a planet smashed into it. The impact was so tremendous that nothing was left of the planet but a few hot splashes thrown back up into space. Within a day of the smash, these splashes had been drawn together by gravity to form the Moon.

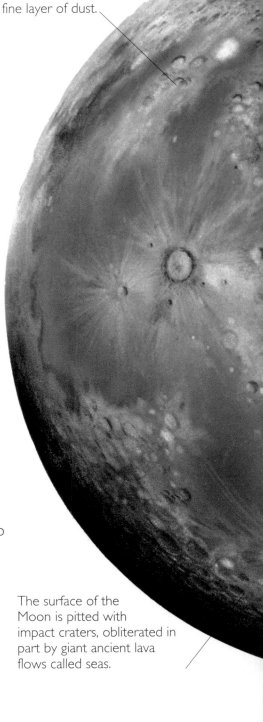

The Moon's surface is covered with a fine layer of dust.

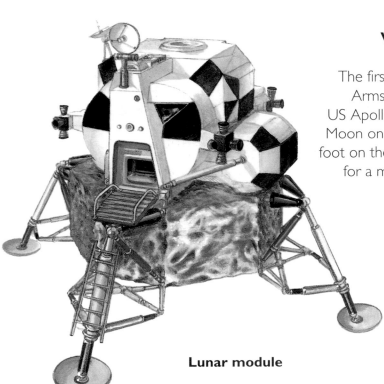

Lunar module

Who were the first men on the moon?
The first men on the Moon were Neil Armstrong and Buzz Aldrin of the US Apollo 11 mission who landed on the Moon on 21 July 1969. (As Armstrong set foot on the Moon, he said: 'This a small step for a man, a giant leap for mankind.')

The lunar module from the Apollo 15 mission was the astronauts' home during their brief stay on the Moon.

The surface of the Moon is pitted with impact craters, obliterated in part by giant ancient lava flows called seas.

What are the Moon's seas?
The large dark patches visible on the Moon's surface are called seas, but in fact they are not seas at all. They are huge plains formed by lava flowing from volcanoes that erupted early on in the Moon's history.

How long is a month?
It takes the Moon 27.3 days to circle the Earth, but 29.53 days from one full moon to the next, because the Earth moves as well. A lunar month is the 29.53 days cycle. Calendar months are entirely artificial.

What is a lunar eclipse?
As the Moon goes round the Earth, sometimes it passes right into Earth's shadow, where sunlight is blocked off. This is a lunar eclipse. If you look at the Moon during this time, you can see the dark disc of the Earth's shadow creeping across the Moon.

What is moonlight?
The Moon is by far the brightest thing in the night sky. But it has no light of its own. Moonlight is simply the Sun's light reflected off the white dust on the Moon's surface.

The Moon's phases

What's inside the Moon?

The Moon's mantle is now very cool compared to the Earth's.

The Moon's outer core is probably solid metal.

The Moon has an inner core of metal, very much smaller in relation to its size than Earth's.

Why does the moon look like cheese?

The moon looks like cheese because it is full of holes, and sometimes appears yellowish too. The holes are craters in the surface created when it was bombarded by huge rocks early on in its history.

The Moon has a crust of solid rock thicker than Earth's – up to 150 km (90 miles) thick on the side away from the Earth.

What is a harvest moon?

The harvest moon is the full moon nearest the autumnal equinox (when night and day are of equal length). This moon hangs bright above the eastern horizon for several evenings, providing a good light for harvesters.

Why does the sea have tides?

The Moon's gravity draws the oceans into an oval around the Earth, creating a bulge of water on each side of the world. These bulges stay beneath the Moon as the Earth spins round and so seem to run around the world, making the tide rise and fall as they pass.

What is a new moon?

THE MOON APPEARS TO CHANGE SHAPE DURING THE MONTH because, as it circles the Earth, we see its bright, sunny side from a different angle. At the new moon, the Moon is between Earth and the Sun, and we catch only a crescent-shaped glimpse of its bright side. Over the first two weeks of the month, we see more and more of the bright side (waxing) until full moon, when we see all its sunny side. Over the next two weeks, we see less and less (waning), until we get back to just a sliver – the old moon.

The phases of the Moon, from left to right: new moon, half moon (waxing), gibbous moon (waxing), full moon, gibbous moon (waning), half moon (waning), old moon.

What is the Sun?

THE SUN IS AN AVERAGE STAR, JUST LIKE COUNTLESS OTHERS IN THE UNIVERSE.
It formed from gas left behind after an earlier, much larger star blew up and now, in middle-age, burns yellow and fairly steadily – giving the Earth daylight and remarkably constant temperatures. Besides heat and light, the Sun sends out deadly gamma rays, X-rays and ultraviolet, as well as infrared and radio waves. Fortunately we are shielded from these by Earth's magnetic field and atmosphere.

What is a solar eclipse?
A solar eclipse is when the Moon comes in between the Sun and the Earth, creating a shadow a few hundred kilometres wide on the Earth.

The photosphere is a sea of boiling gas. It gives the heat and light we experience on Earth.

How big is the Sun?
The Sun is a small to medium-sized star 1,392,000 km (0.86 million miles) in diameter. It weighs just under 2,000 trillion trillion tonnes.

What is the Sun's crown?
The Sun's crown is its corona, its glowing white hot atmosphere seen only as a halo when the rest of the sun's disc is blotted out by the Moon in a solar eclipse.

How hot is the Sun?
The surface of the Sun is a phenomenal 6,000°C (11,000°F), and would melt absolutely anything. But its core is thousands of times hotter at over 16 million°C (29 million°F)!

Sunspot

What makes the Sun burn?
The Sun gets its heat from nuclear fusion. Huge pressures deep inside the Sun force the nuclei (cores) of hydrogen atoms to fuse together to make helium atoms, releasing huge amounts of nuclear energy.

The chromosphere is a tenuous layer through which dart tongues called spicules, making it look like a flaming forest.

The Sun

How old is the Sun?
The sun is a middle-aged star and probably formed about five billion years ago. It will probably burn for another five billion years and then die in a blaze so bright that the Earth will be scorched right out of existence.

What is the solar wind?
The solar wind is the stream of radioactive particles constantly blowing out from the Sun at hundreds of kilometres per second. (The Earth is protected from the solar wind by its magnetic field, but at the Poles the solar wind interacts with Earth's atmosphere to create the aurora borealis or northern lights.)

Beyond the chromosphere is the sun's ultra-thin halo of boiled-off gases called the corona.

Higher above the chromosphere are giant tongues of hot gases called prominences.

What are solar flares?
Flares are eruptions from the Sun's surface that fountain into space with the energy of one million atom bombs for about five minutes. (They are similar to solar prominences, the giant flame-like tongues of hot hydrogen that loop 100,000 km/60,000 miles into space.)

What are sunspots?

SUNSPOTS ARE DARK BLOTCHES SEEN ON THE SUN'S SURFACE. They are thousands of kilometres across, and usually occur in pairs. They are dark because they are slightly less hot than the rest of the surface. As the Sun rotates, they slowly cross its face – in about 37 days at the Equator and 26 days at the Poles. The average number of spots seems to reach a maximum every 11 years, and many scientists believe these sunspot maximums are linked to periods of stormier weather on Earth.

What's frightening about Mars's moons?

One night American astronomer Asaph Hall got fed up with studying Mars and decided to go to bed. But his domineering wife bullied him into staying up – and that night he discovered Mars's two moons. Mocking his fear of his wife, he named the moons Phobos (fear) and Deimos (panic).

Why is Mars red?

Mars is red because it is rusty. The surface contains a high proportion of iron dust, and this has been oxidized in the carbon dioxide atmosphere.

Three quarters of Earth's surface is covered in water, which is why it looks blue.

Earth

Mars

Mars is reddish with shadows visible here and there on the surface of the planet.

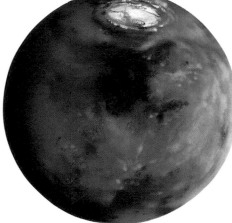

Is there life on Mars?

The Viking landers of the 1970s found not even the minutest trace of life. But in 1996, microscopic fossils of what might be mini-viruses were found in a rock from Mars. So who knows?

The dramatic landscape of Mars has not been worn down by rain or running water.

Martian canyon

What canyon is bigger than the Grand Canyon?

A CANYON ON MARS! THE SURFACE OF MARS IS MORE STABLE THAN EARTH'S, and there is no rain or running water to wear down the landscape. So although it is only half the size of Earth, it has a volcano called Olympus Mons 24 km (15 miles) high – three times as high as Mount Everest. It also has a great chasm, discovered by the Mariner 9 space probe and called the Valles Marineris. This is over 4,000km (25,000 miles) long and four times as deep as America's Grand Canyon.

What is the air on Venus?
Venus's atmosphere would be deadly for humans. It is very deep, so the pressure on the ground is huge. It is made mainly of poisonous carbon dioxide and is also filled with clouds of sulphuric acid.

Why is Venus called the Evening Star?
Venus reflects sunlight so well it shines like a star. But because it is quite close to the Sun, we can only see it in the evening, just after the Sun sets. We can also see it just before sunrise.

What are the inner planets made of?
Each of the inner planets is formed a little bit like an egg – with a hard 'shell' or crust of rock, a 'white' or mantle of soft, semi-molten rock, and a 'yolk' or core of hot often molten iron and nickel.

Could you breathe on Mercury?
Not without your own oxygen supply. Mercury has almost no atmosphere – just a few wisps of sodium vapour – because gases are burned off by the nearby Sun.

How hot is Mercury?
Temperatures on Mercury veer from one extreme to the other because it has too thin an atmosphere to insulate it. In the day, temperatures soar to 430°C (800°F); at night they plunge to −180°C (−290°F).

Venus

Venus is a soft pinkish white ball with no features visible on the surface through its thick atmosphere.

Mercury has virtually no atmosphere and its surface is pitted with craters like the Moon.

Mercury

Sun

What are the inner planets?

THE INNER PLANETS ARE THE FOUR PLANETS IN THE SOLAR SYSTEM that are nearest to the Sun. These planets – Mercury, Venus, Earth and Mars – are small planets made of rock, unlike the bigger planets further out, which are made mostly of gas. Because they are made of rock, they have a hard surface a spaceship could land on, which is why they are sometimes called terrestrial (earth) planets. They all have a thin atmosphere, but each is very different.

What are the giant planets?

JUPITER AND SATURN – THE FIFTH AND SIXTH PLANETS OUT FROM THE SUN – are the giants of the solar system. Jupiter is twice as heavy as all the planets put together, and 1,300 times as big as the Earth. Saturn is almost as big. Unlike the inner planets, they are both made largely of gas, and only their very core is rocky. This does not mean they are vast cloud balls. The enormous pressure of gravity means the gas is squeezed until it becomes liquid and even solid.

How heavy is Saturn?
Saturn may be big, but because it is made largely of liquid hydrogen, it is also remarkably light, with a mass of 600 billion trillion tonnes. If you could find a big enough bath, it would float.

What is the Cassini division?
Saturn's rings occur in broad bands labelled with the letters A to G. In 1675, the astronomer Cassini spotted a dark gap between rings A and B, which is now called after him, the Cassini division.

When it rains on Saturn, it rains drops of liquid helium.

What are the giant planets made of?
Jupiter and Saturn are made largely of hydrogen and helium. On Jupiter, internal pressures are so great that most of the hydrogen is turned to metal.

Saturn

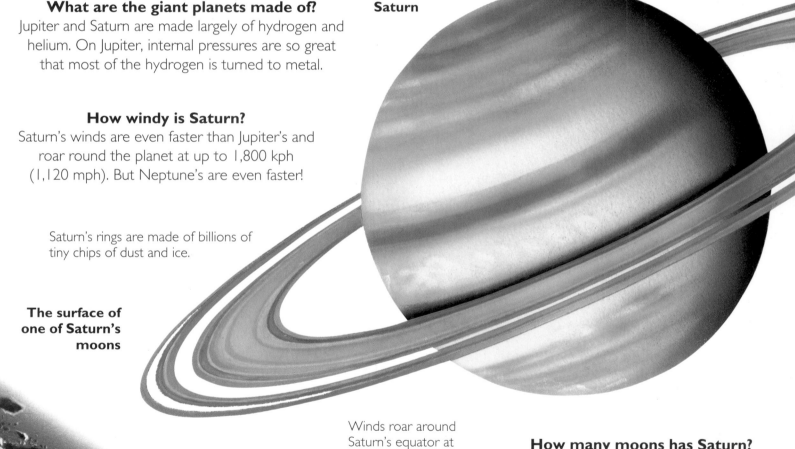

How windy is Saturn?
Saturn's winds are even faster than Jupiter's and roar round the planet at up to 1,800 kph (1,120 mph). But Neptune's are even faster!

Saturn's rings are made of billions of tiny chips of dust and ice.

The surface of one of Saturn's moons

Winds roar around Saturn's equator at 1,800 kph (1,120 mph).

Saturn's moons are all blocks of ice, made dirty with dust and organic compounds, and the surface is barren.

How many moons has Saturn?
Saturn has at least 18 moons, including Iapetus, which is black on one side and white on the other, and Enceladus, which is covered in shiny beads of ice and shimmers like a cinema screen.

Why are astronomers excited about Titan?
Saturn's moon Titan is very special because it is the only moon in the solar system with an atmosphere.

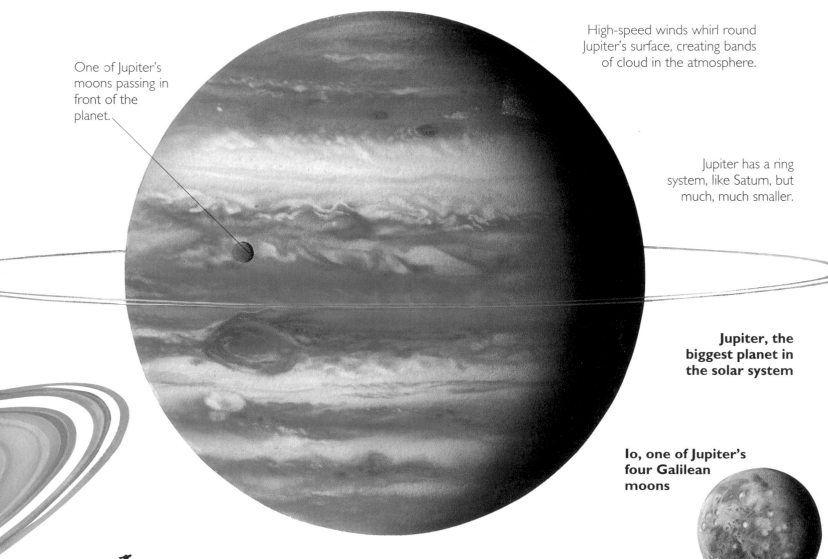

One of Jupiter's moons passing in front of the planet.

High-speed winds whirl round Jupiter's surface, creating bands of cloud in the atmosphere.

Jupiter has a ring system, like Saturn, but much, much smaller.

Jupiter, the biggest planet in the solar system

Io, one of Jupiter's four Galilean moons

Volcanoes erupting sulphur on the surface of Io make it look like a pizza.

What are Saturn's rings?

SATURN'S RINGS ARE THE PLANET'S SHINING HALO, FIRST DISCOVERED IN 1659 by Dutch scientist Christiaan Huygens (1629-95). They are made of countless billions of tiny chips of ice and dust – few bigger than a refrigerator and most the size of ice cubes. The rings are incredibly thin – no more than than 50 m (164 ft) deep – yet they stretch way above Saturn's clouds, 7,000 km (4,350 miles) high, and over 74,000 km (46,000 miles) out into space. One of Saturn's rings is as thin as a piece of tissue paper being stretched over a football pitch.

How many moons has Jupiter?
Jupiter has 16 moons – four big ones, discovered by Galileo as long ago as 1610, and so called after him the Galilean moons, and 12 smaller ones.

What is Jupiter's red spot?
The Great Red Spot or GRS is a huge swirling storm in Jupiter's atmosphere 40,000 km (25,000 miles) across that has gone on in the same place for at least 330 years.

Could you land on Jupiter?
No. Even if your spaceship could withstand the enormous pressures, there is no surface to land on – the atmosphere merges unnoticeably into deep oceans of liquid hydrogen.

How fast does Jupiter spin?
Jupiter spins faster than any other planet. Despite its huge size, it turns right round in just 9.8 hours, which means the surface is moving at 45,000 kph (28,000 mph)!

How big is Jupiter?
Very big. Even though Jupiter is largely gas it weighs 320 times as much as the Earth and is 142,984 km (88,850 miles) in diameter.

What are the outer planets?

THE OUTER PLANETS ARE URANUS, NEPTUNE
and Pluto, and Pluto's companion Charon.
Unlike the other planets, these were
completely unknown to ancient
astronomers. They are so far away, and so
faint, that Uranus was discovered only in
1781, Neptune in 1846, Pluto in 1930 and
Charon as recently as 1978. Uranus and Neptune
are gas giants like Jupiter and Saturn, but Pluto and
Charon are rocky and were probably wandering
asteroids trapped by the Sun's gravity within the
outer reaches of the solar system.

Uranus

What's strange about Uranus?
Unlike any of the other planets, Uranus
does not spin on a slight tilt. Instead it is
tilted right over and rolls round the Sun
on its side, like a giant bowling ball.

Uranus rolls on
its side and is
the seventh
planet out
from the Sun.

**How long is a year
on Neptune?**
Neptune is so far from the Sun –
over four billion km (2,800 million
miles) at maximum – that its orbit
takes 164,79 years. So Neptune's
year is 164,79 of ours.

What's an asteroid?
Asteroids are the thousands of
rocky lumps that circle round the
Sun in a big band between Mars and
Jupiter. The biggest, Ceres, is
1000 km (600 miles) across. Most
are much smaller. Over 3,200
asteroids have been identified so far.

Why is Neptune green?
Neptune is greeny blue because its
surface is completely covered in
immensely deep oceans of liquid
methane (natural gas).

At the heart of a comet
is a nucleus of ice and
dust often shaped like
a lumpy potato, just
a few km across.

What's a comet?

SPECTACULAR COMETS ARE JUST DIRTY
ICEBALLS A FEW KILOMETRES ACROSS.
Normally, they circle the outer reaches of the solar system.
But occasionally, one of them is drawn in towards the Sun.
As it hurtles towards the Sun, it melts and a vast tail of gas
is blown behind it by the solar wind. We may see this
spectacular tail in the night sky shining in the sunlight for a
few weeks until it swings round the Sun and out of sight.
The most recent comet was Hale-Bopp in 1997.

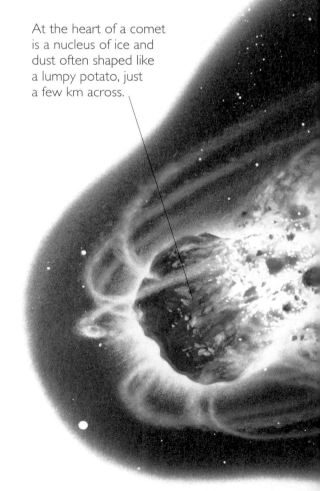

Neptune

Pluto and Charon

Neptune is so far from the Sun that surface temperatures drop to −210°C (−346°F).

How big is Pluto?
Pluto is very small, which is why it was so hard to spot. It is five times smaller than the Earth – just 2,284 km (1,419 miles) across – and 500 times lighter.

Who found Neptune?
Two mathematicians, John Couch Adams in England and Urbain le Verrier in France, predicted where Neptune should be from the way its gravity disturbed Uranus's orbit. Johan Galle in Berlin spotted it on 23 September, 1846.

A tail of ionized atoms is blown out millions of kms behind the comet by the solar wind.

A comet in the night sky

What is a meteorite?
Meteorites are lumps of rock from space big enough to penetrate the Earth's atmosphere and reach the ground without burning up.

Why do some stars throb?
The light from variable stars flares up and down. 'Cepheid' are big young stars that pulsate over a few days or a few weeks. 'RR Lyrae' variables are old yellow stars that vary over a few hours.

How are stars born?
Stars are born when clumps of gas in space are drawn together by their own gravity, and the middle of the clump is squeezed so hard that temperatures reach 10 million°C (18 million°F), so a nuclear fusion reaction starts.

How many stars are there?
It is hard to know how many stars there are in the universe, for the vast majority of them are much too far away to see. But astronomers guess there are about 200 billion billion.

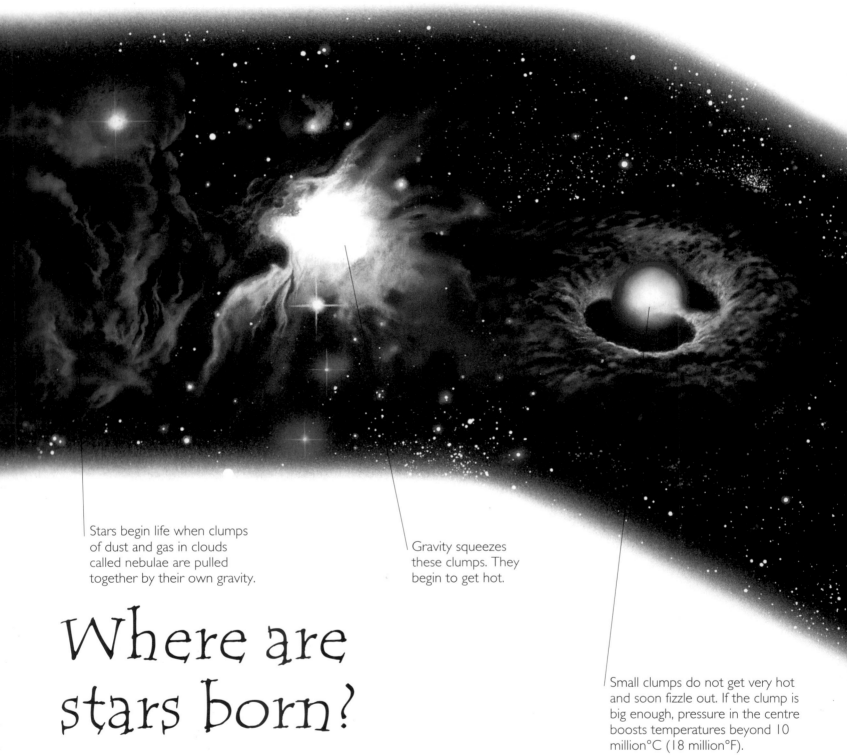

Stars begin life when clumps of dust and gas in clouds called nebulae are pulled together by their own gravity.

Gravity squeezes these clumps. They begin to get hot.

Small clumps do not get very hot and soon fizzle out. If the clump is big enough, pressure in the centre boosts temperatures beyond 10 million°C (18 million°F).

Where are stars born?

STRETCHED THROUGHOUT SPACE ARE VAST CLOUDS OF DUST AND GAS CALLED NEBULAE. These clouds are 99 per cent hydrogen and helium with tiny amounts of other gases and minute quantities of icy, cosmic dust. Stars are born in the biggest of these nebulae, which are called giant molecular clouds. Here temperatures plunge to −263°C −441°F), just 10° short of absolute zero. These nebulae are thin and cold but contain all the materials needed to make a star.

What is the biggest star?
The biggest stars are the supergiants. Antares is 700 times as big as the Sun. There may be a star in the Epsilon system in the constellation of Auriga that is 3 billion km (1,860 million miles) across – 4,000 times as big as the Sun!

What are constellations?

Constellations are small patterns of stars in the sky, each with its own name. They have no real existence, but they help astronomers locate things in the night sky.

What makes stars glow?

Stars glow because the enormous pressure deep inside generates nuclear fusion reactions in which hydrogen atoms are fused together, releasing huge quantities of energy.

What is a star?

STARS ARE GIGANTIC GLOWING BALLS OF GAS, SCATTERED THROUGHOUT SPACE.

They burn for anything from a few million to tens of billions of years. The nearest star, apart from the Sun, is over 40 trillion km (25 trillion miles) away. They are all so distant that we can see stars only as pinpoints of light in the night sky – even through the most powerful telescope. As far as we can see there are no other large objects in the universe.

Nuclear fusion begins as hydrogen atoms fuse together to make helium. The heat from the fusion makes the star shine.

In medium-sized stars, like our Sun, the heat generated in the core pushes gas out as hard as gravity pulls it in, so the star stabilizes and burns steadily for billions of years.

After 10 billion years or so, all the hydrogen in the star's core is burned up, and the core shrinks as it begins to burn helium.

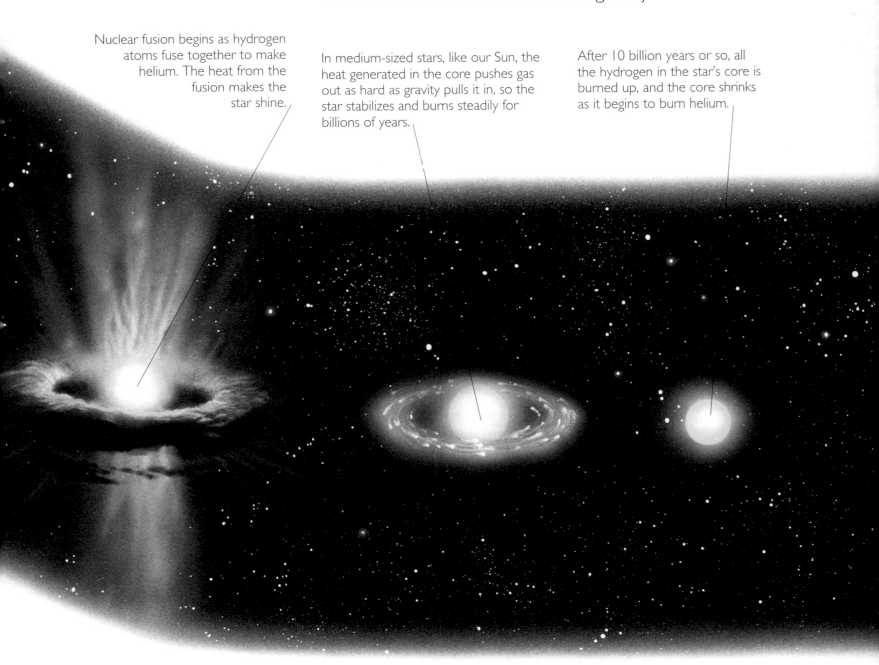

How hot is a star?

The surface temperature of the coolest stars is below 3,500°C (6,300°F); that of the hottest, brightest stars is over 40,000°C (72,000°F).

What makes stars twinkle?

Stars twinkle because the Earth's atmosphere is never still, and starlight twinkles as the air wavers. Light from the nearby planets is not distorted as much, so they don't twinkle.

What colour are stars?

It depends how hot they are. The colour of medium-sized stars varies along a band on a graph called the main sequence – from hot and bright blue-white stars to cool and dim red stars.

What happens when stars die?

STARS DIE WHEN THEY HAVE EXHAUSTED THEIR VAST SUPPLIES OF NUCLEAR FUEL. When the hydrogen runs out, they switch to helium. When the helium runs out, they quickly exhaust any remaining nuclear energy and either blow up, shrink or go cold. Just how long it takes to reach this point depends on the star. The biggest stars have masses of nuclear fuel but live fast and die young. The smallest stars have little nuclear fuel but live slow and long. A star twice as big as the Sun lives a tenth as long. The biggest stars live just a few million years.

What is a pulsar?
Pulsars are stars that flash out intense radio pulses every ten seconds or less as they spin rapidly round. They are thought to be very, very dense dying stars called neutron stars.

How old are the stars?
Stars are dying and being born all the time. Big bright stars live only ten million years. Medium-sized stars like our Sun live ten billion years.

What is a red giant?
Red giants are the huge, cool stars formed as surface gas on medium-sized stars nearing the end of their life swells up.

The outer layers cool off and swell so that the star grows into a cool red giant star.

The biggest stars go on swelling into supergiants. Pressure at the centre becomes so immense that carbon and silicon fuse to make iron.

Once iron forms in its centre, the star does not release energy but absorbs it – the star suddenly and catastrophically collapses in seconds.

What are the oldest stars?
The oldest stars we know of are not stars at all, but simply look like them because they are very bright but very far away. These are 'quasi-stellar radio objects' or quasars. Some are so far away the light we see left them 13 billion years ago.

The remains of a supernova collapses to become a pulsar, a star made mostly of atomic nuclear particles called neutrons.

The collapse of a supergiant triggers an explosion like a huge nuclear bomb, called a supernova.

The pulsar spins rapidly, beaming out pulses of radiation like a lighthouse.

What is a white dwarf?
White dwarfs are the small white stars formed as stars smaller than our Sun lose their surface gas altogether and shrink.

For a few weeks, the exploding supernova shines as brightly as billions of suns.

What is a supernova?

A SUPERNOVA IS A GIGANTIC EXPLOSION. IT FINISHES OFF A SUPERGIANT STAR. For just a brief moment, the supernova flashes out with the brilliance of billions of suns. Supernovae are rare, and usually visible only through a telescope. But in 1987, for the first time in 400 years, one called Supernova 1987A was visible with the naked eye for nine months.

What are neutron stars?
Neutron stars are all that remains of a supergiant star after a supernova explosion. They are tiny unimaginably dense stars that often become pulsars.

What is a light-year?

A light-year is 9,460,000,000,000 km. This is the distance light can travel in a year, at its constant rate of 300,000 km per second.

What is the furthest star we can see?

The furthest objects we can see in space are quasars, which may be over 13 billion light-years away.

What is a parsec?

A parsec is 3.26 light-years. Parsecs are parallax distances – distances worked out geometrically from slight shifts of a star's apparent position as the Earth moves round the Sun.

Distances within the solar system can be given in kilometres or miles.

Distances to nearby stars are measured in light-years.

What is red shift?

When a galaxy is moving rapidly away from us the waves of light become stretched out – that is, they become redder. The greater this red shift, the faster the galaxy is moving away from us.

Distances to the furthest galaxies are measured in billions of light-years.

Are the stars getting further away?

Analysis of red shifts has shown us that every single galaxy is moving away from us. The further away the galaxy, the faster it is moving away from us. The most distant galaxies are receding at almost the speed of light.

Pluto and Charon

Neptune

How far away is the Moon?

AT ITS NEAREST, THE MOON IS 356,410 KM (221,463 MILES) AWAY FROM EARTH; at its furthest, it is 406,697 km (252,710 miles) away. This is measured accurately by a laser beam bounced off mirrors left on the Moon's surface by Apollo astronauts and Soviet lunar probes. The distance is shown by how long it takes the beam to travel to the Moon and back.

Saturn

Uranus

Pluto and its companion Charon (top) are 5,914 million km from the Sun.

Saturn (above) is 1,427 million km from the Sun.
Uranus (left) is 2,871 million km from the Sun.

How did astronomers first estimate the Sun's distance?

Sun

I N 1672, TWO ASTRONOMERS, CASSINI IN FRANCE AND RICHER IN GUIANA, noted the exact position of Mars in the skies. They could work out how far away Mars is from the slight difference between their two measurements. Once they knew this, they could work out by simple geometry the distance from Earth to the Sun. Cassini's estimate was a mere 7 per cent too low.

Mercury

Mercury is 57.9 million km from the Sun.

Venus is 108.2 million km from the Sun.

Venus

How far away is the Sun?
The distance varies between 147 and 152 million km (91 to 94 million miles) from Earth. This is measured very accurately by bouncing radar waves off the planets.

Mars

Earth

How far is it to the nearest star?
The nearest star is Proxima Centauri, which is 4.3 light-years away – 40 trillion km.

Jupiter

The dome rotates, so the telescope can track stars across the sky.

Observatory

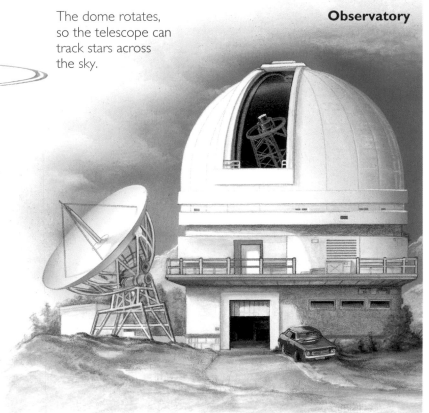

Jupiter is 778.3 million km from the Sun.

How do astronomers measure distance?
For nearby stars, they use parallax (see What is a parsec?). With middle distance stars, they look for standard candles, stars whose brightness they know. The dimmer it looks, compared to how bright it should look, the further away it is.

A spacecraft orbiting Earth

The craft shoots off into space if its forward momentum exceeds the acceleration due to Earth's gravity.

A craft orbiting Earth is effectively falling around it, pulled by the Earth's gravity.

What are orbits?

In space, many objects like planets and moons continually circle round larger objects. An orbit is the path they take. This is usually elliptical rather than perfectly circular in shape.

What did Newton discover?

The discoveries of Isaac Newton (1642-1727) include the three fundamental laws of motion. He also discovered the force called gravity, which holds the Moon in orbit around the Earth, and the planets in orbit around the Sun.

How strong is a planet's gravity?

The more massive the planet – that is the more matter it contains – the more powerful its gravity. Astronauts on the Moon could jump up high in heavy spacesuits, because the Moon is much smaller than the Earth and its gravity is weaker.

A black hole

What is gravity?

G RAVITY IS THE MUTUAL ATTRACTION BETWEEN EVERY SINGLE BIT OF MATTER in the universe. The more matter there is, and the closer it is, the stronger the attraction. A big dense planet pulls much more than a small one, or one that is far away. The Sun is so big, it makes its pull felt over millions of kilometres of space. The Earth is smaller, but big enough to keep the Moon circling around it. The weight of an object is simply how hard gravity is pulling on it.

A giant black hole may exist at the centre of our galaxy.

What happens inside a black hole?
Nothing that goes into a black hole comes out, and there is a point of no return called the event horizon. If you went beyond this you would be 'spaghettified' – stretched long and thin until you were torn apart by the immense gravity.

How big is a black hole?
The singularity at the heart of a black hole is infinitely small. The size of the hole around it depends on how much matter went into forming it. The black hole at the heart of our galaxy may be around the size of the solar system.

How many black holes are there?
No one really knows. Because they trap light they are hard to see. But there may be one at the heart of every galaxy.

The black hole contains so much matter in such a small space that its gravitational pull even drags in light.

We may be able to spot a black hole from the powerful radio signals emitted by stars being ripped to shreds as they are sucked in.

What is a black hole?

IF A SMALL STAR IS VERY DENSE, IT MAY BEGIN TO SHRINK UNDER THE PULL of its own gravity. As it shrinks, it becomes denser and denser and its gravity becomes more and more powerful – until it shrinks to a single tiny point of infinite density called singularity. The gravitational pull of a singularity is so immense that it pulls space into a 'hole' like a funnel. This is the black hole, which sucks in everything that comes near it with its huge gravitational force – including light, which is why it is a 'black' hole.

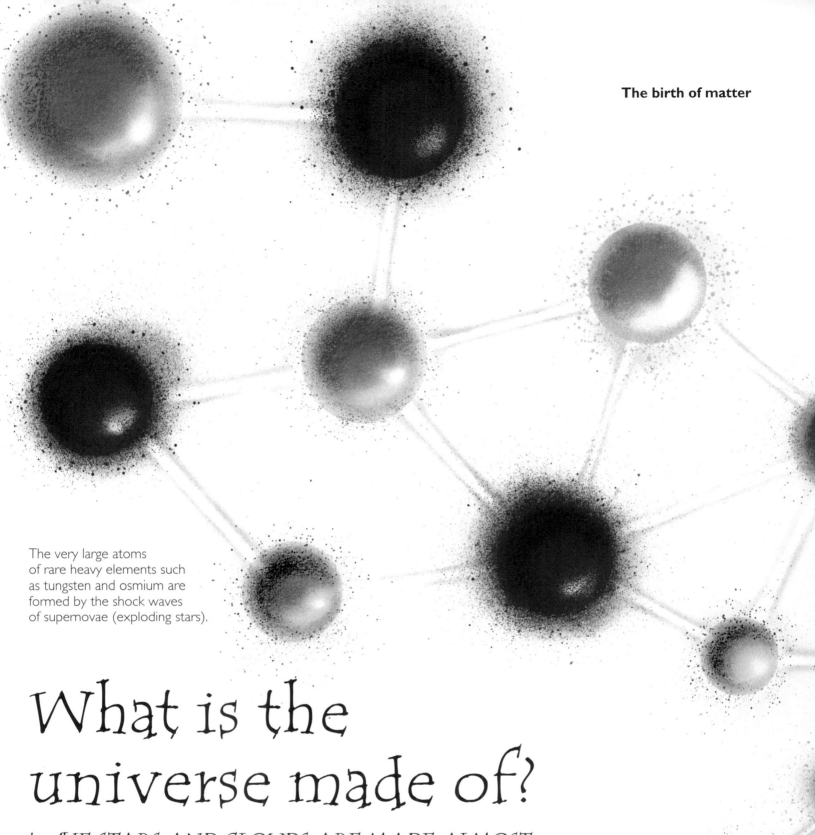

The very large atoms of rare heavy elements such as tungsten and osmium are formed by the shock waves of supernovae (exploding stars).

What is the universe made of?

THE STARS AND CLOUDS ARE MADE ALMOST 100 PER CENT OF HYDROGEN AND HELIUM, the lightest and simplest elements of all. All the other elements are relatively rare. But some, such as carbon, oxygen, silicon, nitrogen and iron can form important concentrations. This happens in the few rocky planets like Earth, where iron, oxygen and magnesium are the most common elements. Carbon, a scarcer element, is the one on which all life forms are based.

Larger atoms such as beryllium, carbon and oxygen are made when nuclear reactions inside stars force the nuclei of helium atoms together.

What are particles?

Particles are the tiny concentrations of energy from which all matter is made up, of which atoms are the largest. There are hundreds of kinds of particles, but all but atoms are too small to see, even with the most powerful microscope.

How were atoms made?

Atoms of hydrogen and helium were made in the early days of the universe when quarks in the matter soup joined together. All other atoms were made as atoms were fused together by the intense heat and pressure inside stars.

How was iron made?

Iron was forged in the heart of supergiant stars near the end of their life when the immense pressures there force carbon atoms together.

What holds everything together?

EVERYTHING IN THE UNIVERSE IS HELD TOGETHER BY FOUR invisible forces. Two of them – gravity and electromagnetism – are familiar in everyday life. The other two – the strong and weak nuclear forces – are unfamiliar because they operate only inside the invisibly small nucleus of the atom, holding it all together.

What was the first element?
The first element to form was hydrogen, which has the simplest and lightest atom of all. It formed within three minutes of the dawn of the universe.

What's the smallest particle?
The smallest particle inside the nucleus is the quark. It is less than 10^{-20} m across – which means a line of ten billion billion of them would be less than a metre long.

What is anti-matter?
Anti-matter is the mirror image of ordinary matter. If matter and anti-matter meet, they annihilate each other. Fortunately, there is very little anti-matter around.

First to form at the birth of the universe were countless particles much smaller than atoms, such as quarks.

Some of these particles fused together to form the first atoms, hydrogen and helium.

In the first few moments of the universe's existence, there was no matter – only seething, incredibly hot space.

Spiral galaxy

Spiral galaxies are spinning Catherine wheel spirals like our Milky Way.

Elliptical galaxy

Elliptical galaxies are shaped like rugby balls and are the oldest galaxies of all.

Barred spiral galaxy

Arms trail from this type of galaxy like water from a spinning garden sprinkler.

What is a galaxy?

OUR SUN IS JUST ONE OF A MASSIVE COLLECTION OF TWO BILLION STARS arranged in a shape like a fried egg, 100,000 light-years across. This collection is called the Galaxy because we see it in the band of stars across the night sky called the Milky Way. (Galaxy comes from the Greek for milky.) But earlier this century it was realized that the Galaxy is just one of millions of similar giant star groups scattered throughout space, which we also call galaxies. The nearest is the Andromeda galaxy.

What is a spiral galaxy?
A spiral galaxy is a galaxy that has spiralling arms of stars like a gigantic Catherine wheel. They trail because the galaxy is rotating. Our Galaxy is a spiral galaxy.

The Milky Way

What is the Milky Way?
The Milky Way is a pale blotchy white band that stretches right across the night sky. A powerful telescope shows it is made of thousands of stars, and is actually an edge-on view of our Galaxy.

Where is the Earth?
The Earth is just over half way out along one of the spiral arms of the Galaxy, about 30,000 light-years from the centre.

What are star clusters?
Stars are rarely entirely alone within a galaxy. Most are concentrated in groups called clusters. Globular clusters are big and round. Galactic clusters are small and formless.

If we could see the Milky Way from above, we would see that it is a giant spiral galaxy.

Irregular galaxies are galaxies that have no particular shape at all.

What exactly are nebulae?

NEBULAE ARE GIANT CLOUDS OF GAS AND DUST SPREAD THROUGHOUT the galaxies. Some of them we see through telescopes because they shine faintly as they reflect starlight. With others, called dark nebulae, we see only inky black patches hiding the stars behind. This is where stars are born. A few – called glowing nebulae – glow faintly of their own accord as the gas within them is heated by nearby stars.

What are double stars?
Our Sun is alone in space, but many stars have one or more nearby companions. Double stars are called binaries.

The Galaxy is whirling rapidly, sweeping the Sun and the other stars round at 100 billion kph (60 billion mph).

The Milky Way is over 100,000 light-years across, 1,000 light-years thick, and contains more than 100 billion stars.

What is the biggest thing in the universe?
The biggest structure in the universe is the Great Wall – a great sheet of galaxies 500 million light-years long and 16 million light-years thick.

How many galaxies are there?
With the largest telescopes and most sensitive detectors, we could probably record about a billion galaxies – there may be many, many more beyond their limits.

How do we know what it was like?

We know partly by mathematical calculations, and partly by experiments in huge machines called colliders and particle accelerators. These recreate conditions in the early universe by using magnets to accelerate particles to astonishing speeds in a tunnel, and then crash them together.

In the beginning there was a ball smaller than an atom. It grew as big as a football as it cooled from infinity to ten billion billion billion °C

How long will the universe last?

It depends how much matter it contains. If there is more than the 'critical density', gravity will put a brake on its expansion, and it may soon begin to contract again to end in a Big Crunch. If there is much less, it may go on expanding forever.

What was there before the universe?

No one has a clue. Some people think there was an unimaginable ocean beyond space and time of potential universes continually bursting into life, or failing. Ours succeeded.

What is inflation?

Inflation was a period in the first few trillionths of a trillionth of a trillionth of a second in the life of the universe, when space swelled up enormously, before there was matter and energy to fill it.

What was the universe like at the beginning?

THE EARLY UNIVERSE WAS VERY SMALL, BUT IT CONTAINED ALL THE MATTER and energy in the universe today. It was a dense and chaotic soup of tiny particles and forces – and instead of the four forces scientists know today, there was just one superforce. But this original universe lasted only a split second. After just three trillionths of a trillionth of a trillionth of a second, the superforce split up into separate forces.

Can we see the Big Bang?

Astronomers can see the galaxies hurtling away in all directions. They can also see the afterglow – low level microwave radiation coming at us from all over the sky, called the microwave background.

After a split second inflation began as space swelled a thousand billion billion billion times in less than a second – from the size of a football to something bigger than a galaxy.

What was the Big Bang?

In the beginning, all the universe was squeezed into an unimaginably small, hot, dense ball. The Big Bang was when this suddenly began to swell explosively, allowing first energy and matter, then atoms, gas clouds and galaxies to form. The universe has been swelling ever since.

Why is the universe getting bigger?

We can tell the universe is getting bigger because every galaxy is speeding away from us. Yet the galaxies themselves are not moving – the space in between them is stretching.

How old is the universe?

How did the first galaxies and stars form?

They formed from curdled lumps of clouds of hydrogen and helium – either as clumps broke up into smaller more concentrated clumps, or as concentrations within the clumps drew together.

WE KNOW THAT THE UNIVERSE IS GETTING BIGGER AT A CERTAIN RATE by observing how fast distant galaxies are moving. By working out how long it took everything to expand to where it is now, we can wind the clock back to the time when the universe was very, very small indeed. This suggests that the universe is between 13 and 15 billion years old. However, studies of globular clusters suggest some stars in our galaxy may be up to 18 billion years old.

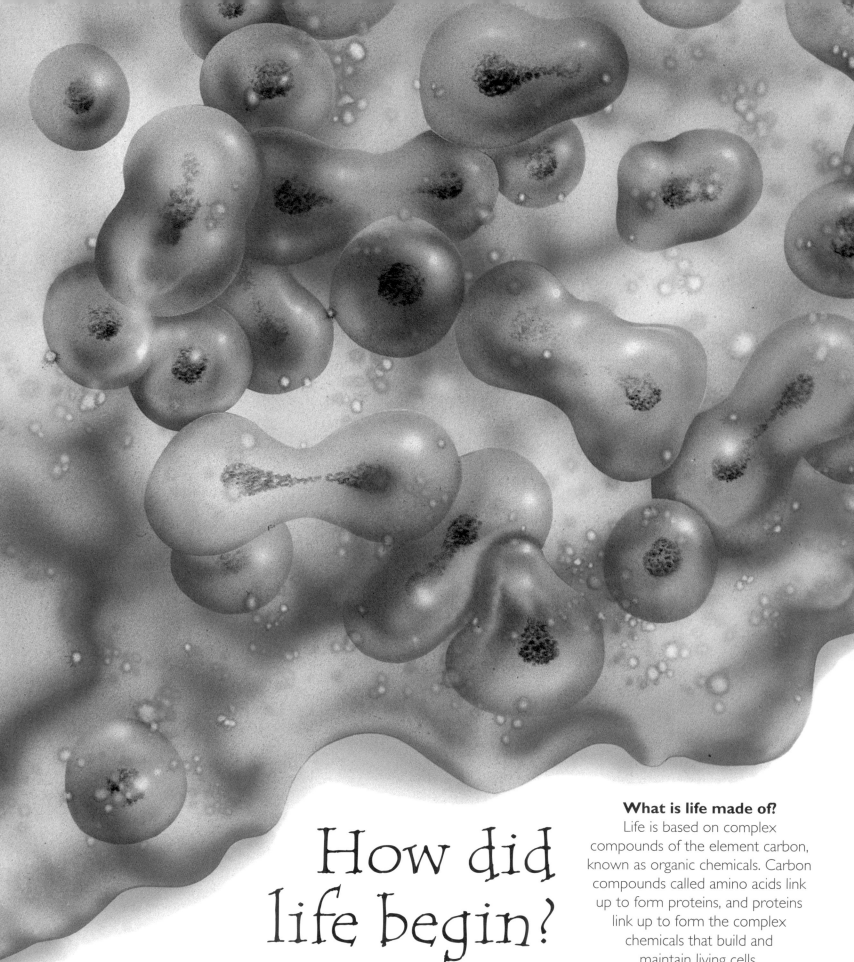

How did life begin?

SCIENTIFIC EXPERIMENTS IN THE 1950s SHOWED HOW LIGHTNING FLASHES might create amino acids, the basic chemicals of life, from the waters and gases of the early Earth. But no one knows how these chemicals joined up to become 'self-replicating' — that is, able to make copies of themselves. This is the key to life — which remains a mystery. However, the first lifeforms were probably tiny bacteria called Archebacteria, which thrive in very hot, chemically rich places.

What is life made of?
Life is based on complex compounds of the element carbon, known as organic chemicals. Carbon compounds called amino acids link up to form proteins, and proteins link up to form the complex chemicals that build and maintain living cells.

Where did the materials of life come from?
It used to be thought that organic chemicals all originated on Earth, but traces of all kinds of organic chemicals have been detected in giant molecular clouds, including formaldehyde, alcohol, and also acetaldehyde, one of the components of amino acids.

Where did life come from?
Most scientists think life on Earth began on Earth – in the oceans or in volcanic pools. But some think the Earth was seeded by micro-organisms from space.

What is SETI?
SETI is the Search for Extra-Terrestrial Intelligence project – designed to continually scan radio signals from space and pick up any signs of intelligence – signals that have a pattern, but are not completely regular like those from pulsating stars.

Why is the universe like it is?
The amazing chance that life exists on Earth has made some scientists wonder if only a universe like ours could contain intelligent life. This is called the weak anthropic principle. Some go further and say that the universe is constructed in such a way that intelligent life must develop at some stage. This is called the strong anthropic principle.

The first lifeforms
The first lifeforms were little more than simple chemical molecules surrounded by a membrane.

What is DNA?
Dioxyribonucleic acid, the most remarkable chemical in the universe – the tiny molecule on which all life is based. It is shaped a bit like a very long rope ladder, with two strands twisted together in a spiral, linked by 'rungs' of four different chemical bases. The order of these bases is a chemical code that provides all the instructions needed for life.

Is there life on other planets?

ORGANIC CHEMICALS ARE WIDESPREAD, AND THE CHANCES ARE THAT IN SUCH a large universe there are many planets, like Earth, suitable for nurturing life. But no one knows if life arose on Earth by a fantastic and unique chain of chance events – or whether it is fairly likely to happen given the right conditions. If the shapes found in Martian rock in 1996 really do prove to be lifeforms, the universe is probably teeming with life.

Are there any other planets like Earth?
There is no other planet like Earth anywhere in the solar system. Recently, though, planets have been detected circling other stars nearby. But they are much too far away for us to know anything about them at all.

How are we looking for extra-terrestrial life?
Since possible fossils of microscopic life were found in Martian rock in 1996, scientists have hunted for other signs of organisms in rocks from space. Future probes to Mars are also being designed to drill into the Martian surface and look for signs of microscopic life below ground.

What does an alien look like?
At the moment, the only aliens we are likely to encounter are very, very small and look like viruses.

Two-mouthed creature from outer space

No one knows what creatures from elsewhere in the universe would look like – but the chances are they would look pretty strange.

Lands and People

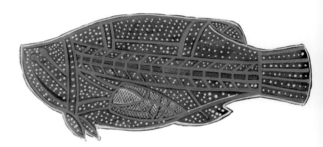

How many people live in the world?
Billions! In 1997 there were about 5,840,000,000 human beings living on our planet. That's more than twice as many as 50 years ago.

6 billion people live on Earth.

Are there more and more people?
Every minute, 167 babies are born around the world. Imagine how they would cry if they were all put together! By the year 2025 there will probably be 8,036,000,000 people in the world.

Have people always lived where they do now?
During history many peoples have moved huge distances, or migrated. The Polynesian people took 2,500 years or more to sail across the Pacific Ocean and settle its islands. People are still on the move today.

Frozen Arctic wastes

Some parts of the world are too harsh, too hot or cold for people to settle.

Why are some lands richer than others?
Some lands have good soil, where crops can grow. Some have oil, which is worth a lot of money. But other countries have poor soil, little rain and no minerals. However hard people work there, they struggle to survive.

Where do people live?

HUMANS LIVE WHEREVER THEY CAN FIND FOOD AND WATER, which they need to stay alive. Nobody at all lives in Antarctica, the icy wilderness at the bottom of the world. Scientists do visit bases there, so that they can study rocks and icebergs and penguins. The Sahara desert in Africa is a land of burning hot sand and rocks. It has just a few places, called oases, where people can get the water they need to survive.

Have humans changed our planet?
Over the ages, humans have changed the face of the world we live in. They have chopped down forests and dammed rivers. They have grown new plants and killed wild animals. They have built big cities and roads.

Clothes from round the world

Is there room for everybody?

Just about! But sometime in the future people may have to live in towns under the ocean or even on other planets. In those places they would need a special supply of air to stay alive.

Which country has the most people?

More people live in China than anywhere else in the world. They number about 1,237,000,000 and most of them live in the big cities of the east and the south. In the far west of China there are empty deserts and lonely mountains.

New York City, USA

Places where many people have chosen to settle have become big cities.

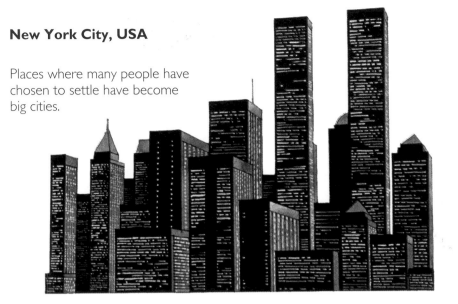

How different are we from one another?

A LL HUMAN BEINGS ARE BASICALLY THE SAME, WHEREVER THEY LIVE. We may speak different languages and have different ideas. We may wear different clothes and eat different foods. Our parents may give us dark or pale skin, blue eyes or brown, or various colours of hair. But in the end we share the same needs, pleasures, hopes and fears. We should not waste our time quarrelling, for we are all members of the same big family.

What is a continent?

The big masses of land that make up the Earth's surface are called continents. The biggest continent of all is Asia, which is home to over 3.5 billion people.

Where are the most crowded places in the world?

Tiny countries and large cities may house many millions of people. The most crowded of the bigger countries is Bangladesh, with over 800 people for every square kilometre of land.

Who are the world's peoples?

Human beings who share the same history or language make up 'a people' or 'ethnic group'. Sometimes many different peoples live in just one country. Over a hundred peoples live in Tanzania, each with its own way of life.

      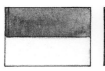

Colourful flags from around the world

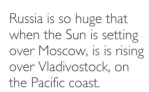

Crossing the world's biggest country, 50 years ago

Which is the biggest country in the world?
The gigantic Russian Federation takes up over 17 million square kilometres of the Earth's surface. It covers two continents, Europe and Asia, and its clocks are set at 11 different times.

How long does it take to cross Russia?
It depends how you travel! These days, trains on the famous Trans-Siberian railway take eight days from Moscow to the Pacific coast.

Russia is so huge that when the Sun is setting over Moscow, is is rising over Vladivostock, on the Pacific coast.

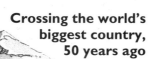

What is a country?

The Trans-Siberian Railway was built over a hundred years ago and opened in 1905.

A COUNTRY IS AN AREA OF LAND UNDER THE RULE OF A SINGLE GOVERNMENT.
A country may be vast, or very small. Its borders have to be agreed with neighbouring countries, although this does sometimes lead to arguments. Countries that rule themselves are called independent. Countries that are ruled by other countries are called dependencies. Sometimes several countries join up to form a single new nation, but countries may also break up into smaller nations, too.

How many dependencies are there in the world ?
Sixty-five of the world's nations are still ruled by other countries. They include many tiny islands in the Caribbean Sea and in the Atlantic and Pacific Oceans.

How many independent countries are there?
There are 192 independent countries in the world today. The number may change from one year to the next.

Swiss Guard, Vatican City

Which country fits inside a town?

The world's smallest nation is an area within the city of Rome, in Italy. It is called Vatican City and is headquarters of the Roman Catholic Church. Only a thousand or so people live there.

Where can you see all the flags of the world?

Rows and rows of flags fly outside the headquarters of the United Nations in New York City, USA. Most of the world's countries belong to this organization, which tries to solve all kinds of problems around the world.

Do all peoples have a land they can call their own?

No, the ancient homelands of some peoples are divided up between other countries. The lands of the Kurdish people are split between Turkey, Iran and Iraq.

What are counties and states?

If you look at the map of a country, you will see that it is divided up into smaller regions. These often have their own local laws and are known as states, provinces, counties or departments.

Refugees are people who have fled their country because of war or hunger.

Kurdish refugees

Why do countries have flags?

FLAGS CAN BE SEEN FLYING FROM BUILDINGS AND FROM BOATS. They show bold patterns and bright colours as they flutter in the wind. Many flags are badges or symbols of a nation, or of its regions. The designs on flags sometimes tell us about a country or its history. The flag of Kenya includes a traditional shield and spears, while the flag of Lebanon includes the cedar tree, which brought wealth to the region in ancient times.

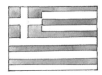
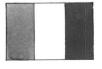

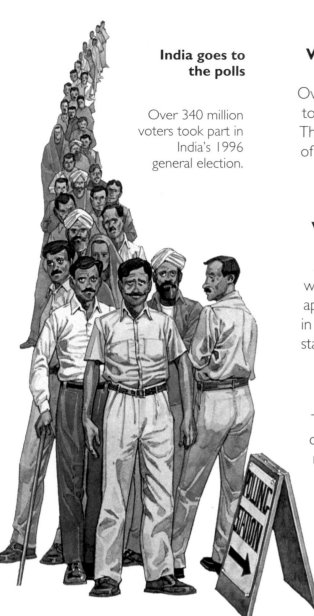

India goes to the polls

Over 340 million voters took part in India's 1996 general election.

Where is the biggest general election?

Over 590 million people are allowed to vote in general elections in India. They can cast their votes at any one of over half a million polling stations set up all over the country.

Which is the world's oldest parliament?

A parliament is a meeting place where new laws are discussed and approved. The oldest parliament is in Iceland. Called the Althing, it was started by Viking settlers in AD930.

What is a head of state?

The most important person in a country is the head of state. This may be a king or a queen or an elected president. The head of state often rides in a big car with a flag on it.

Who invented democracy?

The people of ancient Athens, in Greece, started the first democratic assembly nearly 2,500 years ago. It wasn't completely fair, as women and slaves weren't given the right to vote.

What is a republic?

It's a country that has no king or queen. France is a republic. Over 200 years ago the French king had his head chopped off, during a revolution.

Where do judges wear big wigs?

In Great Britain judges wear wigs, which were in fashion 250 years ago. This old costume is meant to show that the judge is not in court as a private person, but as someone who stands for the law of the land.

An English judge

Governments make the law, but it is up to judges to decide who has broken it.

What are 'Jana-gana-mana' and 'The Star-spangled Banner'?

Both of them are national anthems or songs. The first tune is played to show respect to India, the second to the United States of America. National anthems are played at important occasions, such as the Olympic Games.

Who rules the birds?

Traditionally the king or queen of England owns all the swans on the River Thames, except for those marked in a special ceremony that takes place each summer.

What is a government?

THE MEMBERS OF THE GOVERNMENT ARE THE PEOPLE WHO RUN THE COUNTRY. They pass new laws controlling everything from schools to hospitals and businesses. Countries where the people can choose their government are called democracies. At a general election each person puts a cross on a piece of paper to make their choice known. Then their votes are counted up to see who has won. Some countries do not hold elections or have a choice of political parties. The people who rule these countries are called dictators.

Which is the world's oldest royal family?

The Japanese royal family has produced a long line of 125 reigning emperors over a period of thousands of years.

How do you recognize kings and queens?

For special ceremonies rulers wear glittering crowns and carry symbols of royal power, such as golden sticks called sceptres. The beaded crown and robes shown here were worn by traditional rulers of the Yoruba people, who live in Nigeria.

Traditional robes worn by the Oba (king) of Akure, Nigeria

How does anyone get to be a king or a queen?

NORMALLY YOU HAVE TO BE A PRINCE OR PRINCESS, BORN INTO A ROYAL FAMILY with a king and queen for your mum and dad. About 800 years ago kings were very powerful people. They could have their enemies thrown into some horrible dungeon and then throw away the key. Today kings and queens have to be much nicer to people. They visit hospitals and open new bridges. They travel to meet other heads of state, as a representative of their own country.

How many languages are spoken today?

SOMEWHERE BETWEEN 5,000 AND 10,000 LANGUAGES ARE SPOKEN IN THE WORLD. Some are spoken by very few people. About 200 people in Latvia speak a language called Liv. One African language, Bikya, has only one surviving speaker. The world's most spoken language is Standard Chinese, which is used every day by 1,123 million people. English is the world's most widespread language, spoken by 470 million people.

What has made the world shrink?

Of course the planet hasn't really got smaller, it just seems that way. Today, telephones and faxes make it possible to send messages around the world instantly. Once, letters were sent by ship and took many months to arrive.

Instant communication

Telephones use satellite links to flash messages around the world.

Could we invent one language for all the world?

It's already been done! A language called Esperanto was invented over 100 years ago. Many people have learned how to speak it.

Do we all read left to right?

The Arabic language is read right-to-left, and traditional Japanese top-to-bottom.

Different cities, different signs

CAHKT ΠΕΤΕΡΟΥΡR
ST PETERSBURG

Many languages are related to each other and have words that sound similar.

አዲስ አበባ
ADDIS ABABA

What was that you whistled?

In some parts of Central America, Turkey and the Canary Islands, people worked out a way of communicating using whistles instead of words.

Can we talk without words?

People who are unable to hear or speak can sign with their hands. Various sign languages have been developed around the world, from China to the USA.

How do we talk through space?

Satellites are machines sent into space to circle the Earth. They can pick up telephone, radio or television signals from one part of the world and beam them down to another.

Should I stay or should I go?

Movements of the head and hands can be a kind of language. Be careful! In some countries wagging the hand palm down means 'come here', but in others it means 'go away'. Shaking the head can mean 'yes' in some countries and 'no' in others.

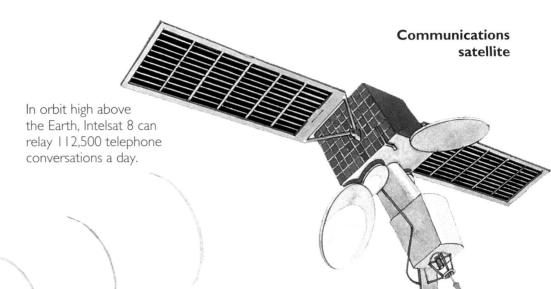

In orbit high above the Earth, Intelsat 8 can relay 112,500 telephone conversations a day.

Each language has its own culture and traditions.

What's in a name?

In Scandinavia there's a village called Å. In New Zealand there's a place called Taumatawhakatangihangakoa-uauotamateaturipukakapikim-aungahoronukupokaiwhenuaki-tanatahu.

Does everybody in one country speak the same language?

Not often. For example, families from all over the world have made their homes in London, the capital city of England. Their children mostly speak English at school, but at home may speak one of 275 other languages, from Turkish to Urdu.

Methods of writing, such as alphabets, are called scripts.

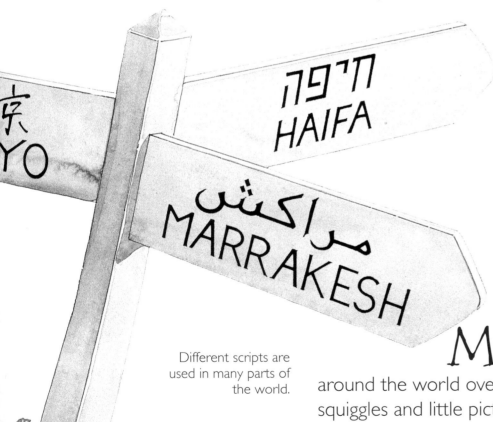

Different scripts are used in many parts of the world.

Do we use different ways of writing?

MANY DIFFERENT KINDS OF WRITING HAVE GROWN UP around the world over the ages, using all sorts of lines and squiggles and little pictures. This book is printed in the Roman alphabet, which has 26 letters and is used for many of the world's languages. Chinese writers normally use around 5,000 different symbols, or characters, although ten times as many can be used. The Khmer alphabet, used in Cambodia, has 74 letters, while the Rotokas alphabet, used on the island of Bougainville, has only 11 letters.

What are houses made from?

MUD, STONE, SLATE, BOULDERS, BRICKS, BRANCHES, REEDS, STEEL GIRDERS sheets of iron, concrete, glass, timber planks, straw, scrap metal, turf, frozen snow, bamboo, animal hides, packing cases, cardboard boxes – you name it! All over the world people make use of whatever materials they can find or produce in order to build shelters and homes. Today many modern buildings look much the same wherever they have been built, from Brasília to Singapore. However, all sorts of local types of houses can still be seen as well.

Where do they build mud huts?
Thatched huts with walls of dried mud can still be seen in parts of Africa, such as Mali. They are cheap to build, cool to live in and they often look beautiful too.

Why were skyscrapers invented?
So that more people could fit into a small area of city. High-rise flats and offices were first built in Chicago, USA, about 120 years ago. By 1887 new high-speed lifts were saving people a very long climb upstairs!

A Dogon village, Mali

Mud huts and grain stores are built around a yard, or compound.

What are houses like in the Arctic?
Today the Inuit people of Canada mostly live in modern houses and cabins made of wood. Traditionally, their houses were made of stone and turf. They also made overnight shelters out of blocks of snow.

Which people live in caravans?
Many of Europe's Gypsies live in caravans, moving from one campsite to another. The Gypsies, who are properly known as Roma, Sinti or Manush, arrived in Europe from India about 1,000 years ago.

Why do people live underground?
To stay cool! At Coober Pedy in Australia it is so hot that miners digging for opals built houses and even a church underground.

Bedouin nomads use camels to move from one part of the desert to another.

Houses must shelter people from cold and heat, rain and snow, storms and floods.

Where do people live in caves?

The first human beings often took shelter in caves. Even today, some people in Turkey and in China still make their homes in caves. These are not cold and dripping, like Stone Age dwellings. They can be snug and very comfortable.

Why do chalets have big roofs?

In the mountains of Switzerland, the wooden houses have broad roofs, designed for heavy falls of snow each winter.

Reeds are used for building from South America to Southwest Asia. They are also used to thatch cottages in parts of England.

Why do people live in tents?

IN MANY PARTS OF THE WORLD PEOPLE DO NOT LIVE IN THE SAME PLACE all year round. They are nomads, following their herds of sheep and goats from one desert oasis to another, or from lowland to mountain pastures. The Bedouin are nomads who live in the dry lands of North Africa and the Near East. Their tents are woven from camel hair. Today some Bedouin have settled in towns.

Why build houses with reeds?

It makes sense to use the nearest building material to hand. Tall reeds grow in the marshes and wetlands of southern Iraq – so the Marsh Arabs who live there use them to build beautiful houses.

A tent can be packed up easily and moved from one place to another.

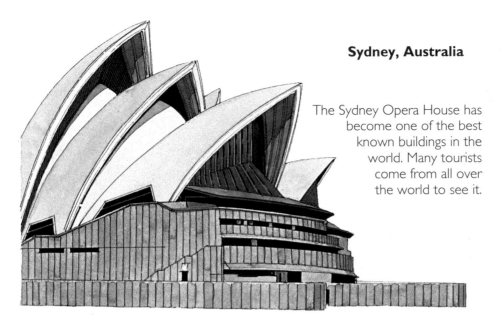

Sydney, Australia

The Sydney Opera House has become one of the best known buildings in the world. Many tourists come from all over the world to see it.

Which famous building looks like a sailing boat?
Sydney Opera House is in Australia. Its roofs rise from the blue waters of the harbour like the sails of a big yacht.

Why are landmarks useful in a city?
Each city has eye-catching buildings and monuments, which help you find your way around. Paris, in France, has the Eiffel Tower. Berlin, in Germany, has the Brandenburg Gate.

Which country has three capitals?
The most important city in a country is called the capital. South Africa has three of them! Cape Town is the home of the National Assembly. Pretoria is where the government offices are. Bloemfontein is the centre for the law.

Where are the biggest cities in the world?

IN JAPAN, WHERE BIG CITIES HAVE SPREAD AND JOINED UP TO MAKE GIANT CITIES! Japan is made up of islands that have high mountains, so most people live on the flat strips of land around the coast. In order to grow, large cities have had to stretch out like ribbons until they merge into each other. Over 27 million people live in and around the capital, Tokyo. It's still growing today. On the other side of the world, Mexico City is catching up fast.

Ancient Çatal Hüyük, Turkey

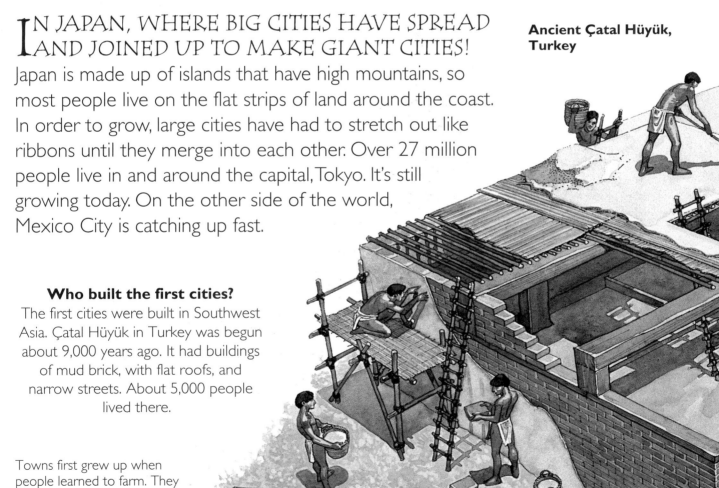

Who built the first cities?
The first cities were built in Southwest Asia. Çatal Hüyük in Turkey was begun about 9,000 years ago. It had buildings of mud brick, with flat roofs, and narrow streets. About 5,000 people lived there.

Towns first grew up when people learned to farm. They no longer had to run after herds of wild animals for their food. They could stay in one place.

What problems do cities cause?

CITIES CAN BE EXCITING PLACES TO LIVE IN. THEY ARE FULL OF HUSTLE AND BUSTLE. But they often have big problems, too. So many people in one place need a lot of looking after. They need water and electricity and proper drains, fire engines and ambulances and police cars. Too much traffic often blocks up the roads and fills the air with fumes. In some countries people pour into the cities from the countryside. They cannot find work and have to live in poor conditions.

Where is the world's tallest building?
The Petronas Towers in Kuala Lumpur, Malaysia, look like two gigantic space rockets. They soar to nearly 452 metres (1,483 ft), making up the tallest building in the world.

Which is the world's oldest capital?
Damascus, capital of Syria, has been lived in for about 4,500 years.

How does this ancient town differ from a modern one?

Cities became centres of trade, where people made pottery, baskets, food, tools and clothes.

Where is the Big Apple?
This is a nickname for New York City, in the eastern United States. Take a bite!

Who lives at the ends of the Earth?
One of the world's most northerly settlements is Ny-Alesund, in the Arctic territory of Svalbard. The southernmost is Puerto Williams in Tierra del Fuego, Chile.

Which is the highest city?
Lhasa stands 3,684 metres (12,086 ft) above sea level. It is the capital city of Tibet, a region in the Himalaya Mountains that is governed by China. Tibet is sometimes called the 'roof of the world'.

Why was London Bridge falling down?
Children today still sing a rhyme that says 'London Bridge is falling down.' It's a very old song. The ancient bridge over the River Thames was pulled down by a Viking called Olaf the Stout – nearly a thousand years ago!

Which city is named after a goddess?
Athens, the capital of Greece, shares its name with an ancient goddess called Athene. Her beautiful temple, the Parthenon, still towers over the modern city. It was built in 438BC.

How do you cross the Arctic snow?

You could always ride on a sled pulled by a team of dogs, as in the old days. But most people today ride snowmobiles, which are a bit like motorcycles with runners instead of wheels.

In Siberia, snowmobiles can use solid frozen rivers as roads during the winter months.

Crossing the Russian Arctic

Where can you catch a train into the sky?

In the Andes mountains of South America. One track in Peru climbs to 4,818 metres (15,807 ft) above sea level. In Salta, Argentina. you can catch another high-rise locomotive, known as the 'Train to the Clouds'.

Where was a hot-air balloon first flown?

The place was Paris, the capital of France, and the year was 1783. The passengers were, believe it or not, a sheep, a dog and a duck! Later, people tried out the balloon for themselves.

What is the world's longest road?

THE PAN-AMERICAN HIGHWAY. IT STARTS AT THE TOP OF THE WORLD, IN THE CHILLY AMERICAN state of Alaska. It then heads on through Canada and the USA to the steamy forests of Central America. There is still a bit missing in the middle, but the road starts up again and carries on all the way down through South America to Chile, looping round to Argentina and Brazil. The total distance ? Well over 24,000 kilometres (14,914 miles)!

Chinese junk

Where is the world's biggest airport?

Riyadh airport in Saudi Arabia is bigger than some countries. It covers 225 square kilometres (87 square miles) of the Arabian desert.

Where are boats used as buses?

In the beautiful Italian city of Venice, there are canals instead of roads. People travel from one part of the city to another by boat.

Who rides in a caravan?

No, not one pulled by a car! This kind of caravan is a group of traders who cross the desert by camel. Camels can carry people across the Sahara for six days without needing a drink of water.

Where are the longest trucks?

In the outback, the dusty back country of Australia, the roads are long and straight and pretty empty. Trucks can hitch on three or four giant trailers to form a 'road train'.

Australian road train

A road train speeds across the Nullarbor Desert in southern Australia.

Traditional wooden boats still sail along the Hong Kong waterfront.

How can you travel underneath the Alps?

THE ALPS ARE SNOWY MOUNTAINS THAT RUN ACROSS FRANCE, ITALY, Switzerland and Austria. They soar to 4,810 metres (15,800 ft) above sea level at Mont Blanc. In the days of ancient Rome a general called Hannibal tried to cross the Alps with 34 war elephants! Today, tunnels carry trains and cars through the heart of the mountains. The St Gotthard tunnel in Switzerland is the world's longest road tunnel, over 16 kilometres (10 miles) long.

Many countries still use wooden boats. Dhows sail off Arabia and East Africa, and feluccas are used on the River Nile.

What is a junk?

It is a big wooden ship, traditionally built in China. Its big sails are strengthened by strips of wood. Junks aren't as common as they used to be, but they can still be seen on the South China Sea.

African mask

This mask is worn at special ceremonies in Baluba, Africa.

Where is the capital of fashion?

Milan, London, New York and many other cities stage fantastic fashion shows each year. But Paris, in France, has been the centre of world fashion for hundreds of years.

What is batik?

This is a way of making pretty patterns on cloth. Wax is put on the fibre so that the dye sinks in only in certain places. This method was invented in Java, Indonesia.

Do people still wear national costume?

Most people in the world today wear T-shirts and jeans, skirts or suits. Only on special occasions do they still put on traditional costumes of their region. In some countries, however, people still wear their local style of dress every day.

Clothes today may be made from natural fibres such as wool, silk or cotton, or from artificial fibres such as nylon and plastic.

How do people dress in hot countries?

IN HOT COUNTRIES PEOPLE PROTECT THEIR HEADS FROM THE SUN WITH all kinds of broad-brimmed hats, from the Mexican sombrero to the cone-shaped straw hats worn by farm workers in southern China and Vietnam. They may wear robes like the Arabs, or loose fitting cotton trousers. In desert lands people may cover their heads with cloths, to keep out the sand. The Tuareg of the Sahara wrap scarves around the face until only the eyes can be seen. Their name means 'the veiled people'.

Which ladies wear tall lace hats?

The Breton people of northwest Europe are proud of their costume, which they wear for special occasions. The men wear waistcoats and big black hats. The women wear lace caps, some of which are high and shaped like chimneys.

Where do Panama hats come from?

Actually, Panama hats were first made in Ecuador, where they were plaited from the leaves of the jipijapa palm. They were first exported, or shipped abroad, from Panama, which is why they are now called Panama hats.

Today it is not always easy to tell where people come from by the clothes they wear.

How do we keep warm and dry?

SINCE PREHISTORIC TIMES, PEOPLE HAVE USED FUR AND ANIMAL SKINS TO KEEP out the cold. In the Arctic today, the Inuit people still often wear traditional clothes made from fur, sealskin or caribou (reindeer) hide. The Saami people of northern Finland also use their reindeer herds to provide leather goods. Wool, woven into textiles or pressed into felt, is used wherever the weather is cold. It is a good warm fibre, and the natural oils in it keep out the rain – that's why sheep don't shrink!

Who invented silk?

The Chinese were the first people to make silk, from the cocoons of silkworms, thousands of years ago. Today silk may be used to make beautiful Indian wraps called saris and Japanese robes called kimonos.

Where do soldiers wear skirts?

Guards of honour in the Greek army are called Evzónes. Their uniform is based on the old-fashioned costume of the mountain peoples – a white kilt, woollen leggings and a cap with a tassel.

Who are the true cloggies?

A hundred years ago wooden shoes, or clogs, were worn in many parts of Europe. The most famous clogs were the Dutch ones, which are still often worn today by farmers and market traders in the Netherlands.

Who wears feathers to a singsing?

A singsing is a big festival, Papua New Guinea style. Men paint their faces and wear ornaments of bone and shell and bird-of-paradise feathers. Traditional dress may include skirts made of leaves and grass.

Who are the Gauchos?

The cowboys of the Pampas, which are the grasslands of Argentina. Once the Gauchos were famous for their wild way of life. Today they still round up the the cattle on big ranches called estancias.

Where are the world's biggest ranches?

The world's biggest sheep and cattle stations are in the Australian outback. The best way to cross these lands is in a light aircraft.

How can barren deserts be turned green?

Water can be piped into desert areas so that crops will grow there. But this irrigation can be very expensive and the water can also wash salts from the soil, making it difficult to grow plants.

Where do farmers grow coconuts?

Coconut fruits are big and green – the bit we buy in shops is just the brown seed inside. The white flesh inside the nut may be dried and sold as copra. Coconut palms grow best on the shores of the Indian and Pacific Oceans.

Which were the first all-American crops?

Six hundred years ago, nobody in Europe had ever seen potatoes, maize or tomatoes. These important food crops were first developed by the peoples who lived in the Americas before European settlers arrived there.

What grows best in floods and soggy wet mud?

RICE KEEPS THE WORLD ALIVE. BILLIONS OF PEOPLE EAT IT EVERY DAY, ESPECIALLY in Asia. Grains of rice are the seeds of a kind of grass that grows wild in wet river valleys. To cultivate it, farmers plant out the seedlings in flooded fields called paddies. In hilly lands, terraces are cut in the hillsides and the water flows down channels in the muddy soil.

Terraced rice fields

Some rice terraces, like these in the Philippines, are thousands of years old.

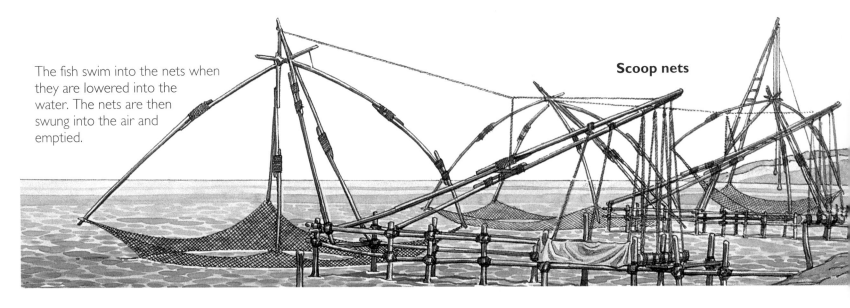

The fish swim into the nets when they are lowered into the water. The nets are then swung into the air and emptied.

Scoop nets

What is a cash crop?

It is any crop that is sold for money. Many small farmers around the world can only grow enough food to feed themselves and their families, without having any to spare.

Where do fishermen use hoops and scoops?

Giant fishing nets like these can be lowered from the shore into lakes and seas. They are often used in China and India.

Are there enough fish in the sea?

Modern boats catch so many fish that in many places fish have become scarce. Some of the richest fishing grounds were off Newfoundland, in the North Atlantic Ocean. Fishing there has now been banned until the numbers recover.

Combine harvester

Basic foods such as wheat (above) and rice are called staple crops.

What is the sweetest crop of all?

Sugar cane is grown on many islands in the Caribbean region. In Barbados, the end of the cane harvest is marked by Cropover, a grand celebration with music, dancing and parades.

Modern types of rice can produce several harvests a year. They can be planted by machines, but these are too expensive for many farmers.

Where are the world's bread baskets?

IMPORTANT WHEAT-PRODUCING AREAS OF THE WORLD ARE CALLED 'BREAD BASKETS' because they provide us with the bread we eat each day. Wheat is a kind of grass, and so it grows best in areas which were once natural grasslands. These include the prairies of Canada and the United States and the steppes of Ukraine and southern Russia. Huge combine harvesters move across the prairies for days and weeks on end, cutting the wheat and separating out the grain.

How do we keep food fresh?

TODAY, BUTTER CAN BE SENT TO EUROPE ALL THE WAY FROM NEW ZEALAND – kept cool by refrigeration. The first ever refrigerator ship was invented in 1877 to carry beef from Argentina. But how did people keep food fresh before that? The old methods were simpler – pickling, smoking or drying. The Native Americans dried meat in the sun and mixed it with fruit to make pemmican for their travels. Traditional methods are still used today to produce some of the world's tastiest foods – Indian pickles and chutneys, Irish smoked salmon, or Italian sun-dried tomatoes.

How much seaweed can you eat?
Various seaweeds are eaten in Japan, and in South Wales seaweed makes up a dish called laverbread. A seaweed called carrageen moss is often used to thicken ice cream and milk puddings. Seaweed is also found in toothpaste!

How do you eat with chopsticks?
Chopsticks are popular in China and Japan. Hold one stick between the thumb and the bottom of the first two fingers. Hold the other stick further along the first two fingers and support it with the third. It's easy!

The food people eat depends not just on the crops they can grow, the animals they can raise or the fish they can catch, but also on their traditional customs and religious beliefs.

Who invented noodles?
Which noodles came first – Italian spaghetti or Chinese chow mein? Some people say that the traveller Marco Polo brought the secret of noodle-making back to Italy from China in the Middle Ages. No! say others – the Romans were making pasta in Italy long before that. Maybe it was invented in both places.

Fresh foods from around the world

What is caviare?
One of the most expensive foods in the world. It is made of eggs from a fish called the sturgeon, which lives in lakes and rivers in Russia and other northern lands.

What is yerba maté?
It is a bitter but refreshing hot drink, made from the leaves of the Paraguay holly. It is sipped from a gourd (a kind of pumpkin shell) through a silver straw, and is very popular in Argentina.

Many southern Indian dishes are vegetarian. Some people in other parts of the world also prefer not to eat meat.

Who wrote a poem to his haggis?

Robert Burns, Scotland's greatest poet, who lived in the 1700s. The haggis is a traditional dish from Scotland. It is made up of lamb's heart, liver and lungs, suet, onions and oatmeal cooked inside – guess what – a sheep's stomach!

What is jambalaya?

Rice for a start, then prawns and peppers, all in an amazing hot spicy sauce. Where is this served up? New Orleans, in the steamy southern United States.

Where do you buy milk by the kilo?

In the Russian Arctic it is so cold in winter that milk is sold in frozen chunks rather than by the litre.

What is the most delicious food?

HAUTE CUISINE IS FRENCH, AND IT MEANS HIGH-QUALITY COOKING. People all over the world love French food. But is it really the most delicious food in the world? Chinese cooking is also thought to be a fine art. But really, which food we like or dislike is just a question of personal taste. Sheeps' eyeballs, insect grubs, snakes and pigs' ears can all be found on menus in one part of the world or another – and many people find them absolutely mouthwatering.

Preparing an African meal

African dishes are often based on cornmeal, and served with spicy vegetables, fish or meat.

Who makes the world's hottest curries?

The people of southern India. A mouthwatering recipe might include fiery spices such as red chilli pepper and fresh hot green chillies, ginger, garlic, turmeric and curry leaves.

Where were banknotes invented?
Paper money was first used in China, a thousand years ago.

More and more people around the world use plastic cards to pay for goods.

What are currencies?
A currency is a money system, such as the Japanese yen, the US dollar, the Mongolian tugrik or the Bhutan ngultrum. The exchange rate is what it costs to buy or sell one currency for another.

Plastic, a new form of money

Where is the Silk Road?
This is an ancient trading route stretching all the way from China through Central Asia to the Mediterranean Sea. Hundreds of years ago, silk, tea and spices were transported along this road to the West by camel and pony trains.

Who catches smugglers?
If you wish to take some goods from one country to another, you might have to pay a tax to the government. Customs officers may check your luggage to see that you are not sneaking in – or smuggling – illegal goods.

Who makes the most money?
The mint – that's the place where coins and banknotes are made. The United States treasury in Philadelphia produces billions of new coins each year.

Why sell stamps on Pitcairn?
Only 50 or so people live on remote Pitcairn Island, in the Pacific Ocean. So why do the islanders print so many postage stamps? Well, they sell them to stamp collectors and this make them a lot of money.

Where do people do business?

IN NIGERIA, MONEY CHANGES HANDS EVERY DAY IN THE BUSY TOWN MARKET.
Laid out on the ground are batteries, watches, embroidered hats, peanuts, yams and cans of fish. The customers haggle with the women selling the goods, arguing about the price. In England trading might take in a big supermarket, packed with Saturday morning shoppers. In Switzerland bankers watch their computer screens to check their profits. In the New York stock exchange, traders grab their telephones as they buy and sell shares in companies. It's all in a day's work.

Where do you buy your food? At a city store or in a traditional street market?

All kinds of objects have been used as money

What can people use as money?

TODAY EVERY COUNTRY IN THE WORLD USES COINS AND PAPER BANK NOTES, although goods may still be swapped rather than bought in many regions. Over the ages all kinds of other things have been used as money around the world – shells, large stones, beads, salt, tobacco, blocks of tea, sharks' teeth or cocoa beans. These had no value in themselves, but then neither do the metal, paper or plastic we use today. They are just tokens of exchange.

Where in the world are there floating markets?

In Thailand and other parts of Southeast Asia, traders often sell vegetables, fruit, flowers and spices from small boats called sampans, which are moored along river banks and jetties.

Street market, India

An Indian trader waits for customers to buy her fresh produce. Among her wares are okra, tomatoes, beans, cauliflower, mooli, peppers and lemons.

What are the five 'K's'?
Sikh men honour five religious traditions. Kesh is uncut hair, worn in a turban. They carry a Kangha, or comb, a Kkara or metal bangle, and a Kirpan or dagger. They wear an under-garment called a Kaccha.

Which city is holy to three faiths?
Jerusalem is a holy place for Jews, Moslems and Christians. Sacred sites include the Western Wall, the Dome of the Rock and the Church of the Holy Sepulchre.

Stained glass window
This round window – called a rose window – in Lincoln Cathedral, England, is made of beautiful stained glass.

Where do young boys become monks?
In Myanmar a four year-old boy learns about the life of Buddha at a special ceremony. He is dressed as a rich prince and is then made to wear the simple robes of a Buddhist monk.

Where do pilgrims go?

PILGRIMS ARE RELIGIOUS PEOPLE WHO TRAVEL TO HOLY PLACES AND SHRINES around the world. Moslems try to travel to the sacred city of Mecca, in Saudi Arabia, at least once in their lifetime. Hindus may travel to the city of Varanasi, in India, to wash in the holy waters of the River Ganges. Christians travel to Bethlehem, the birthplace of Jesus Christ, or to the great cathedrals built in Europe during the Middle Ages, such as Santiago de Compostela in Spain.

What is Diwali?
This is the time in the autumn when Hindus celebrate their new year and honour Lakshmi, goddess of good fortune. Candles are lit in windows and people give each other cards and presents.

The lamps of Diwali

Lighted candles mark the feast of Diwali. The Hindu religion grew up in India many thousands of years ago.

Why do people fast?

IN MANY RELIGIONS PEOPLE FAST, OR GO WITHOUT FOOD, AS PART OF THEIR WORSHIP. If you visit a Moslem city sich as Cairo or Algiers during Ramadan, the ninth month of the Islamic year, you will find that no food is served during daylight hours. Many Christians also give up eating certain foods during Lent, the days leading up to Holy Week, when they think about the death of Jesus. In Spain, during Holy Week, Christians carry crosses and religious statues in street processions.

Why is Mount Athos important?
This rocky headland in northern Greece is holy to Christians of the Eastern Orthodox faith. Monks have worshipped here since the Middle Ages. They wear beards, tall black hats and robes.

Which country has the most Moslems?
Indonesia is the largest Islamic country in the world, although some parts of it, such as the island of Bali, are mostly Hindu.

Moslem prayers
Moslems pray to God (Allah) five times a day. The most important worship is at noon on Friday.

What is the Tao?
It is said 'dow' and it means 'the way'. It is the name given to the beliefs of the Chinese thinker Lao Zi, who lived about 2,600 years ago. Taoists believe in the harmony of the universe.

Who was Confucius?
This is the English name given to the Chinese thinker Kong Fuzi, who lived at the same time as Lao Zi. His beliefs in an ordered society and respect for ancestors became very popular in China.

What is Shinto?
This is the ancient religion of Japan. At its holy shrines people pray for happiness and to honour their ancestors. Many Japanese people also follow Buddhist beliefs.

What is Hanukkah?
This Jewish festival of light lasts eight days. Families light a new candle each day on a special candlestick called a menorah. Hanukkah celebrates the recapture of the temple in Jerusalem in ancient times.

Which priests cover their mouths?
Some priests of the Jain religion, in India, wear masks over their mouths. This is because they respect all living things and do not wish to harm or swallow even the tiniest insect that might fly into their mouths.

What are Parsis?
The Parsi religion began long ago in ancient Persia, now Iran. Many of its followers fled to India over 1,000 years ago and are now found in many countries around the world.

Light and fire are important symbols of the holy spirit in many religions.

Aboriginal art, Australia

Like dance and theatre, art often has its origins in religious and magical rituals.

Who paints pictures of the dreamtime?

Australia's Aborigines look back to the dreamtime, a magical age when the world was being formed, along with its animals and peoples. They paint wonderful pictures of it.

Where do they dance like the gods?

Kathakali is a kind of dance drama performed in Kerala, southern India. Dancers in masks and gorgeous costumes act out ancient tales of gods and demons.

Why do people love to dance?

DANCING IS A VERY DRAMATIC WAY OF EXPRESSING FEELINGS OF EVERY KIND.
In Spain, passionate flamenco dancers stamp and click their fingers to guitar music. In England, morris dancers happily jingle bells tied to their legs and wave sticks. In Africa there are important dances for growing up and for funerals. The first dances of all were probably designed to bring good fortune to prehistoric hunters, where a priest put on the skins and horns of the animal his people wanted to kill.

Who sings in Beijing?

Beijing opera is quite a performance! Musicians bang cymbals together and actors sing in high voices. They take the part of heroes and villains in ancient Chinese tales. Their faces are painted and they wear beautiful costumes with long pheasant feathers.

Where is the world's biggest art gallery?

At St Petersburg in Russia. It is made up of two great buildings, the Hermitage and the Winter Palace, and these hold millions of exhibits.

Mbuti dancers

Young Mbuti people from Zaire decorate their bodies with white make-up for a dance to celebrate the beginning of adulthood.

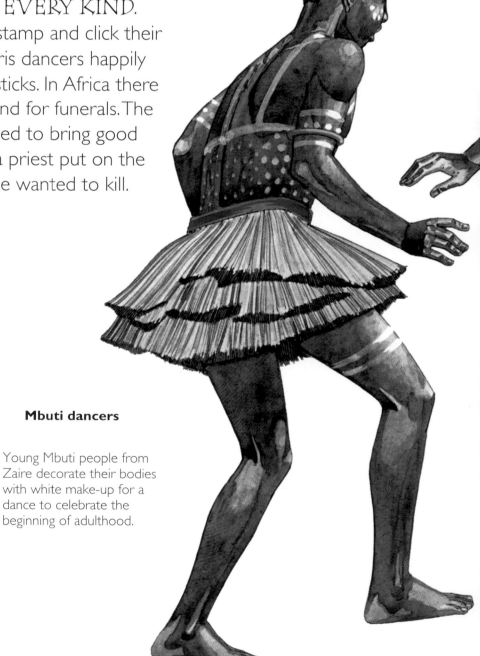

Where do drums talk?

The tama is nicknamed the 'talking drum'. Its tightness can be varied while it is being played, to make a strange throbbing sound. It is played in Senegal and the Gambia, in Africa.

Where is the world's very oldest theatre?

THE OLDEST THEATRE STILL IN USE TODAY IS CALLED THE TEATRO OLIMPICO and it is at Vicenza, in Italy. It opened over 400 years ago. But people were going to see plays long, long before that. In ancient Greece people went to see masked actors appear in some of the funniest and saddest plays ever written, at open-air theatres made of stone. These can still be seen today all over Greece.

What is kabuki?
Kabuki is an exciting type of drama that became popular in Japan in the 1600s and may still be seen today. The actors wear splendid make-up and costumes.

Kabuki – Japanese theatre

In kabuki, all the parts are played by male actors, some dressed up as beautiful women.

Who dances a hakka?
In New Zealand young Maori people have kept alive many of their traditional dances. The hakka was a dance for warriors, to bring them strength to face the battles ahead.

Who plays the 'pans'?
People in the Caribbean, at carnival time. The 'pans' are the steel drums, which can produce beautiful dance rhythms and melodies.

Where is Stratford?
Well, there are two Stratfords. Four hundred years ago, Stratford-upon-Avon, in England, was the home of one of the most famous playwrights who ever lived, William Shakespeare. The other Stratford in Ontario, Canada, holds a drama festival every year in his honour.

Who makes pictures from sand?
The Navaho people of the southwestern United States make beautiful patterns using many different coloured sands.

Fireworks were invented long ago in China.

What is a pow-wow?
It means 'get-together' in Algonkian. The Native American peoples of the United States and the First Nations of Canada meet up at pow-wows each year to celebrate their traditions with dance and music.

Where is the bun festival?
On the Chinese island of Cheung Chau, near Hong Kong, there is a big festival each May, with parades and religious ceremonies. During the celebrations people climb up huge towers made of buns.

What is carnival?

IN ANCIENT ROME THERE WAS A ROWDY WINTER FESTIVAL CALLED SATURNALIA. People copied this idea in the Middle Ages. They feasted and had fun before the dark, cold days of Lent began, when Christians had to give up eating meat. People still celebrate carnival today. In Germany there are wild parties and in Venice, Italy, people wear elegant masks and cloaks. In New Orleans, in the United States, jazz bands parade in the streets. In Trinidad and in Rio de Janeiro, Brazil, people dance wearing sparkling fancy dress and let off spectacular fireworks.

Who rides to the Feria?
Each April the people of Seville, in Spain, ride on horseback to a grand fair on the banks of the River Guadalquivir. They wear traditional finery and dance all night.

Who gets to sit in the leader's chair?
In Turkey, 23 April is Children's Day. A child even gets the chance to sit at the desk of the country's prime minister! There are puppet shows, dances and a kite-flying competition.

Dragon dance

At the Chinese New Year people parade through the streets wearing the skin of a mighty dragon.

Where do dragons dance?

WHEREVER CHINESE PEOPLE GET TOGETHER TO CELEBRATE their New Year or Spring Festival. The lucky dragon weaves in and out of the streets, held up by the people crouching underneath its long body. Firecrackers go bang, to scare away evil spirits. The festival is a chance for families to get together, give each other presents and wish each other good fortune for the year ahead.

The festival of Holi

Hindu children throw coloured powder over each other at the spring festival.

Who wears green on St Patrick's Day?

St Patrick's Day, on 17 March, is the national day of Ireland. It is celebrated wherever Irish people have settled over the ages, from the United States to Australia. People wear green clothes or put green shamrock leaves in their buttonholes.

Who remembers the fifth of November?

People in Great Britain. The date recalls the capture of Guy Fawkes, who plotted to blow up the Houses of Parliament in London nearly 400 years ago. The night is marked by blazing bonfires, fireworks and home-made toffee.

Where is New Year's Day always wet?

In Myanmar people celebrate the Buddhist New Year by splashing and spraying water over their friends!

History

This tent is made with the skin and bones of the woolly mammoth.

Who walked to America?

THE FIRST AMERICANS! FOR MILLIONS OF YEARS, NORTH AND SOUTH AMERICA were cut off from the world by deep, stormy oceans. No one lived there. Then, during the last Ice Age, the oceans froze and parts of the sea-bed were uncovered. A 'land-bridge' of dry sea-bed linked America and Northeast Asia. Many wild animals lived on the land-bridge, so groups of hunters roamed across it in search of food. Eventually, they reached America, and settled there. Historians are not sure exactly when this happened, but it was probably about 18,000 years ago.

Who lived in huts made of bones?
Groups of nomads who lived on the plains of Eastern Europe about 15,000 years ago. They hunted woolly mammoths, ate the meat, and made shelters from the skin and bones.

Did people live in caves?
Yes, but not all the time. Nomad hunters built temporary shelters in cave entrances and used inner caves as stores. On hunting expeditions they camped in shelters made of branches, brushwood, dry grass and bracken.

What were the first houses like?
Small, single-storey and made of sun-dried mud. They were built in Middle Eastern lands around 11,000 years ago. The first villages were built close to streams and ponds, to ensure a steady water supply.

When did people start to live in towns?
Jericho in Jordan (built around 10,000 years ago) and Çatal Hüyük in Turkey (built around 8,000 years ago) are the world's first big towns. They were centres of trade and craftwork, and were surrounded by strong walls.

What did prehistoric people wear?
In cold countries, they wore leggings and tunics made from furs and skins, sewn together using bone needles and sinews for thread. In hot countries, they wore skin loincloths – or nothing at all!

Hungry nomads set out from Siberia on the long trek to America.

**Ape:
Australopithecus**

This early human ancestor lived about 3 million years ago.

**Hominid:
Homo habilis**

The first toolmaker lived about 2 million years ago.

Human: Homo sapiens sapiens

Modern men and women first developed around 200,000 years ago.

How do we know about apes who lived millions of years ago?

From fossil remains. Fossils are made when chemicals in the soil soak into dead bodies and turn the bones to stone. After many years, the soil turns into rock with fossils hidden inside.

Where were the first farms?

In the Middle East. About 11,000 years ago, people there noticed that wild grains they had accidentally scattered on the ground sprouted and grew into plants. So they cleared plots of land, scattered more grain, and harvested it when it was ripe.

How did modern humans develop?

OUR DISTANT ANCESTORS ARE A GROUP OF ANIMALS KNOWN AS PRIMATES.
Primates first appeared on earth about 50 million years ago, and looked rather like squirrels. Over millions of years they changed and grew, as the environment changed around them and they learned new skills to adapt to it. Slowly, they developed into apes, then into hominids (almost-humans), then into modern human beings.

The first Americans

Who were the Neanderthals?

A type of human who lived in Europe and Asia from around 200,000 to 35,000 years ago. Neanderthals were short and stocky with low, ridged brows. They died out – no one knows why – and were replaced by modern humans, who originated in Africa.

When did people start to read and write?

About 6,000 years ago. The Sumerians (who lived in present-day Iraq) were the first people to invent writing. They used little picture-symbols scratched on to tablets of soft clay. Only specially trained scribes could read them.

What did the first Americans carry with them?

Everything they needed to survive – spears and nets for hunting; seeds, berries and dried meat to eat; furs to use as cloaks or blankets, and skin coverings for tents.

69

Where are the pyramids?

In Egypt, in North Africa. They stand on the west bank of the River Nile. The Egyptians believed this was the land of the dead, because the Sun set there. They built their homes on the east bank of the river – the land of sunrise and living things.

How old are the pyramids?

The first true pyramid was built around 2575 BC. Before then, people were buried under flat-topped mounds, called 'mastabas', and in pyramids with stepped sides. The last pyramid was built around 1570 BC.

What were Egyptian houses like?

Small and simple, with flat roofs that served as extra rooms and courtyards where people worked. Rich people's homes were large and richly decorated, with fine furniture, gardens and pools.

How was a pyramid built?

By man-power! Thousands of labourers worked in the hot sun to clear the site, lay the foundations, drag building stone from the quarry, and lift it into place. Most of the labourers were ordinary farmers, who worked as builders to pay their taxes. Expert craftsmen cut the building stone into blocks and fitted them carefully together.

What are the pyramids made of?

Of hard, smooth limestone. Top quality stone was used for the outer casing; poor quality stone and rubble were used for the inner core.

Why were the pyramids built?

THE PYRAMIDS ARE HUGE MONUMENTAL TOMBS FOR PHARAOHS AND NOBILITY. The Egyptians believed that dead people's spirits could live on after death if their bodies were carefully preserved. It was specially important to preserve the bodies of dead pharaohs (Egyptian kings) and other nobles. Their spirits would help the kingdom of Egypt to survive. So they made dead bodies into mummies, and buried them in these splendid tombs along with clothes, jewels and models of everything they would need in life after death.

A pyramid's shape was important. It represented the rays of the Sun. The Egyptians believed that dead pharaohs were carried to heaven by the Sun's rays.

Were all corpses mummified?

Egyptian coffin

NO, BECAUSE MAKING A MUMMY WAS A COMPLICATED AND EXPENSIVE PROCESS.
First, soft, internal organs like the stomach, lungs and brain were removed, then the body was packed in natron (soda) for 40 days to dry out. Finally, it was wrapped in resin-soaked linen bandages, and placed in a beautifully decorated coffin. Most ordinary people were buried in simple coffins made of reeds, or sometimes just in shallow graves in the desert.

Carved scarab

Why did Egyptian people carry carved stone scarabs?
Scarabs (dung-beetles) collected animal dung and rolled it into little balls. To the Egyptians, these dung balls looked like the life-giving Sun, so they hoped that scarabs would bring them long life.

How many different boats might you see on the Nile?
Rafts made from papyrus reed, flat-bottomed punts, big, heavy cargo boats, splendid royal barges, and funeral boats carrying bodies across the river to pyramid tombs.

Why was the River Nile so important?
Because Egypt got hardly any rain. But every year the Nile flooded the fields along its banks, bringing fresh water and rich black silt, which helped crops grow. Farmers dug irrigation channels to carry water to distant fields.

The beautifully painted coffin protects the fragile mummy inside. Often, coffins were decorated with portraits of the dead person they contained.

Did the Greeks invent money?

No. The first coins were made in Lydia (part of present-day Turkey) around 600 BC. But the Greeks soon copied the Lydians and made coins of their own.

The owl was the symbol of the city of Athens.

Greek coins

What were the original Olympic sports?

At first, running was the only sport. Later, boxing, wrestling, chariot races, horse races and pentathlon (running, wrestling, long-jump, discus and javelin) were added.
There were also music, poetry and drama competitions.

What were Greek coins made of?

Silver and gold. They were decorated with symbols of the cities where they were made, or with portraits of heroes and gods.

Could women take part in the Olympic Games?

No. Women were banned from the whole site during the games. But once every four years, there were special games for women only. They were held in honour of Hera, wife of the god Zeus.

Did the Greeks go to war?

Yes. In 490 BC and 479 BC, the Greeks defeated Persian invaders, on land and at sea. From 431 BC to 362 BC, there were many civil wars. In 338 BC, Greece was conquered by the Macedonians, and Greek power ended.

Were there games in other Greek cities?

Yes. There were over 200 different sports festivals in Greece and the lands round the Mediterranean Sea.

Why did the Greeks build so many temples?

BECAUSE THEY WORSHIPPED SO MANY DIFFERENT GODDESSES AND GODS!
The Greeks believed each god and goddess needed a home where their spirit could live. So they built splendid temples to house them, with beautiful statues inside. Each god and goddess had special powers, which visitors to the temple prayed for. Zeus was the god of the sky, Ares the god of war, and Aphrodite the goddess of love.

The Parthenon, Athens

The Parthenon (built 447–438 BC) was one of the finest temples in Ancient Greece.

Why did Greek temples have so many columns?

Because their design was copied from ancient Greek royal palaces, which had lots of wooden pillars to hold up the roof.

The original Olympic Games

Who were the Barbarians?
Foreigners – people who did not speak Greek. The Greeks thought their words sounded like 'baa, baa'.

What took place outside temples?
Sacrifices. Animals and birds were killed and burnt on altars outside temples as offerings to the gods. People also made offerings of wine, called 'libations'.

What were Greek warships like?

LONG, NARROW AND FAST. THEY HAD A SHARP BATTERING RAM AT THE PROW, and were powered by 170 oarsmen and huge square linen sails. Sea battles were fought by ships smashing into one another, or by sailing close enough for men to jump across and fight on deck with swords and spears.

The Parthenon was dedicated to the goddess Athene.

After a sacrifice, priests gave portions of roasted meat from the altar to worshippers. They left the fat and bones for the gods!

73

Who wanted to rule the world?

ABOUT 400 BC THE ROMANS SET OUT TO CONQUER THEIR ITALIAN NEIGHBOURS. By 272 BC they controlled all of Italy – but they didn't stop there! After defeating their rivals in Carthage (Northwest Africa), they invaded lands all around the Mediterranean Sea. In 31 BC they conquered the ancient kingdom of Egypt. They invaded Britain in 55–54 BC. By AD 117, in Emperor Trajan's reign, the mighty Roman Empire stretched from Scotland to Syria and to Iraq.

Who joined the Roman army?

Young men from all over the empire. Recruits had to be fit, tall and strong, aged under 25, and (preferably) able to read and write. Roman citizens became legionary (regular) soldiers. Men from other nations enrolled as auxiliary (helper) troops.

What did Roman soldiers wear?

A uniform designed to keep them safe and warm: armour made of metal strips over a wool or linen tunic, tough leather sandals, a thick cloak, a padded leather helmet, and short trousers or woollen underpants.

How long did Roman soldiers serve?

For about 25 years. After that, they retired. They were given a lump sum of money, or a pension, and a certificate recording their service.

Who attacked Rome with elephants?

General Hannibal, leader of the Carthaginians, who lived in North Africa. In 218 BC he led a large army, including war-elephants, through Spain and across the Alps to attack Rome.

Roman centurion

Centurions were senior army officers. They dressed for parade in a beautifully decorated metal breastplate and a helmet topped with a crest of horsehair.

Why did the Romans spend so long in the bath?

Because Roman baths were great places to relax and meet your friends. Most big towns had public bath-houses, with steam baths, hot and cold swimming pools, sports facilities and well trained slaves giving massages and beauty treatments.

How else did the Romans relax?

By eating and drinking in taverns, gambling, going to the theatre, and watching chariot races and gladiator fights.

Romans rubbed oil on to their skin, then scraped the oil and the dirt off with metal strigils (scrapers) before getting into the bath.

Olive oil jar and strigils

Did the Romans have central heating?

Yes. They invented a system called the 'hypocaust'. Hot air, heated by a wood-burning furnace, was circulated through brick-lined pipes underneath the floor.

Were the Romans expert engineers?

Yes – among the best in the world! They built roads, bridges, aqueducts (raised channels to carry water), long networks of drains and sewers, and the first-ever blocks of flats.

Where did Roman soldiers live?

In goatskin tents, while on the march, or in big barrack blocks inside strongly built forts. Groups of eight ordinary soldiers shared a single room, fitted with bunk beds. Centurions (officers) had a room of their own.

How long did Roman power last?

The Romans first became powerful around 200 BC. By 100 AD, they ruled a very large empire. Roman power collapsed after the city of Rome was attacked by warlike tribesmen from Asia around 500–400 BC.

Why did Hadrian build a wall?

To MARK THE FRONTIERS OF THE ROMAN EMPIRE AND GUARD THEM FROM ATTACK. Roman emperor Hadrian (ruled AD 117–138) made many visits to frontier provinces, such as England, to inspect the defences and to encourage the Roman troops stationed there. The Roman Empire reached its greatest size during his reign.

Hadrian's Wall in the north of England is 120 km (75 miles) long. Roman soldiers patrolled the wall, looking out for Celtic raiders. The Celts wore checked trousers, or went into battle naked, after painting their bodies blue.

Hadrian's Wall

When were the Vikings powerful?

Viking raiders first sailed south to attack the rest of Europe around AD 800. They continued raiding until around AD 1100.

Viking brooch

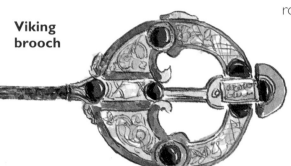

What were Viking ships made of?

Narrow, flexible strips of wood, fixed to a solid wooden backbone called a keel. Viking warships were long and narrow, and could sail very fast. They were powered by men rowing, or by the wind trapped in big square sails.

Where were the Viking homelands?

The countries we call Scandinavia today – Norway, Sweden and Denmark. The word Viking comes from the old Scandinavian word vik, which means a narrow bay beside the sea. That's where the Vikings lurked, ready to set off on raids.

What did the Vikings seize on their raids?

All kinds of treasure. Churches were a favourite target for attack, because they were full of gold crosses and holy books covered with jewels. The Vikings also attacked farms and villages, and kidnapped the people to sell as slaves.

Who were the raiders from the sea?

Viking raiders

VIKINGS! BOLD, BRAVE, BLOODTHIRSTY WARRIORS WHO TERRORIZED ALL THE PEOPLE OF EUROPE. The Vikings made raids from Scotland to Italy, killing, burning and carrying away all they could. It was hard to make a living in the cold Viking homelands, so Viking men sailed off to seek adventure, hoping to get rich by raiding wealthier lands. However, not all Vikings were raiders. Many were peaceful hunters and farmers, who spent most of their lives at home.

Were the Vikings good sailors?

Yes. They sailed for thousands of miles across the icy northern oceans in small wooden boats that were completely open to the elements. They learned how to navigate by observing shoals of fish, birds in flight, sea currents, waves and stars.

Did the Vikings reach America?

Yes, around 1000 AD. A bold adventurer named Leif Ericsson sailed westwards from Greenland until he reached 'Vinland' (present-day Newfoundland). He built a farmstead there, but quarrelled with the local people, and decided to return home.

Why did the Vikings comb their beards?

Viking comb

The handle of this Viking comb is made from an elk antler.

BECAUSE THEY WANTED TO LOOK GOOD ENOUGH TO ATTRACT GIRLFRIENDS! At home, all Viking people liked to look good and keep clean. They combed their hair and took sauna baths in steam produced by pouring water over red-hot stones. Viking men and women proudly wore the best clothes they could afford. Both sexes liked to wear fine jewellery and eye make-up and painted their cheeks a glowing red.

Who led the Vikings on their raids?
Usually, the most powerful people in Viking society: kings, earls and thegns (landowners). But sometimes, Viking raiders were led by wild law-breakers, who had been expelled from their local community for fighting and causing trouble.

Who helped Viking raiders and settlers?
The Vikings prayed to many different gods. Thor sent thunder and protected craftsmen. Woden was the god of wisdom and war. Kindly goddess Freya gave peace and fruitful crops.

Viking raiders leap from their longboats and rush up the beach to make a surprise attack.

Who were the Incas?
A people who lived high in the Andes mountains of South America (part of present-day Peru). They ruled a mighty empire from AD 1438 to 1532.

How did the Incas keep records of past events?
On bundles of knotted string, called quipus. The pattern of knots formed a secret code, which no one knows how to read today.

What was the Golden Garden?
A courtyard next to the Great Temple in the Incas' capital city of Cuzco. It contained lifesize models of animals and plants, made of real silver and gold. They were offerings to the gods.

Inca gold

Incas gave gold offerings – like this model of a llama – to their gods.

Why were llamas so important?
Because they could survive in the Incas' mountain homeland, over 3,000 metres (10,000 ft) above sea level. It was cold and windy there, and few plants grew. The Incas wove clothes and blankets from llamas' soft, warm fleece, and used llamas to carry heavy loads up steep mountain paths.

Who spat into their beer?
Inca women. They made a special beer, called chicha, by chewing maize to a pulp, spitting it out into big jars, mixing it with water and leaving it to ferment.

Who was the 'Son of the Sun'?
The Inca ruler – a king who was worshipped and feared. The Inca people believed he was descended from Inti, the Sun god. The greatest Inca leader was Pachachuti Yupanqui (ruled 1438–1471), who conquered many neighbouring lands.

Who climbed up stairways to gaze at the stars?

This tall tower was built around 600 AD on top of the splendid Mayan royal palace at Palenque. Scribes and priests climbed to the top, to study the stars.

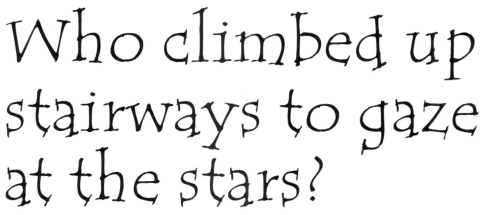

PRIESTS AND SCRIBES BELONGING TO THE MAYA CIVILIZATION, which was powerful in Central America between around 200 and 900 AD. They built huge, step-sided pyramids, with temples and observatories on top. The Mayans were expert astronomers and mathematicians. They worked out very accurate calendars, and invented a system of numbers using just three symbols – shells, bars and dots.

What was a huaca?

An Inca holy place. Inca people believed that powerful spirits lived in huacas in mountains, rivers and caves. They left offerings there, to bring good luck. Rich nobles left food or clothes. Poor people left blades of grass, drops of water – or just an eyelash.

Who wrote in pictures?

Mayan and Aztec scribes. The Mayans invented the first writing in America, using a system of picture symbols called glyphs. Mayans and Aztecs both wrote in zig-zag folding books, called codexes, using paper made from fig-tree bark.

Who were the Aztecs?

The Aztecs were wandering hunters who arrived in Mexico around AD 1200. They fought against the people already living there, built a huge city on an island in a marshy lake, and soon grew rich and strong.

Who invented chocolate?

Aztec cooks. They made a sweet, frothy chocolate drink from ground-up cocoa beans and honey, flavoured with spices. We still use a version of the Aztec name for this drink – 'chocolatl' – today.

Who was the great Feathered Serpent?

An important Aztec god – his real name was Quetzalcoatl. The Aztecs believed that one day, he would visit their homeland and bring the world to an end. Quetzalcoatl was portrayed in many Aztec drawings and sculptures. He was worshipped and feared by many other South American peoples, too.

Feathered god

Quetzalcoatl drawn by an Aztec scribe.

How did the Mayas, Aztecs and Incas lose their power?

They were conquered by soldiers from Spain, who arrived in America in the early 16th century, looking for treasure – especially gold.

Mayan palace, Palenque

Who fought the Flowery Wars?

FIERCE AZTEC SOLDIERS, ARMED WITH BOWS AND ARROWS, KNIVES AND CLUBS. During the 15th and early 16th centuries, they fought against other tribes who lived in Mexico, in battles called the Flowery Wars. The Aztecs believed that the blood of their enemies fertilized the land and enabled flowers and crops to grow. They sacrificed prisoners of war and offered their hearts to the gods.

What were Mayan palaces made of?

Great slabs of stone, or sun-dried mud brick, covered with a layer of plaster, then decorated with pictures of gods and kings. Mayan temples were built in the same way, but were painted bright red.

The massive stairway leads to the royal apartments, its doorways flanked by carvings of gods and kings.

Who lived in a circular city?

THE CITIZENS OF BAGHDAD, FOUNDED IN 762 AD BY RULER CALIPH AL-MANSUR, the most powerful Muslim of his time. He employed the best builders and architects to create a huge circular city, surrounded by strong walls. His royal palace was at the centre of the circle, with government offices and army barracks nearby. There were mosques, hospitals, schools, libraries, markets, fountains and gardens. Craftworkers and all kinds of traders lived on the outer rim of the city. Poor people and farmworkers lived outside the walls. Today the modernized city of Baghdad is the capital of Iraq.

What were the Crusades?
A series of wars fought between Christian and Muslim soldiers for control of the area around Jerusalem (in present-day Israel), which was holy to Muslims, Christians and Jews. The Crusades began in 1096, when a Christian army attacked. They ended in 1291 when Muslim soldiers forced the Christians to leave.

Crossing the desert

Muslim merchants led camel trains laden with valuable goods across the deserts of Arabia. They carried frankincense (a perfumed gum from an Arabian tree), pearls and fine glassware.

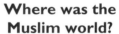

Samarra's spiral tower

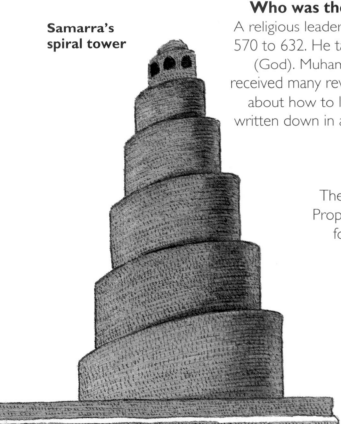

Who was the Prophet Muhammad?
A religious leader who lived in Arabia from AD 570 to 632. He taught people to worship Allah (God). Muhammad reported that he had received many revelations (messages) from God about how to lead a good life. These were written down in a holy book called the Qur'an.

What is Islam?
The religious faith taught by the Prophet Muhammad. People who follow the faith of Islam are called Muslims.

Who were the Mongols?
Tribes of nomads who roamed over the vast plains of Central Asia, tending their horses, sheep and goats. They lived in felt tents, called yurts.

Where was the Muslim world?
From around 700 to 1200 AD the Muslim world included southern Spain, North Africa, Northwest India, Central Asia and almost all the Middle East. It was ruled by Muslim princes and governed by Muslim laws. The scientists and scholars of the Muslim world wrote books in Arabic, and all across this vast area the ordinary people shared many traditions and beliefs.

Loose robes keep people cool in the desert heat and turbans and scarves protect against windborne sand.

Where is this spiral tower?
At Samarra, in present-day Iraq. It is a part of a mosque (place of worship) built for the caliphs of Baghdad around 848 AD. Five times a day, a muezzin (caller) climbed to the top of the tower to summon Muslim people to prayer.

When did the Mongols attack?
In AD 1206, all the separate Mongol tribes united under a warlike leader, called Temujin. He took the title Genghis Khan (supreme ruler) and set out to conquer the world. His armies destroyed Baghdad in 1258. By 1279, they controlled a vast empire, stretching from China to eastern Europe.

Where did Muslim traders sail?
All round the Mediterranean, down the east coast of Africa, across the Indian Ocean and on to Indonesia and the lands nearby. They traded Middle Eastern silver, glass and perfumes for cloth, slaves, herbs and spices.

Who invented astrolabes?
Muslim scientists who lived and worked in the Middle East, round about 800 AD. Astrolabes were scientific instruments that helped sailors find their position when they were out of sight of land. They worked by measuring the height of the sun above the horizon.

Astrolabe

What were ships of the desert?

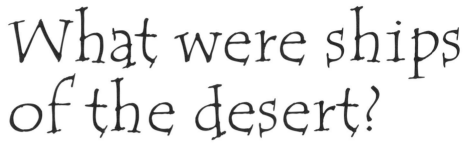

CAMELS BELONGING TO TRAVELLING MERCHANTS WHO LIVED IN ARABIA. They were the only animals that could survive long enough without food and water to make exhausting journeys across the hot, dry desert, laden with valuable goods to sell. They stored enough nourishment in their humps to last for ten days. Camels were smelly and bad-tempered, but they were highly prized.

Which rulers claimed descent from the Sun goddess?

The emperors of Japan. The first Japanese emperor lived around 660 BC; his descendants ruled until AD 1192. After that, army generals, called shoguns, ran the government, leaving the emperors with only religious and ceremonial powers.

Who made laws about cartwheels?

Qin Shi Huangdi, the first Chinese emperor, who united the country, made strict new laws, reformed the coinage and burned all books he disagreed with. He ruled from 221 to 207 BC, and was buried with 6,000 terracotta warriors guarding his tomb. He wanted to stop carts crashing on rutted roads, so gave orders that they should all have wheels the same distance apart. That way, they could follow the same track.

Who wrote one of the world's first novels?

Lady Murasaki, who lived at the elegant, cultured Japanese court around AD 1015. Japanese nobles loved music, poetry, painting, graceful buildings and exquisite gardens. They lived shut away from ordinary people, who had harsh, rough lives.

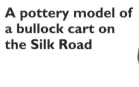

A pottery model of a bullock cart on the Silk Road

Carts were made of wood and woven bamboo, with strong wooden wheels.

Where did the Silk Road run?

From rich Chinese cities, across the Gobi desert, through the mountains of Central Asia to trading ports in the Middle East and around the Mediterranean Sea. European merchants travelled for years along the Silk Road to bring back valuable goods, especially silk and porcelain.

Who valued honour more than life?

Japanese warriors, called samurai, who were powerful from around AD 1200. They were taught to fight according to a strict code of honour. They believed it was better to commit suicide rather than face defeat.

When was the world's first book printed?

No one knows for certain, but it was probably between AD 600 and 800, in China. The world's oldest surviving book is 'The Diamond Sutra', a collection of religious texts, also printed in China, in AD 868.

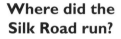

Where was the Middle Kingdom?

THE CHINESE BELIEVED THEIR COUNTRY TO BE AT THE VERY CENTRE OF THE WORLD, which is why they called it the Middle Kingdom. Certainly, for many centuries, China was one of the largest, richest and most advanced civilizations anywhere on Earth. Under the Tang and Song dynasties (ruled AD 618–1279), for example, Chinese cities like Chang'an (present-day Xi'an) and Kinsai (present-day Huangzhou) were the biggest in the world, and very prosperous. At the same time, Chinese scientists and inventors made many important discoveries, including printing, porcelain, paper-making, rockets, gunpowder, banknotes and clockwork.

Ming vase

Chinese potters left clay to weather for up to 40 years before firing (baking) at very high temperatures, until it was smooth as glass.

How did China get its name?

From fine pottery and porcelain, produced by Chinese workers, which was admired and valued in many parts of the world. Chinese potters pioneered many new techniques and designs. Some of their most famous pieces were decorated with blue-and-white glazes, like this tall jar, made around AD 1350.

What was China's best-kept secret?

How to make silk. For centuries, no one else knew how. Chinese women fed silk-moth grubs on mulberry leaves, and the grubs spun thread and wrapped themselves in it, to make cocoons. Workers steamed the cocoons to kill the grubs, unwound the thread, dyed it, and wove it into cloth.

Men worked for hours at this endless-chain machine. It forced water to flow uphill, pushed by wooden squares, to irrigate the fields.

What made China so prosperous?

THE INVENTIONS OF CHINESE FARMERS AND ENGINEERS MADE THE LAND PRODUCTIVE, and this made China wealthy. In the Middle Ages, the Chinese made spectacular strides in agriculture. They dug networks of irrigation channels to bring water to the rice fields. They built machines like the foot-powered pump (below) to lift water to the fields from canals. They also worked out ways of fertilizing fruit and vegetable plots with human manure.

Foot-powered water pump

Who did battle in metal suits?

KINGS, LORDS AND KNIGHTS WHO LIVED IN EUROPE DURING THE MIDDLE AGES. In those days, men from noble families were brought up to fight and lead soldiers into battle. It was their duty, according to law. Around AD 1000, knights wore simple chain-mail tunics, but by around 1450, armour was made of shaped metal plates, carefully fitted together. The most expensive suits of armour were decorated with engraved patterns or polished gold.

Which Russian Tsar was terrible?

Ivan IV, who became Tsar in 1533, when he was only three years old. He was clever but ruthless, and killed everyone who opposed him. He conquered vast territories in Siberia, and passed laws turning all the Russian peasants into serfs – unfree people, like slaves.

What was the Ancien Regime?

The system of government in many parts of Europe between AD 1600 and 1800. That was when kings and queens ruled without consulting the ordinary people in their lands. The result was that royalty and nobility were very rich and powerful, while almost everyone else was powerless and poor.

Who farmed land they didn't own?

People from poor peasant families. Under medieval law, all land belonged to the king, or to rich nobles. They let the peasants live in little cottages in return for rent or for work on their land. Sometimes, the peasants protested about this arrangement, or tried to run away.

How much were war horses worth?

A knight's war horse was his most valuable possession. It cost him as much as a small private plane or a top-of-the-range luxury car today.

Which French king lost his head?

Louis XVI. Under his oppressive rule, the poor French rose up in protest. In 1789, the French Revolution began. Three years later, Louis was sent to the guillotine and beheaded.

Who was the Virgin Queen?

Elizabeth I of England, who reigned from 1556 to 1603 – at a time when many people believed that women were too weak to rule. Elizabeth proved them wrong. Under her leadership, England grew stronger. She decided not to marry, because she could not find a husband who did not want to take over her power.

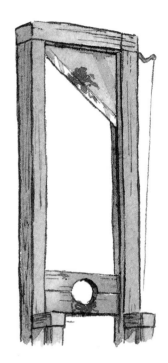

The guillotine

For fun, and to practise their skills, knights fought mock battles called tournaments or jousts.

Who built castles and cathedrals?

KINGS, QUEENS AND RICH NOBLES WHO LIVED IN EUROPE IN THE MIDDLE AGES. The first castles were just rough wooden forts. Later, they were built of stone, and became impressive homes. They were decorated with carvings, paintings and fine furniture. Some even had flower gardens outside. Cathedrals were very big churches, in cities or towns. Merchants, master-craftsmen and other rich citizens gave money to help build them. They wanted to worship there – and also to create a beautiful building that brought honour to their town.

What job was fit for a lady?

When knights went into battle, their ladies ran the castle. They supervised the household and discussed business and politics with important guests. Some women also fought to defend their castles against attack.

Knights jousting

When were the Middle Ages?

Some say the Middle Ages began around AD 500, others say around AD 1000. But everyone agrees that they ended round about AD 1500.

Who prayed the day away?

Monks and nuns spent a third of their lives at prayer. They promised never to marry and devoted their lives to God.

Taj Mahal

One of the most beautiful buildings in the world,
the Taj Mahal, near Agra in India, was built in 1653.

Who built his wife a beautiful tomb?

Mughal emperor Shah Jehan (ruled 1627–1658).
He was so sad when his wife Mumtaz Mahal
died giving birth to their 14th child that he built
a lovely tomb for her, called the Taj Mahal. It is
made of pure white marble decorated with gold
and semi-precious stones.

Who founded a new religion in India?

Guru Nanak, a religious teacher who lived in
Northwest India from 1469–1539. He taught
that there is One God, and that people should
respect one another equally, as brothers and
sisters. His followers became known as Sikhs.

Who conquered a kingdom aged only 14?

PRINCE BABUR, WHO WAS DESCENDED FROM THE
GREATEST MONGOL WARRIOR GENGHIS KHAN.
He captured the rich Central Asian city of Samarkand in 1497, and
made it his own private kingdom. He invaded Afghanistan, and
conquered northern India in 1526. Babur was a good scholar and
administrator, as well as a soldier. He founded a new empire in India,
and a new dynasty of rulers. They became known as the Mughals,
which was the North Indian way of writing Mongols.

Who was the Tiger King?

Tippu Sultan, king of the southern
Indian state of Mysore from 1785 to
1799. Tippu means tiger, and he
fought as fiercely as a tiger to
defend his land against British and
Mughal soldiers.

Who lived in a rose-covered palace?

The rulers of Vijayanagar, a kingdom
in southern India. Their royal palace
was covered in carvings of roses and
lotus flowers, and surrounded by
lakes and gardens. Vijayanagar was
conquered by the Mughals in 1565.

Grain was stored in
the tall towers. The
houses were made of
earth and roofed with grass
thatch held up on wooden poles.

Why did British merchants go to India?

To make their fortunes! They knew
that Indian goods – especially
cotton cloth, drugs and dyestuffs –
fetched high prices in Europe. In
1600 they set up the East India
Company, to organize trade. The
Company grew very rich, and had
its own private army. By 1757, it
controlled the richest parts of India
and almost all Indian trade.

How long did the Mughals rule?

For more than three centuries –
from 1526 to 1858. But from
around 1750, Mughal emperors
were weak and powerless. The last
Mughal emperor was turned off his
throne when the British government
took control of India after Indian
soldiers working for the British East
India Company rebelled in 1857.

Who swapped salt for sandalwood and gold?

Merchants from the north coast of
Africa who travelled across the
Sahara desert to trade with people
living in the West African kingdoms
of Ghana, Mali and Songhay, which
were powerful from around
AD 700 to 1600. Flakes of gold
were found among gravel in West
African rivers and streams; sweet
smelling sandalwood came from
tropical trees.

Who was the Great She Elephant?

This was a title of respect given to the Queen Mother in southern African kingdoms, now part of present-day Botswana and neighbouring lands. It honoured her status as mother of the king, and showed her power.

Which African city had a famous university?

Timbuktu, in present-day Mali, West Africa. The city was founded in the 11th century and became a great centre of learning for Muslim scholars from many lands. Timbuktu also had many mosques and markets, a royal palace, and a library.

Who made wonderful statues of brass and bronze?

Artists and craftworkers living in the great rainforest kingdom of Benin (part of present-day Nigeria), which was powerful from around 1400 to 1900. The statues were used to decorate the royal palace, and were placed on family altars in honour of dead ancestors.

The fortress city of Great Zimbabwe

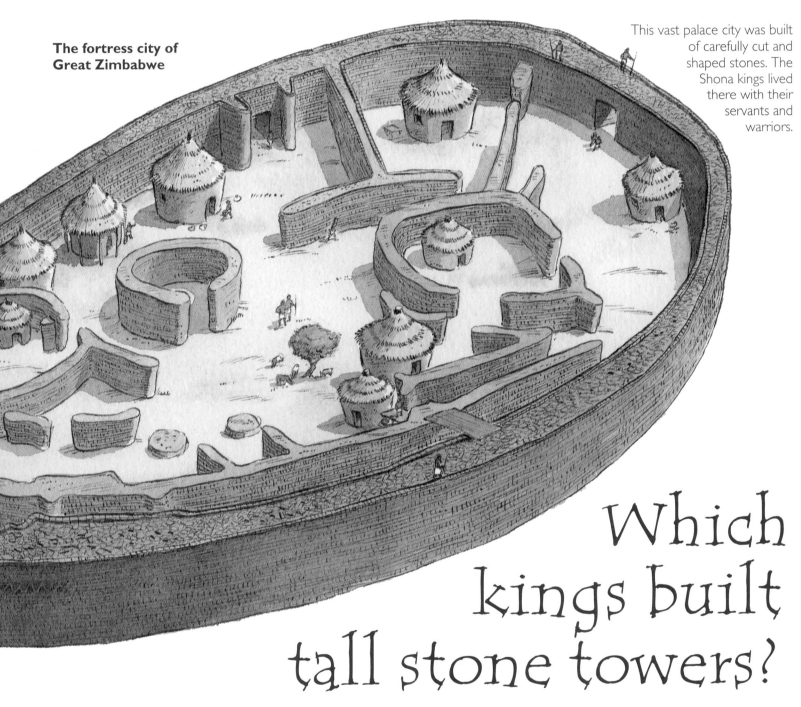

This vast palace city was built of carefully cut and shaped stones. The Shona kings lived there with their servants and warriors.

Which kings built tall stone towers?

SHONA KINGS OF SOUTHEAST AFRICA, WHO BUILT A CITY CALLED GREAT ZIMBABWE. Zimbabwe means Stone Buildings – and the city was also a massive fortress. From inside this fortress, the Shona kings ruled a rich empire AD 1200–1600. The Shona were originally farmers, growing millet and raising cattle. Later they became skilled miners and metal workers. They traded gold, copper, iron, ivory and leather with Arab merchants living on the East African coast. In return they bought glass and fine porcelain.

Where did dhows sail to trade?

Dhows were ships built for rich merchants living in trading ports like Kilwa, in East Africa. They sailed to the Red Sea and the Persian Gulf to buy pearls and perfumes, across the Indian Ocean to India to buy silks and jewels, and to Malaysia and Indonesia to buy spices.

87

Did the Aboriginals always live in Australia?

No, they probably arrived there from Southeast Asia around 50,000 BC, at a time when the sea surrounding Australia was much shallower than today. Historians think they travelled in log rafts or boats made of dug-out tree trunks.

How did the Maoris cross the vast Pacific Ocean?

By sailing and paddling big outrigger canoes. They steered by studying the waves and the stars, and made maps out of twigs and shells to help themselves navigate.

Who were the first people to discover New Zealand?

The Maoris. They migrated from other Pacific Islands around AD 950 and landed on the coast of New Zealand, which had been uninhabited until then. By around AD 1400, Maori families had settled throughout the land.

What were dingoes used for?

Dingoes are a type of dog. They were brought to Australia by Indian Ocean traders around 2000 BC. They were used as guard dogs – and to keep Aboriginal people warm as they slept around campfires in the desert, which gets very cold at night.

Who explored the eastern seas?

Muslim explorer Ibn Battuta, who was born in Tangiers, North Africa, sailed to India and China in the 14th century. He was followed by Cheng Ho, a Chinese admiral, who made seven long voyages between 1405 and 1433. Cheng explored the seas around India, Arabia and the east coast of Africa. He sailed south to Malaysia and Indonesia, and may even have sighted Australia.

Who arrived in America by mistake?

Italian explorer Christopher Columbus. In 1492, he sailed westwards across the Atlantic Ocean from Spain. He hoped to reach China or India, but arrived instead in America. He did not know it was there!

Which pirate became an explorer, too?

Sir Francis Drake, an English sailor who grew rich and famous by robbing Spanish ships. In his ship the 'Golden Hind', Drake made the second voyage round the world between 1577 and 1580. In 1588, Drake became a war-hero, when he led an English fleet to fight against the invading Spanish Armada.

Aboriginal hunters

Aboriginals used spears to kill kangaroos for food.

Who lives in the Australian desert?

THE ABORIGINAL PEOPLE HAVE LIVED IN THE DESERT FOR THOUSANDS OF YEARS. In that time, they have made valuable discoveries about the desert environment, and developed special survival skills. They learned how to find underground water, and to dig up nourishing roots hidden deep in the earth. They discovered which seeds, berries, grubs and animals are poisonous, and which are good to eat. They perfected the use of wild herbs in natural remedies. They found out how to use fire to scorch the earth and encourage wild food plants to grow. In addition, they invented throwing sticks called boomerangs for hunting kangaroos, and nets and traps for catching birds.

A brief history of exploration across the oceans of the world

1304–1377 Ibn Battuta sails to India and China.
1405–1433 Cheng Ho's voyages to Africa and Indonesia.
1419 Portuguese explorers begin to sail along the west coast of Africa.
1492 Columbus sails by mistake to America.
1497 Vasco Da Gama sails round Africa to reach India.
1519–1522 Magellan's ship sails round the world.
1577–1580 Drake sails round the world.
1642 Tasman sails to Australia.
1768–1779 Captain Cook explores the Pacific.

Who sailed round the world?

THE FIRST ROUND-THE-WORLD TRIP WAS MADE BY SAILORS in the ship 'Vittoria', owned by Ferdinand Magellan, a Portuguese explorer. In 1519, he sailed eastwards from Europe, but was killed fighting in the Philippines. Most of his crew died too, from hunger or disease. A few survivors, led by sea-captain Sebastian del Cano, managed to complete Magellan's planned voyage, and returned home to Europe, weak but triumphant, in 1522.

How did sailors help science?
By observing the plants, fishes and animals as they travelled – and by bringing specimens home with them. When Captain Cook explored the Pacific Ocean he took artists and scientists with him, to study and record what they saw.

The 'Vittoria'

Magellan set off from Europe with a fleet of five ships, but only the 'Vittoria' survived.

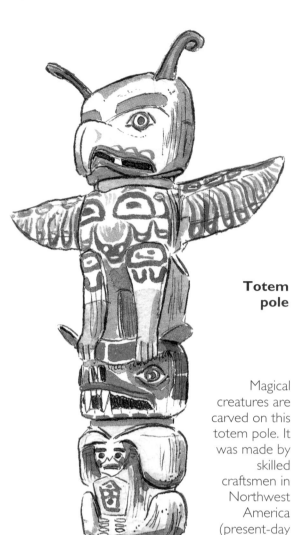

Totem pole

Magical creatures are carved on this totem pole. It was made by skilled craftsmen in Northwest America (present-day Canada).

Who lived in tents on the Great Plains?

Native American hunters, like the Sioux/Dakota and the Cheyenne. They spent summer and autumn moving across the wide, rolling grasslands of the Great Plains, following herds of buffalo, which they killed for meat and skins. In winter time, they camped in sheltered valleys or woods. Before Europeans settled in America, bringing horses with them, Great Plains hunters travelled vast distances on foot. They had no animals to ride – the Native American horse died out around 10,000 BC.

What stories do totem poles tell?

Native American people who lived in the forests of Northwest America carved tall totem poles to record their family's history, and to re-tell ancient legends about the powerful spirits that lived in all rocks, mountains, wild animals and trees.

Who or what were the Three Sisters?

Beans, maize and squash (pumpkin) – three essential foodcrops that Native American farmers grew wherever they could.

Who built strange shaped mounds?

The Hopewell Native American people, who lived on the banks of the Ohio River around AD 200–550. They buried their dead under huge heaps of earth, and created massive earth-mound sculptures, to honour their gods. The biggest, Great Serpent Mound, is about 400 metres (1330 ft) long.

Home on the Plains

A Native American woman and her child prepare to say goodbye to a hunter outside their tipi (tent) on the Great Plains. The hunter rides bareback – without a saddle.

Who were the first Europeans to settle in America?

Spanish missionaries, who settled in present-day Florida and California from around 1540, and French and English farmers, who built villages in present-day Virginia, on the east coast, from 1584.

Why did the Pilgrims leave home?

The Pilgrims were a group of English families with strong religious beliefs. They quarrelled with church leaders in England, and with the government, too. In 1620, they sailed for America in their ship 'Mayflower'. They wanted to build a new community, ruled by their own religious laws.

Did Native Americans live in big cities?

Yes, some of them. The people who lived in the Mississippi valley around AD 700–1200 built huge cities as centres of farming and trade. Their biggest city was called Cahokia – about 10,000 people lived there.

How did nomads move their tipis?

First, they unwrapped the skin covering of the tipi, and bundled it up. They packed up floor mats and rugs, too. Then they tied the tipi poles together to make a big A-shaped frame, called a travois, and loaded the bundles on top. The heavy travois was pulled along by women or dogs as the nomads moved from one camp to the next.

Moving camp, and setting it up again, was women's work. Working together, nomad women could clear a whole campsite in a morning.

Soldiers in the American Civil War

A Confederate soldier from the southern states, supporting slavery.

A Union soldier from the northern states, opposing slavery.

Why did a civil war break out in America?

THE AMERICAN CIVIL WAR WAS CAUSED MAINLY BY A QUARREL OVER SLAVERY. The war lasted from 1861 to 1865 and was fought between the southern and northern states of the USA. The economy of the southern states relied on black slaves shipped from Africa to work in the cotton plantations and on the farms of wealthy white owners. The northern states knew that slavery was wrong, and wanted it banned. There were also disagreements about law-making, politics and trade. After four years of heavy fighting, the northern states finally won, and most of the slaves were set free.

Who went to the Boston Tea Party?

European settlers in America attended this famous demonstration. In 1773, they poured tonnes of tea imported from Britain into the waters of Boston harbour. They were protesting against paying taxes to help the British government fund the wars it was fighting in far-away Europe. They wanted to ban all British taxes, and campaigned for the freedom to rule their own land.

When did the USA become independent?

On 4 July 1776, 13 English colonies (the land where most Europeans in America had chosen to settle) proclaimed a Declaration of Independence. In it they refused to be ruled by Britain any longer. They became a new nation – the United States of America. Britain sent troops to fight the USA and try and win the colonies back, but was defeated in 1783.

Late 19th-century lavatory

By 1900 many ordinary homes had lavatories, but only the rich could afford a polished wooden seat and an elaborately painted pottery pan like this.

Why were drains and lavatories so important?
Because without them, deadly diseases carried in sewage could spread very quickly through crowded industrial towns. Pottery-making was one of the first mass-production industries. Machines in 19th-century pottery factories produced millions of cups, plates – and lavatory pans.

What was the Industrial Revolution?

IT WAS A BIG CHANGE IN THE WAY PEOPLE WORKED AND GOODS WERE PRODUCED. It began around 1775 in Britain and spread to Belgium, Germany, northern Italy, France and – after 1850 – to Japan and the USA. Machines in huge factories replaced the craftworkers who used to make all kinds of goods slowly, one by one, at home. People had to learn new jobs operating machines that could mass-produce very large quantities of clothes, shoes, paper, metal and wooden goods more quickly and cheaply than the hand-workers could.

'The Rocket', built by George and Robert Stephenson in 1829

Did new industries make people rich?

They made some inventors and factory owners very rich indeed. This angered many ordinary workers, who often earned barely enough to stay alive. They joined together to form Trades Unions, to campaign for better pay and conditions.

When did the first trains run?

Horse-drawn railway wagons had been used to haul coal trucks in mines since the 1600s, but the first passenger railway was opened by George Stephenson in the north of England in 1825. Its locomotives were powered by steam. People rode standing in open carriages.

Did children lead better lives?

No. Many worked 16 hours a day in factories and down mines. Large numbers were killed in accidents with machinery, or died from breathing coal dust, cotton fibres or chemical fumes. But after 1830, governments began to pass laws to protect child workers, and conditions slowly improved.

How did railways change people's lives?

They helped trade and industry grow, by carrying raw materials to factories, and finished goods from factories to shops. They carried fresh foods from farms to cities. They made it easier for people to travel and encouraged a whole new holiday industry.

Who worked in the first factories?

THOUSANDS OF POOR, HUNGRY, UNEMPLOYED MEN AND WOMEN moved from the countryside to live in fast-growing factory towns. They hoped to find regular work and more pay. Wages in factories were better than those on farms, and some people enjoyed the excitement and bustle of living in a town. But working conditions in factories were often dirty and dangerous, and houses in factory towns were crowded, noisy and full of disease.

Who fought and died in the trenches?

Millions of young men during the First World War (1914–1918). Trenches were ditches dug deep into the ground. They were meant to shelter soldiers from enemy gunfire, but offered little protection from shells exploding overhead. Soon, the trenches filled up with mud, water, rats and dead bodies, and many soldiers drowned in them, or died from disease.

Who dropped the first atomic bomb?

ON 6 AUGUST 1945 THE USA BOMBED HIROSHIMA, JAPAN, KILLING OR WOUNDING 150,000 PEOPLE. By using this terrible new weapon on Japan, the USA, together with its allies in Britain and Russia, hoped to bring the Second World War (1939–1945) to an end. Japan was the strongest ally of Adolf Hitler, ruler of Nazi Germany. Hitler's invasions of European nations and his persecution of the Jewish people had led to the war breaking out in 1939. On 14 August Japan surrendered after the Americans dropped another atom bomb on the city of Nagasaki. The war was at an end.

Mao Zhedong

In 1966 Mao started a Cultural Revolution among the younger generation in China. He wrote down his thoughts in the 'Red Book'.

Who shot the Russian Tsar?

Russian rebels, called Bolsheviks. During the Russian Revolution of 1917 they killed the whole Russian royal family and set up a communist government instead.

Who made Five Year Plans?

Joseph Stalin, Russian communist leader who ruled from 1924–1953. He reorganized the country in a series of Five Year Plans. He built thousands of new factories, took land away from ordinary people and divided it into vast collective farms. Many of Stalin's schemes did not succeed; he used brutal punishments to silence his critics.

What was the Long March?

A gruelling march by Chinese communist soldiers through wild, rocky countryside in 1934. They escaped from land held by their enemies and set up a communist state of their own. They were led by Mao Zhedong, who became ruler of all China in 1949.

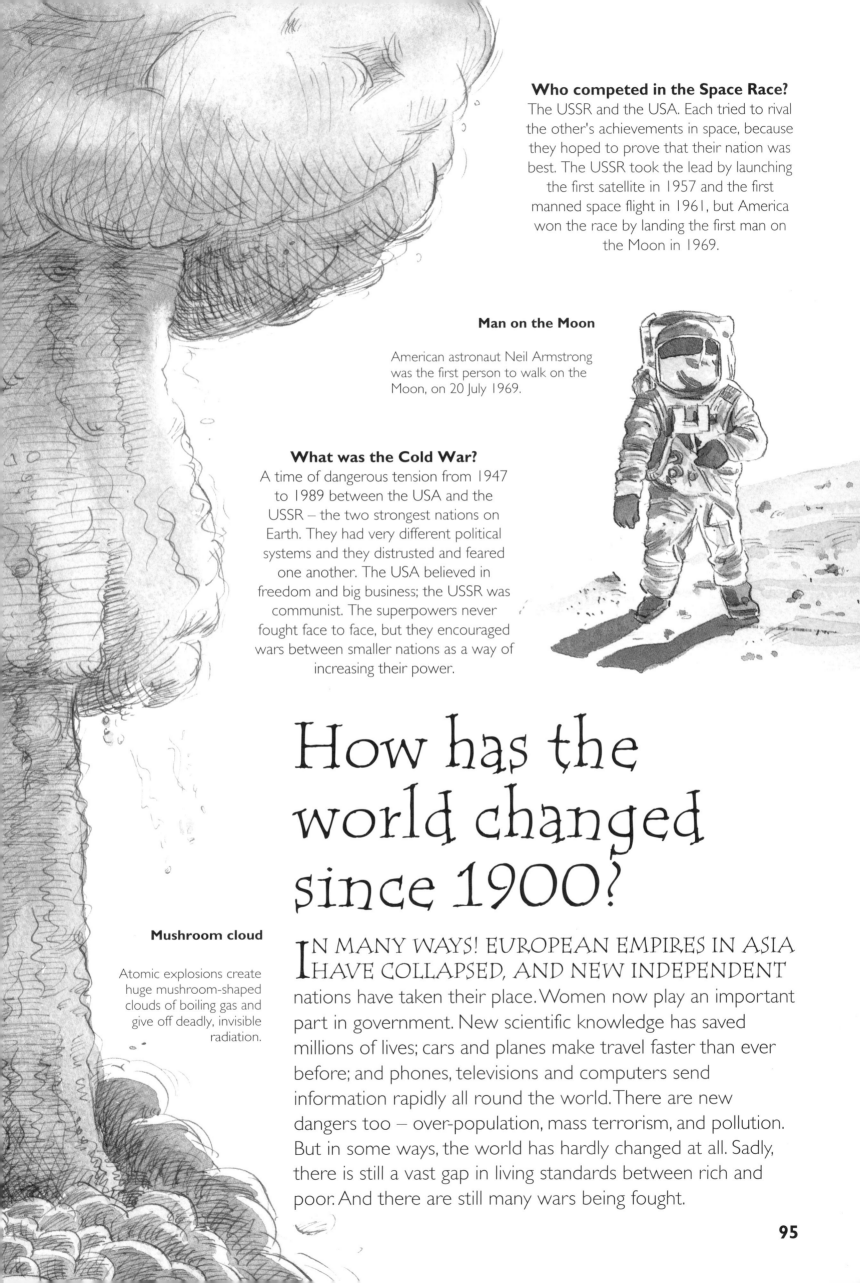

Who competed in the Space Race?
The USSR and the USA. Each tried to rival the other's achievements in space, because they hoped to prove that their nation was best. The USSR took the lead by launching the first satellite in 1957 and the first manned space flight in 1961, but America won the race by landing the first man on the Moon in 1969.

Man on the Moon

American astronaut Neil Armstrong was the first person to walk on the Moon, on 20 July 1969.

What was the Cold War?
A time of dangerous tension from 1947 to 1989 between the USA and the USSR – the two strongest nations on Earth. They had very different political systems and they distrusted and feared one another. The USA believed in freedom and big business; the USSR was communist. The superpowers never fought face to face, but they encouraged wars between smaller nations as a way of increasing their power.

How has the world changed since 1900?

IN MANY WAYS! EUROPEAN EMPIRES IN ASIA HAVE COLLAPSED, AND NEW INDEPENDENT nations have taken their place. Women now play an important part in government. New scientific knowledge has saved millions of lives; cars and planes make travel faster than ever before; and phones, televisions and computers send information rapidly all round the world. There are new dangers too – over-population, mass terrorism, and pollution. But in some ways, the world has hardly changed at all. Sadly, there is still a vast gap in living standards between rich and poor. And there are still many wars being fought.

Mushroom cloud

Atomic explosions create huge mushroom-shaped clouds of boiling gas and give off deadly, invisible radiation.

Science

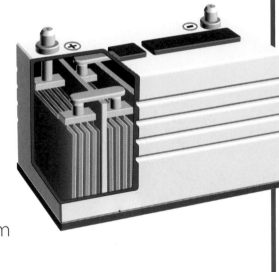

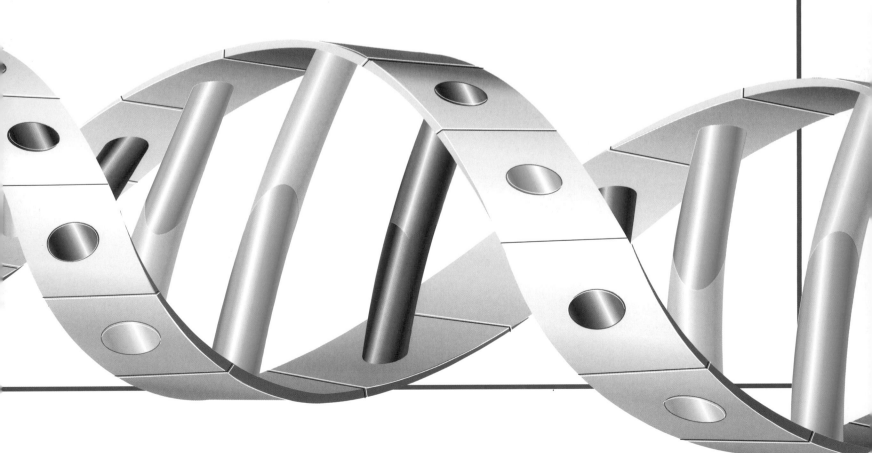

What are solids?

SUBSTANCES CAN BE EITHER SOLID, LIQUID OR GAS – THE THREE 'STATES OF MATTER'. Substances move from one state to another when they are heated or cooled – boosting or reducing the energy of the particles they are made of. In solids, particles are locked together, so solids have a definite shape and volume. In liquids, particles move around a bit, so liquids can flow into any shape – but stay the same volume. In gases, particles zoom about all over the place, so gases spread out to fill containers of any size or shape. When a substance is normally a liquid but turns into a gas, this is called a vapour.

What is a plasma?
A plasma is the rare fourth state of matter. It occurs only when a gas becomes so hot its particles break up. This happens inside the Sun and stars and in lightning, and in gas neon tubes. Plasmas are good conductors of electricity.

When do things freeze?
Things freeze from liquid to solid when they reach the freezing point, which is the same as melting point. Most substances get smaller when they freeze as the particles pack closer together. Water gets bigger as it turns to ice, which is why frozen pipes burst in winter.

What substance has the highest melting point?
The metal with the highest melting point is tungsten, which melts at 3,420°C (6,188°F). But the highest melting point of any substance belongs to carbon, which melts at 3,530°C (6,386°F).

What substance has the lowest freezing point?
Mercury has the lowest freezing point of any metal –38.87°C (–37.96°F). Helium has the lowest freezing point of all substances – –272.2°C (–457.96°F), less than 1° above absolute zero.

When do things boil?
Things boil from liquid to gas when they reach boiling point, which is the maximum temperature a liquid can reach. For water this is 100°C (212°F). An increase in pressure increases boiling point, which is why pressure cookers allow things to cook at higher temperatures.

Water as solid, liquid and gas

Solids do not keep their shape completely. The ice in glaciers can flow very slowly.

When do things melt?
Things melt from solid to liquid on reaching a temperature called the melting point. Each substance has its own melting point. Water's is 0°C (32°F); lead's is 327.5°C (621.5°F).

Thunderclouds

Large thunderclouds are made from water droplets and ice crystals.

What happens in evaporation and condensation?

E VAPORATION HAPPENS WHEN A LIQUID IS WARMED UP AND CHANGES TO A VAPOUR. Particles at the liquid's surface vibrate so fast they escape altogether. Condensation happens when a vapour is cooled down and becomes liquid. Evaporation and condensation take place not only at boiling point, but also at much cooler temperatures.

What is pressure?
Pressure is the amount of force pressing on something. Air pressure is the force with which air presses. The force comes from the bombardment of the moving air particles. The more particles there are, and the faster they are moving, the greater the pressure.

How does pressure change?
If you squeeze a gas into half the space, the pressure doubles (as long as the temperature stays the same). This is Boyle's law. If you warm a gas up, the pressure rises in proportion (as long as you keep it the same volume). This is the Pressure law.

Clouds form when rising air gets so cold that the water vapour it contains condenses into water droplets.

What is an atom?

ATOMS ARE WHAT EVERY SUBSTANCE IS MADE OF. ATOMS ARE THE SMALLEST recognizable bit of any substance. They are so small that they are visible only under extremely high-powered microscopes – you could fit two billion atoms on the full stop at the end of this sentence. Yet atoms are largely composed of empty space – empty space dotted with even tinier clouds of energy called sub-atomic particles.

What is the nucleus?
Most of an atom is empty space, but right at its centre is a very tiny area that is densely packed with particles much bigger than electrons. This is the nucleus, and it usually contains two kinds of nuclear particle – neutrons with no electrical charge, and protons with a positive electrical charge (opposite to the negative charge of electrons).

How big are atoms?
Atoms are about a ten millionth of a millimetre across and weigh 100 trillionths of a trillionth of a gram. The smallest atom is hydrogen; the biggest is meitnerium. (Since they are so small, atoms are measured in terms of 'moles', which is a quantity of the substance containing the same number of atoms as 12 grams of a form of carbon called Carbon 12.)

What are electrons?
Electrons are the very tiny electrically charged particles that whizz round inside an atom. They were discovered by the English physicist J.J. Thomson (1856–1940) in 1879 during some experiments with cathode ray tubes. (Computer and TV screens are cathode ray tubes, and cathode rays are actually streams of electrons.)

What is a molecule?
Quite often, atoms cannot exist by themselves, and must always join up with others – either of the same kind, or with other kinds to form chemical compounds. A molecule is the smallest particle of a substance that can exist on its own.

What is an ion?
An ion is an atom that has either lost one or a few electrons, making it positively charged (cation) or gained a few, making it negatively charged (anion). Ions usually form when substances dissolve in a liquid.

Inside a proton

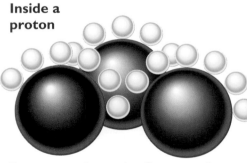

Protons may be made of even smaller particles – quarks joined by gluons.

What holds atoms together?
Electrons are held to the nucleus by electrical attraction – because they have an opposite electrical charge to the protons in the nucleus. The particles of the nucleus are held together by a force called the strong nuclear force.

What are electron shells?

ELECTRONS BEHAVE AS IF THEY ARE STACKED AROUND THE NUCLEUS AT different levels, like the layers of an onion. These levels are called shells, and there is room for only a particular number of electrons in each shell. The number of electrons in the outer shell determines how the atom will react with other atoms. An atom with a full outer shell, like the gas argon, is unresponsive. An atom with room for one or more extra electrons in its outer shell, like oxygen, is very reactive.

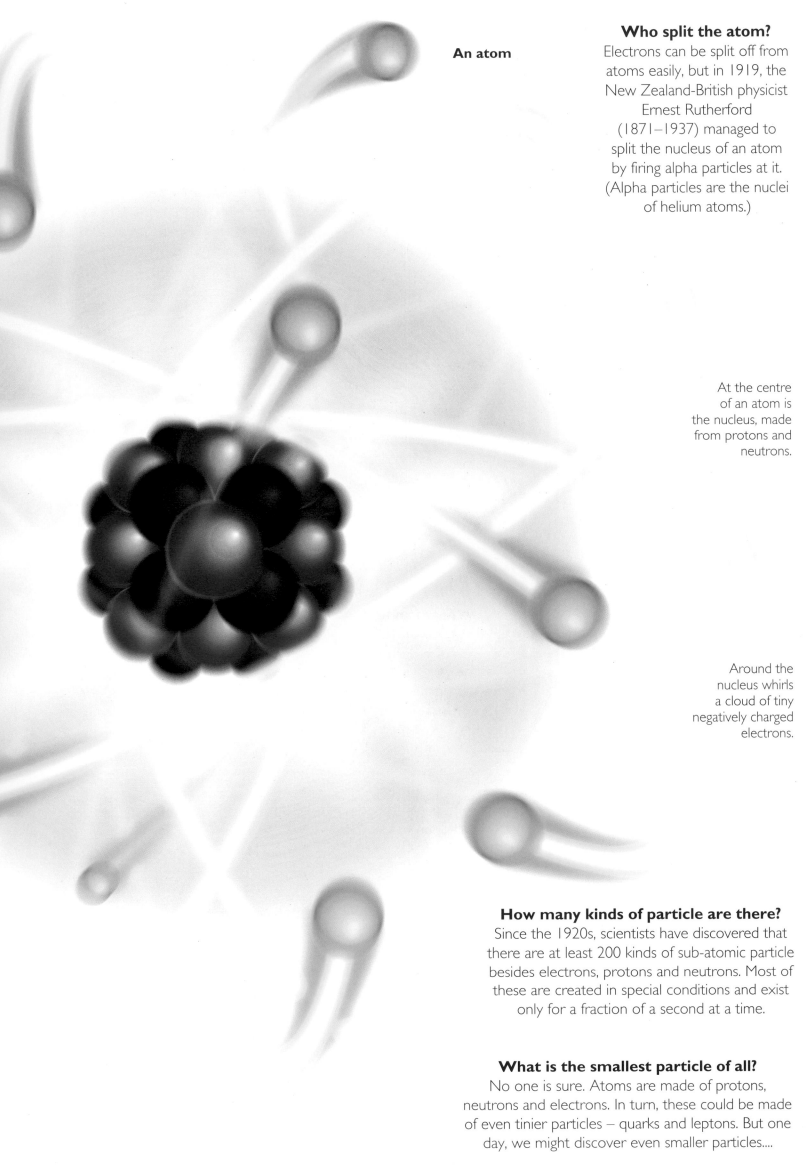

An atom

Who split the atom?
Electrons can be split off from atoms easily, but in 1919, the New Zealand-British physicist Ernest Rutherford (1871–1937) managed to split the nucleus of an atom by firing alpha particles at it. (Alpha particles are the nuclei of helium atoms.)

At the centre of an atom is the nucleus, made from protons and neutrons.

Around the nucleus whirls a cloud of tiny negatively charged electrons.

How many kinds of particle are there?
Since the 1920s, scientists have discovered that there are at least 200 kinds of sub-atomic particle besides electrons, protons and neutrons. Most of these are created in special conditions and exist only for a fraction of a second at a time.

What is the smallest particle of all?
No one is sure. Atoms are made of protons, neutrons and electrons. In turn, these could be made of even tinier particles – quarks and leptons. But one day, we might discover even smaller particles....

How many elements are there?

New elements are discovered every so often, but the total number identified so far is 112.

Fluorine

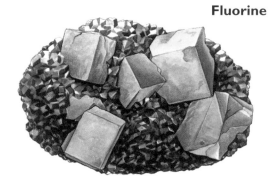

What are noble gases?

Group 0 is the furthest right-hand column of the periodic table. This group is called the noble gases, because they have full-up outer electron shells and so nobly stay aloof from any reaction with 'base' metals or any other substance. They are sometimes called inert gases.

Why are some elements reactive?

Elements are reactive if they readily gain or lose electrons. Elements on the left of the periodic table, called metals, lose electrons very easily – the further left they are, the more reactive they are. So Group I metals (called the alkali metals) including sodium, potassium and francium are very reactive.

What is the heaviest element?

The heaviest is hahnium. It has 105 protons and 157 neutrons in its nucleus. The atomic mass of hahnium is 262.

What are the transition metals?

Transition metals are the metals in the middle of the periodic table, such as chromium, gold and copper. They are generally shiny and tough, but easily shaped. They conduct electricity well and have high melting and boiling points.

What is a metal?

Most people can recognize a metal. It is hard, dense and shiny, and goes 'ping' when you strike it with something else made of metal. It also conducts both electricity and heat well. Chemists define a metal as an electropositive element, which basically means that metals easily lose negatively charged electrons. It is these lost, 'free' electrons that make metals such excellent conductors of electricity.

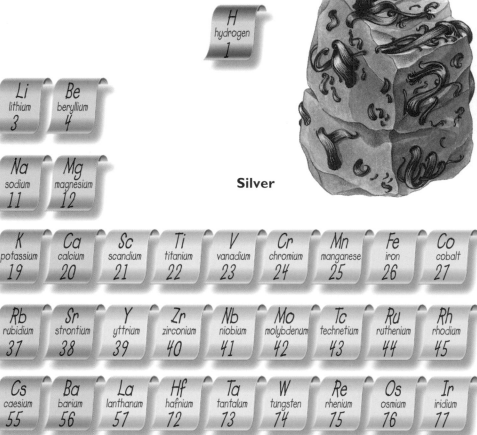

Silver

What is an element?

IT IS A SUBSTANCE THAT CANNOT BE SPLIT UP INTO OTHER SUBSTANCES.
Water is not an element because it can be split into the gases oxygen and hydrogen. Oxygen and hydrogen are elements because they cannot be split. Every element has its own atomic number. This is the number of protons in its nucleus, which is balanced by the same number of electrons.

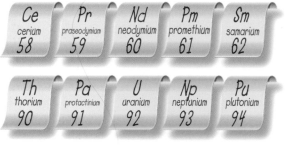

Uranium

What is the periodic table?

ALL THE ELEMENTS CAN BE ORDERED ACCORDING TO THEIR PROPERTIES, forming a chart called the periodic table. Columns are called groups, rows are called periods. Elements in the same group have the same number of electrons in the outer shell of their atoms and similar properties.

Copper

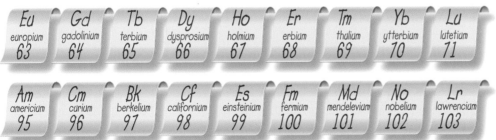

The actinides are a group of 15 elements at the bottom of the periodic table that take their name from actinium. They include radium and plutonium and are all very radioactive.

What is the lightest element?
The lightest element is hydrogen. It has just one proton in its nucleus and has an atomic mass of just one. The heaviest is osmium, which is 10 times denser than lead.

Why is carbon so special?
Carbon is the most friendly element in the Universe. With four electrons in the outer shell of its atom (and so four gaps), carbon atoms link very readily with other atoms.

Who discovered radium?
The Polish-French physicist Marie Curie (1867–1934), born Marya Sklodowska, is the only woman to have won two Nobel prizes – one in 1903 for her part in the discovery of radioactivity, and one in 1911 for her discovery of the elements polonium and radium.

What is atomic mass?
Atomic mass is the 'weight' of one whole atom of a substance – which is of course very tiny! It includes all the particles in the atom – protons, neutrons and electrons.

Sulphur

What are the lanthanides?
The lanthanides are a group of 15 elements in the middle of the periodic table that take their name from lanthanum. They are all shiny silvery metals and often occur naturally together. They all have two electrons in their outer electron shells. This makes them chemically similar – they are all very reactive.

Gold

How do batteries work?

Batteries create electric currents from the reaction between two chemicals, one forming a positive electrode and the other a negative. The reaction creates an excess of electrons on the negative electrode, producing a current. Chemicals used include zinc chloride, strong alkaline chemicals and lithium.

What is electrolysis?

Electrolysis is a chemical reaction caused when an electric current is passed through a solution – the electrolyte. The effect is to make positive ions (or cations) move to the negative terminals (the cathode) and negative ions (or anions) move to the positive terminal (the anode).

What is a mixture?

Mixtures are substances that contain several chemical elements or compounds mixed in together but not chemically joined. The chemicals intermingle but do not react with each other, and with the right technique can often be separated. An example of a mixture is milk.

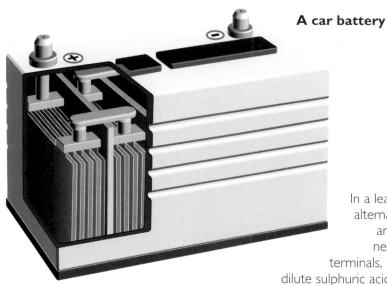

A car battery

In a lead-acid car battery, alternating plates of lead and lead oxide form negative and positive terminals, linked by a bath of dilute sulphuric acid – the electrolyte.

What is a chemical formula?

A chemical formula is a shorthand way of describing an atom, an ion or a molecule. Initial letters (sometimes plus an extra letter) usually identify the atom or ion; a little number indicates how many atoms are involved. The formula for water is H_2O, because each molecule consists of two hydrogen atoms and one oxygen atom.

What are compounds?

THEY ARE SUBSTANCES MADE FROM TWO OR MORE ELEMENTS JOINED TOGETHER. Every molecule in a compound is the same combination of atoms. Sodium chloride, for instance, is one atom of sodium joined to one of chlorine. Compounds have different properties to the elements that make them up. Sodium, for instance, spits when put in water; chlorine is a thick green gas. Yet sodium chloride is ordinary table salt!

What's the sea made of?

The sea is water with oxygen, carbon dioxide, nitrogen and various salts dissolved in it. The most abundant salt is common salt (sodium chloride). Others include Epsom salt (magnesium sulphate), magnesium chloride, potassium chloride, potassium bromide and potassium iodide.

What's the air made of?

Pure air is 78.9% nitrogen, 20.95% oxygen. There are traces of argon (0.93%), carbon dioxide (0.03%), helium (0.0005%), neon (0.018%), krypton (0.001%), xenon (0.0001%) and radon.

How do chemicals react?

WHEN SUBSTANCES REACT CHEMICALLY, THEIR ATOMS, IONS AND MOLECULES interact to form new combinations – separating elements from compounds or joining them together to form different compounds. Nearly all chemical reactions involve a change in energy – usually heat – as the bonds between particles are broken and formed.

How do things dissolve?

When solids dissolve in liquid, it may look as if the solid disappears. Its atoms, ions or molecules are, in fact, still intact – but are separated and evenly dispersed throughout the liquid.

Fire

Fire is a chemical reaction in which one substance gets so hot that it combines with oxygen in the air.

Nuclear fission

A nucleus splits, and each part makes another nucleus split, and so on, in a fission chain reaction.

Why is nuclear power awesome?

THE ENERGY THAT BINDS TOGETHER AN ATOMIC NUCLEUS IS ENORMOUS, even though the nucleus itself is so small. In fact, as Einstein showed in 1905 with his theory of Special Relativity, the particles of the nucleus can also be regarded as pure energy. This enables nuclear power stations to generate huge amounts of power with just a few tonnes of nuclear fuel. It also gives nuclear bombs a massive and terrifying destructive power.

What is nuclear fusion?

Nuclear energy is released by fusing or joining together small atoms like those of deuterium (a form of hydrogen). Nuclear fusion is the reaction that keeps stars glowing and provides energy for thermonuclear warheads. Scientists hope to find a way of harnessing nuclear fusion for power generation.

What is nuclear fission?

Nuclear fission releases nuclear energy by splitting big atomic nuclei – usually those of uranium. Neutrons are fired at the nuclei. As the neutrons smash into the nuclei they split off more neutrons, which bombard other nuclei, setting off a chain reaction.

What is an atomic bomb?

An atomic bomb or A-bomb is one of the two main kinds of nuclear weapon. An A-bomb relies on the explosive nuclear fission of uranium-235 or plutonium-239. Hydrogen bombs, also called H-bombs or thermonuclear weapons, rely on the fusion of hydrogen atoms to create explosions a thousand times more powerful.

How do nuclear power stations work?

Inside the reactor there are fuel rods made from pellets of uranium dioxide, separated by spacers. When the station goes 'on-line', a nuclear fission chain reaction is set up in the fuel rods. This is slowed down by control rods, which absorb the neutrons so that heat is produced steadily to drive the steam turbines that generate electricity.

A nuclear power station

A containment building houses the reactor vessel, keeping in heat, radioactivity and other energy.

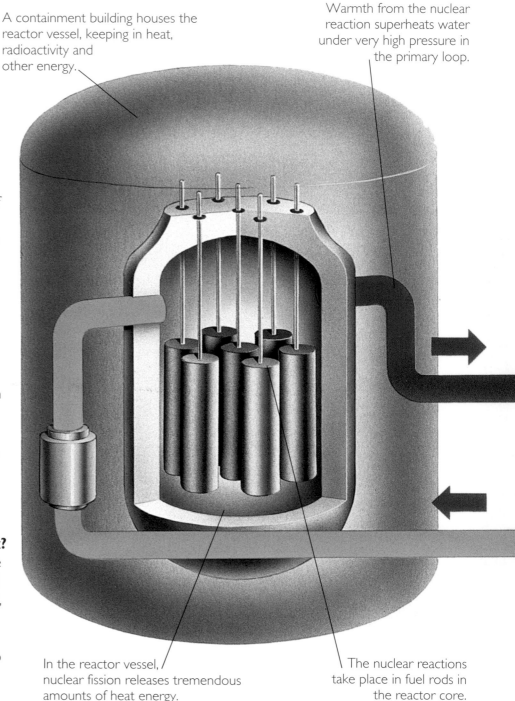

Warmth from the nuclear reaction superheats water under very high pressure in the primary loop.

In the reactor vessel, nuclear fission releases tremendous amounts of heat energy.

The nuclear reactions take place in fuel rods in the reactor core.

What does radiation do to you?

It causes radiation sickness. With a very high dose, the victim dies in a few hours from nerve damage. With a less high dose, the victim dies after a week or so from damage to the gut or a complete collapse of the body's resistance to disease. Lower doses of radiation can cause cancer (including leukaemia) and defects in new-born babies.

How can radioactivity be used to indicate age?

Radioactivity proceeds at a very steady rate. So by measuring how much of a substance has decayed radioactively, you can tell how old it is. With once-living things, the best radioactive isotope to measure is carbon-14. This form of dating is called carbon dating.

What exactly is radioactivity?

THE ATOMS OF AN ELEMENT MAY COME IN SEVERAL DIFFERENT FORMS OR ISOTOPES. Each form has a different number of neutrons in the nucleus, indicated in the name, as in carbon-12 and carbon-14. The nuclei of some of these isotopes – the ones scientists call radioisotopes – are unstable, and they decay (break up), releasing radiation, consisting of streams of particles called alpha, beta and gamma rays. This is what radioactivity is.

Who invented the atomic bomb?

The first atomic bombs were developed in the USA towards the end of the Second World War by a brilliant team of scientists under the leadership of Robert Oppenheimer (1904–1967). His colleagues included Leo Szilard (1898–1964) and Otto Frisch (1904–1979). Together they created the first two A-bombs, which were dropped on Hiroshima and Nagasaki in Japan in 1945 with devastating effect.

What is half-life?

No-one can predict when an atomic nucleus will decay. But scientists can predict how long it will take for half the particles in a substance to decay. This is its half-life. Strontium-90 has a half-life of 9 minutes. Uranium-238 has a half-life of 4.5 billion years.

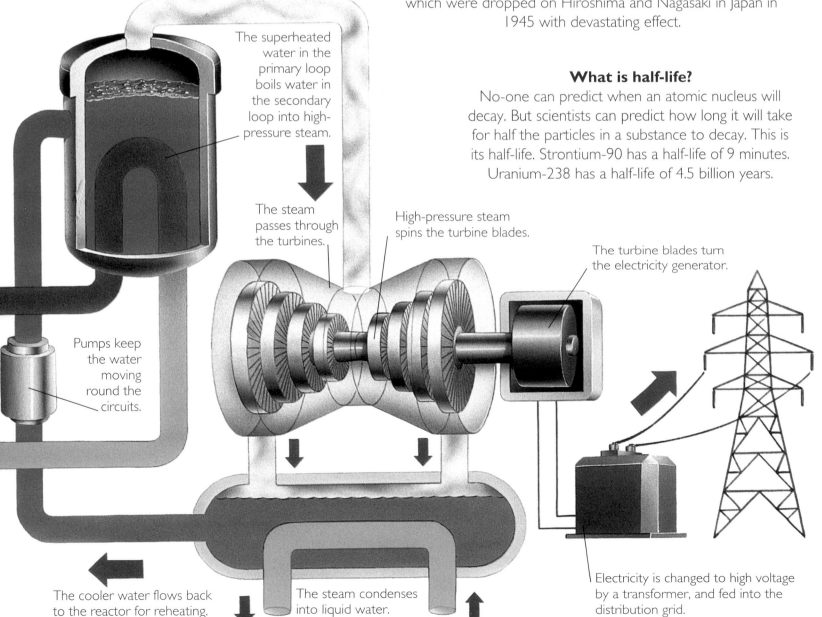

The superheated water in the primary loop boils water in the secondary loop into high-pressure steam.

The steam passes through the turbines.

High-pressure steam spins the turbine blades.

The turbine blades turn the electricity generator.

Pumps keep the water moving round the circuits.

The cooler water flows back to the reactor for reheating.

The steam condenses into liquid water.

Electricity is changed to high voltage by a transformer, and fed into the distribution grid.

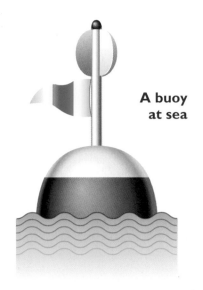

A buoy at sea

What's so special about water?

WATER IS SPECIAL IN MANY WAYS, AND IS ESSENTIAL TO ALL LIVING THINGS. Water is chemically neutral, yet dissolves many substances, which is why it is so important for life. It is denser as a liquid than a solid and so expands when it freezes. Water is found naturally in all of its three states of matter – solid ice, liquid water and gaseous water vapour. This is unusual, because of the strong bonds between its two hydrogen atoms and one oxygen atom. When cooled, most substances with similar sized atoms to water do not freeze until –30°C (–22°F). Water freezes at a much higher temperature, 0°C (32°F).

Why do things float?

When an object is immersed in water, the weight of the object pushes it down. But the water around it pushes it back up with a force equal to the weight of water displaced (pushed out of the way). The object sinks until its weight is equalled by the upthrust, then floats.

Hydroelectric dam

Hydroelectric power depends on the fact that water is drawn downwards by gravity to turn the turbine that generates electricity.

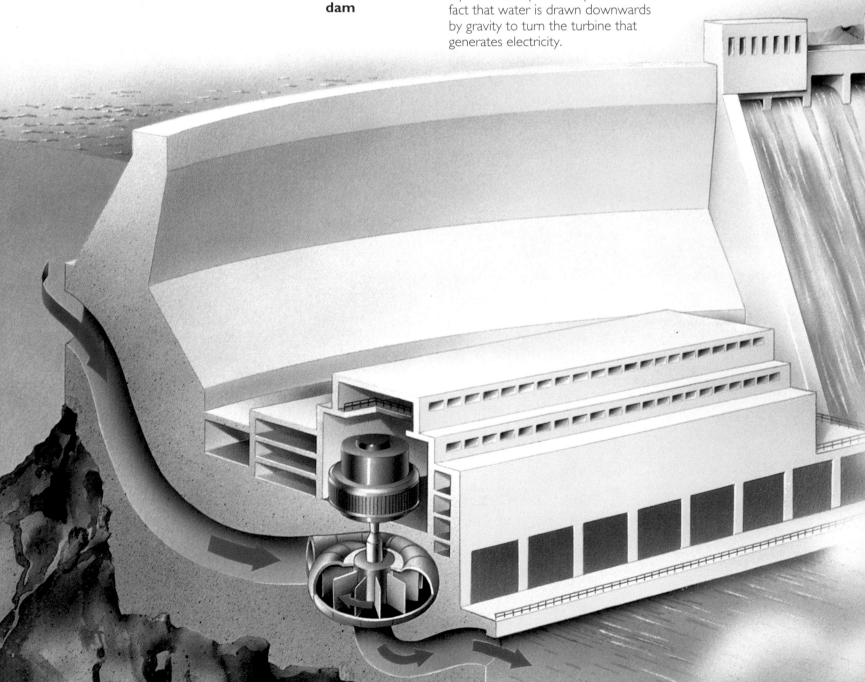

What is hydraulic power?

Fluids like water are incompressible – that is, they cannot be squashed. So if you push fluid through a pipe, it will push out the other end. Hydraulic power uses fluid-filled pipes working like this to drive things very smoothly. Hydraulic means water, but most hydraulic systems use oil to avoid rust problems

What is heavy water?

Heavy water is deuterium oxide – water that is a little heavier than ordinary water because it contains the hydrogen isotope deuterium rather than ordinary hydrogen. Heavy water is used in the nuclear industry to slow down nuclear reactions.

How much water is there in the body?

Water is found in nearly every cell of the body, which is why human bodies are almost three-quarters water. Women's bodies have slightly less water than men's, and children's bodies slightly less than women.

Hydraulic lift truck

Slowly releasing the fluid lets the load back down.

Pumping fluid into the forklift truck's hydraulic pipes raises the load.

Why do plants need water?

Plants contain an even higher proportion of water than the human body. Plants need water for building cells, and also for transporting nutrients from the roots to the leaves where they are needed.

Why does sweating keep you cool?

Because sweat is nearly all water, and water needs warmth to turn to vapour – which we call 'drying'. Watery sweat dries from the skin by taking warmth from the body. This makes the body cooler.

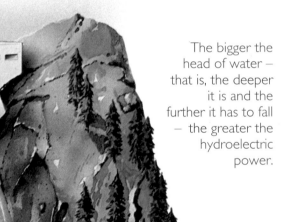

The bigger the head of water – that is, the deeper it is and the further it has to fall – the greater the hydroelectric power.

What is hydroelectric power?

Hydroelectric power or HEP is electricity generated by turbines turned by falling water. Typically, hydroelectric power stations are sited inside dams built to create a big fall or 'head' in the water.

Who made the first waterwheels?

Nobody knows for sure, but wheels turned by water to generate power were described by Ancient Greek writers over 2,000 years ago.

Why do icebergs float in the sea?

WHEN MOST THINGS GET COLDER, THEY CONTRACT, AND WHEN MOST LIQUIDS freeze they get very much smaller. Water is unique in that it contracts only down to a certain temperature, 4°C (39.2°F). If it gets colder still, it begins to expand, because the special bonds between the hydrogen atoms in the water begin to break down. When it freezes, water expands so much that ice is actually lighter (less dense) than water, so ice floats. But it is only a little lighter, so icebergs float with almost nine-tenths below the water line – which is why they are so dangerous to ships.

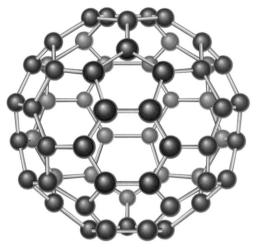

Carbon buckyball

This is one molecule of buckminster fullerene made from dozens of carbon atoms linked together in a ball.

What are buckyballs?
Before 1990, carbon was known in two main forms or allotropes – diamond and graphite. In 1990, a third allotrope was created. Its molecule looks like a football or the domed stadium roofs created by American architect Buckminster Fuller. And so this allotrope is called, after him, a buckyball.

Who discovered the shape of DNA?
The discovery in 1953 that every molecule of DNA is shaped like a twisted rope ladder or 'double helix' was one of the great scientific breakthroughs of the 20th century. Maurice Wilkins and Rosalind Franklin did the groundwork for the discovery. Francis Crick and James Watson, two young researchers at Cambridge University, UK, had the inspiration and won the Nobel Prize.

What is a polymer?
Polymers are substances made from long chains of thousands of small carbon-based molecules, called monomers, strung together. Some polymers occur naturally, such as wool and cotton, but plastics such as nylon and polythene are man-made polymers.

How is oil refined?
Oil drilled from the ground, called crude oil, is separated into different substances, mainly by distillation. This means the crude oil is heated until it evaporates. The substances are then drawn off and condensed from the vapour at different temperatures. The molecules of heavier oils may then be 'cracked' by heating under pressure.

What is DNA?

DNA IS DEOXYRIBONUCLEIC ACID. THIS IS THE AMAZING LONG DOUBLE-SPIRAL molecule that is found inside every living cell. It is made up of long chains of sugars and phosphates linked by pairs of chemical 'bases'– adenine, cytosine, guanine and thymine. The order in which these bases recur provides in code form the instructions for all the cell's activities, and for the lifeplan of the entire organism.

DNA molecule

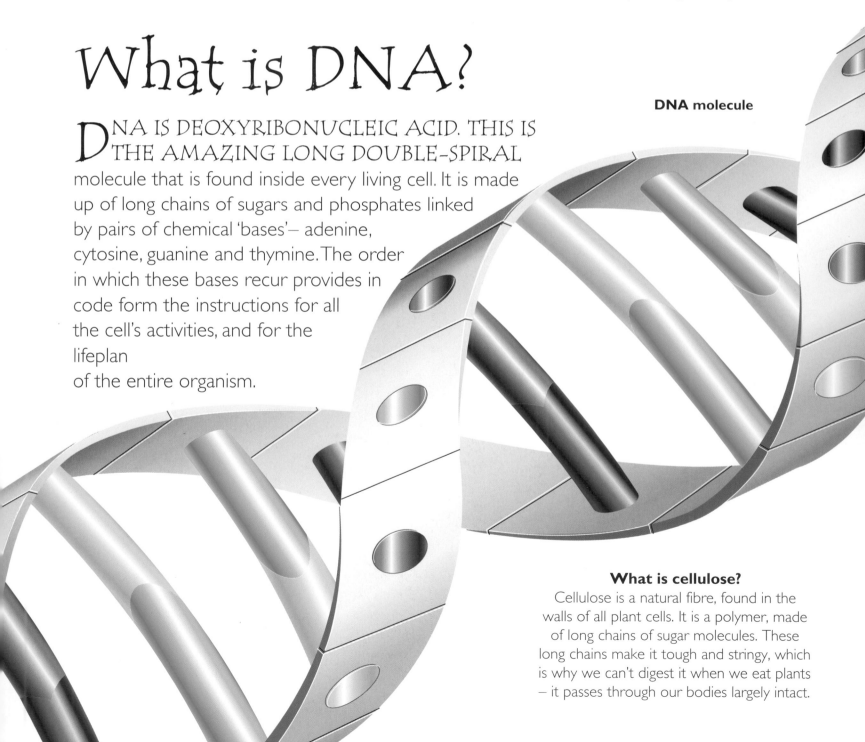

What is cellulose?
Cellulose is a natural fibre, found in the walls of all plant cells. It is a polymer, made of long chains of sugar molecules. These long chains make it tough and stringy, which is why we can't digest it when we eat plants – it passes through our bodies largely intact.

How is natural oil made?

Oil is formed from tiny plants and animals that lived in warm seas millions of years ago. As they died, they were slowly buried beneath the sea-bed. As the sea-bed sediments hardened into rock, the remains of the organisms were turned to oil and squeezed into cavities in the rock.

What is oil?

Oils are thick liquids that won't mix with water. Mineral oils used for motor fuel are hydrocarbons – that is, complex organic chemicals made from hydrogen and carbon.

The 'ropes' of the DNA molecule are alternating groups of chemicals called sugars and phosphates.

The 'rungs' of DNA are pairs of chemicals called bases, linked together by chemical bonds.

How is plastic made?

Most plastics are made from ethene, one of the products of cracked oil. When heated under pressure, the ethene molecules join in chains 30,000 or more long. These molecules get tangled like spaghetti. If the strands are held tightly together, the plastic is stiff. If the strands can slip easily over each other, the plastic is bendy, like polythene.

What is organic chemistry?

ORGANIC CHEMISTRY IS THE CHEMISTRY OF CARBON AND ITS COMPOUNDS. Carbon's unique atomic structure means it links atoms together in long chains, rings or other shapes to form thousands of different compounds. These include complex molecules – such as DNA – that are the basis of life, which is why carbon chemistry is called organic chemistry.

What is a carbon chain?

Carbon atoms often link together like the links of a chain to form very long thin molecules – as in the molecule of propane, which consists of three carbon atoms in a row, with hydrogen atoms attached.

What are aromatics?

Benzene is a clear liquid organic chemical found in coal tar. It can be harmful, but has many uses, for example as a cleaning fluid and in manufacturing dyes. It has distinctive hexagonal molecules made of six carbon atoms and six hydrogen atoms and called a benzene ring. It also has a distinctive aroma, which is why chemicals that have a benzene ring are called aromatics.

What is the carbon cycle?

Carbon circulates like this: animals breathe out carbon as carbon dioxide. Plants take in carbon dioxide from the air, convert it into carbohydrates – and when animals eat plants, they take in carbon again.

What are carbohydrates?

Carbohydrates are chemicals made only of carbon, hydrogen and oxygen atoms – including sugars, starches and cellulose. Most animals rely on carbohydrate sugars such as glucose and sucrose for energy.

The knock-on effect

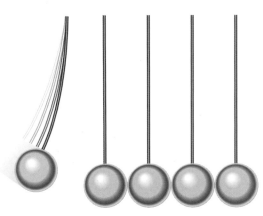

In this toy, each swinging ball knocks into the next, passing momentum along.

What is a knock-on effect?

When two objects collide, their combined momentum remains the same, if nothing else interferes. So if one object loses momentum, this momentum must be passed on to the other object, making it move. This is essentially a knock-on effect.

What is a turning force?

When something fixed in one place, called a fulcrum, is pushed or pulled elsewhere, it turns around the fulcrum. When you push a door shut, that push is the turning force, and the hinge is the fulcrum.

When your toboggan hits a rock, your hat carries on without you. Its momentum throws it forwards.

What was Newton's breakthrough?

Sir Isaac Newton's breakthrough, in 1665, was to realize that all movement in the Universe is governed by three simple rules, which we now called Newton's Laws of Motion. The First is about inertia and momentum. For his three Laws of Motion, read on.

What's the difference between inertia and momentum?

Inertia is the tendency of things to stay still unless they are forced to move. Momentum is the tendency for things to keep going once they are moving, unless forced to stop or slow. This is the First Law of Motion.

What is acceleration?

Acceleration is how fast something gains speed. The larger the force and the lighter the object, the greater the acceleration. This is Newton's Second law of Motion.

What happens with every action?

This is Newton's Third Law of Motion – for every action, there is an equal and opposite reaction. Which means that whenever something moves, there is a balance of forces pushing in opposite directions. When you push your legs against water to swim, for instance, the water pushes back on your legs equally hard.

How do things get moving?

THINGS ONLY MOVE IF FORCED TO MOVE.
SO WHEN SOMETHING STARTS MOVING,
there must be a force involved – whether it is visible, like someone pushing, or gravity, which makes things fall. But once they are moving, things will carry on moving at the same speed and in the same direction, until another force is applied – typically friction.

Why do things go round?

IF ONLY ONE FORCE IS INVOLVED, THINGS WILL ALWAYS MOVE IN A STRAIGHT LINE. This is called linear motion. Things go round when there is more than one force involved. A ball loops through the air because gravity is pulling it down while its momentum is pushing it on – less and less strongly. A wheel goes round on its axle because there is one force trying to make it carry on in a straight line and another keeping it the same distance from the axle.

A toboggan ride, courtesy of the force of gravity

What is uniform motion?
Uniform motion is when an object carries on travelling at exactly the same speed in exactly the same direction.

Once gravity has overcome your toboggan's inertia and got you swishing downhill, its momentum will keep it going until something stops it.

What's the difference between velocity and speed?
Speed is how fast something is going. Velocity is how fast something is going and in which direction. Speed is therefore called a scalar quantity; velocity a vector.

What is Special Relativity?
The theory of Special Relativity shows how both space and time can be measured only relatively – that is, in comparison to something else. This means that time can speed up or slow down, depending on how fast you are moving.

Who was Einstein?
Albert Einstein (1897–1955) was the scientific genius who transformed science with his two big theories – Special Relativity (1905) and General Relativity (1915). The theory of Special Relativity was developed while he was working in the Swiss Patent Office in Bern.

What's the fastest thing in the Universe?
Light, which travels at 300,000 km (186,000 miles) per second. This is the one speed in the universe that is constant – that is, it always the same no matter how fast you are going when you measure it.

113

How a rocket works

A typical rocket has fuel tanks of liquid propellant fuel and liquid oxygen.

The rocket motors burn the propellant fuel and liquid oxygen. As the fuel burns, it expands in a high-speed stream of water vapour.

Although the water vapour is light, its high speed means it has enormous momentum.

In accordance with Newton's Law of Motion, the momentum of the gas gives the rocket an equal momentum in the opposite direction, thrusting it upward.

What is a force?

A FORCE IS WHAT MAKES SOMETHING MOVE – BY PUSHING IT OR PULLING IT in a particular direction. It may be an invisible force, like gravity, or a visible force like a kick, but it always causes something to either accelerate or decelerate or change shape. Forces always work in pairs – whenever a force pushes, it must push against something else equally – which is why guns kick back violently when fired.

What's the difference between mass and weight?
Mass is the amount of matter in an object. It is the same wherever you measure it, even on the Moon. Weight is a measure of the force of gravity on an object. It varies according to where you measure it.

What is power?
Power is the rate at which work is done – a high-powered engine is an engine that can move a great deal of weight very quickly. Power is also the rate at which energy is transferred – a large amount of electric power might be needed to heat a large quantity of water.

What is gravity?
Gravity is the invisible force of attraction between every bit of matter in the Universe. Its strength depends on the mass of the objects involved and their distance apart.

What did Galileo do on the Tower of Pisa?
The Italian scientist and astronomer Galileo Galilei (1564–1642) is said to have dropped metal balls of different weights from the Leaning Tower of Pisa to show that they all fall at the same speed.

What did a great scientist learn from an apple?
The mathematician and physicist Sir Isaac Newton is said to have developed his ideas about gravity while sitting one day under an apple tree. As he watched an apple fall to the ground, it occurred to him in a flash that the apple was not merely falling but was being pulled towards the ground by an invisible force. This is the force he called gravity.

How is force measured?
Force is measured in newtons, in honour of Sir Isaac Newton. A newton is the force needed to accelerate 1 kilogram by 1 metre per second every second.

What is friction?
Friction is the force between two things rubbing together, which may be brake pads on a bicycle wheel or air molecules against an aeroplane. Friction tends to slow things down, making them hot as their momentum is converted into heat.

How fast does a stone fall?
At first, the stone falls faster and faster at a rate of 9.8 metres (32 ft) per second at every second. But as the stone's speed accelerates, air resistance increases until it becomes so great that the stone cannot fall any faster. It now continues to fall at the same velocity, called the terminal velocity.

Why can you jump higher on the Moon?

The Moon is much smaller than the Earth, so its gravity is much weaker. Astronauts weigh six times less on the Moon than they do on Earth – and can jump much higher!

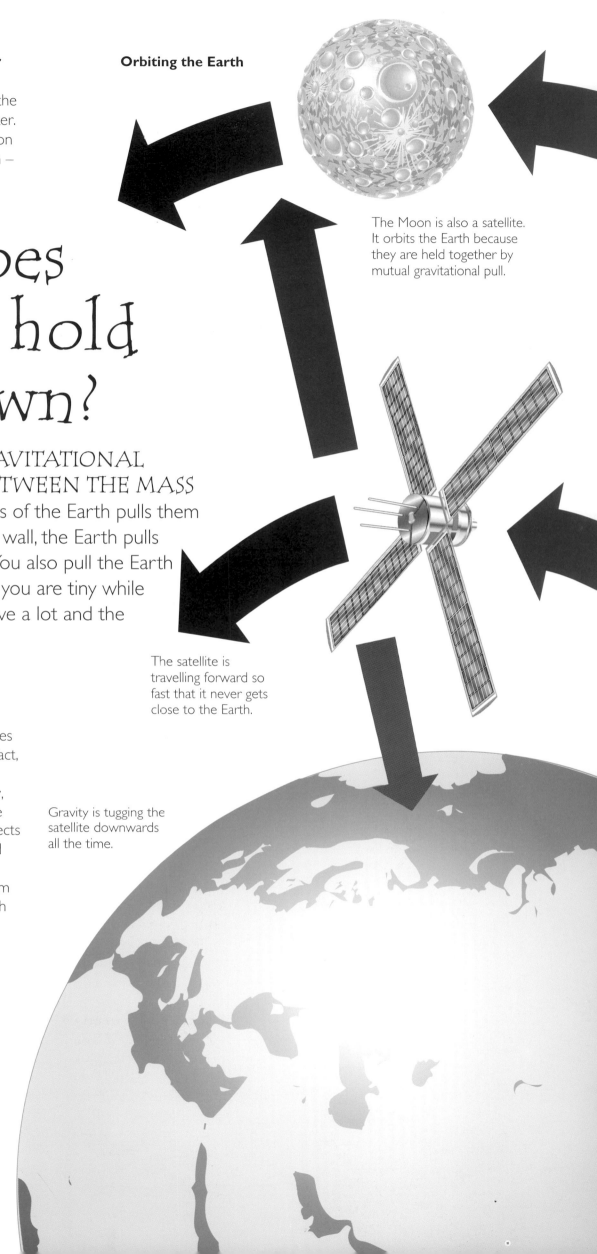

The Moon is also a satellite. It orbits the Earth because they are held together by mutual gravitational pull.

How does gravity hold you down?

THE MUTUAL GRAVITATIONAL ATTRACTION BETWEEN THE MASS of your body and the mass of the Earth pulls them together. If you jump off a wall, the Earth pulls you towards the ground. You also pull the Earth towards you, but because you are tiny while the Earth is huge, you move a lot and the Earth barely moves at all.

The satellite is travelling forward so fast that it never gets close to the Earth.

Does gravity vary?

An object's gravitational pull varies with its mass and its distance. In fact, gravity diminishes precisely in proportion to its distance away, squared. You can work out the force of gravity between two objects by multiplying their masses and dividing by the square of the distance between them. This sum works all over the Universe with pinpoint accuracy.

Gravity is tugging the satellite downwards all the time.

Why do satellites go round the Earth?

Satellites are whizzing through space at exactly the right height for their speed. The Earth's gravity tries to pull them down to Earth, but they are travelling so fast that they go on zooming round the Earth just as fast as the Earth pulls them in.

How is energy conserved?

Energy can be neither created nor destroyed. When energy is converted from one form to another, there is always exactly the same amount of energy afterwards as there was before. In this way energy is conserved, even when converted into a different form.

What is energy efficiency?

Some machines waste a great deal of energy, while others waste very little. The energy efficiency of a machine is measured by the proportion of energy it wastes. Waste energy is usually lost as heat.

How are energy and mass linked?

Energy is a form of mass; mass is a form of energy. In nuclear reactions, tiny amounts of mass are changed into huge quantities of energy.

What's absolute zero?

Absolute zero is the coldest possible temperature, the temperature at which atoms stop moving altogether. This happens at −273.15°C (−459.67°F), or 0 on the Kelvin scale.

What is conduction?

Conduction is one of the three ways in which heat moves. It involves heat spreading from hot areas to cold areas as moving particles knock into one another. The other ways are convection, in which warm air or water rises, and radiation, which is rays of invisible infrared light.

What is energy?

ENERGY TAKES MANY FORMS. HEAT ENERGY BOILS WATER, KEEPS US WARM and drives engines. Chemical energy fuels cars and aeroplanes. Electrical energy drives many small machines and keeps lights glowing. Almost every form of energy can be converted into other forms. But whatever form it is in, energy is essentially the capacity for making something happen or, as scientists put it, 'doing work'.

How fossil fuels were formed

Millions of years ago, plants absorbed the Sun's energy and converted it into new fibres as they grew.

The stored energy in the plant fibres was concentrated into coal as the fibres were buried and squeezed beneath layers of sediment over millions of years.

Where does our energy come from?

NEARLY ALL OF OUR ENERGY COMES TO US ULTIMATELY FROM THE SUN. Some we get directly via solar power cells. Most comes indirectly via fossil fuels (coal and oil), which got their energy from the fossilized plants (and other organisms) of which they are made. The plants got their energy directly from the sun by a process called photosynthesis.

400 million°C (720 million°F) is the highest temperature ever measured – in a nuclear fusion experiment in USA.

The highest air temperature ever recorded is 58°C (136°F) in Libya.

Earth's lowest air temperature ever measured is −88°C (−190°F) in Antarctica.

The lowest temperature ever measured is almost −273.15°C (−459.67°F) in a Finnish laboratory.

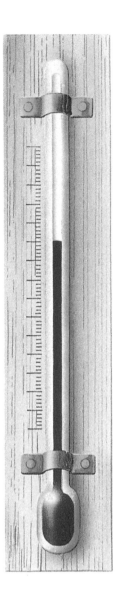

Spirit thermometer for measuring normal air temperatures

What's the difference between heat and temperature?

Heat is molecules moving. It is a form of energy – the combined energy of all the moving molecules. Temperature, on the other hand, is simply a measure of how fast all the molecules are moving.

How do you convert Fahrenheit to Celsius?

You can convert from Fahrenheit to Celsius by subtracting 32 then dividing by nine and multiplying by five. You can convert from Celsius to Fahrenheit by dividing by five, multiplying by nine and adding 32.

How is temperature measured?

Temperature is usually measured with a thermometer. Some thermometers have a metal strip that bends according to how hot it is. But most contain a liquid, such as mercury, in a tube. As it gets warmer, the liquid expands, and its level rises in the tube. The level of the liquid indicates the temperature.

The deepest coal (called anthracite) is squashed to almost pure black carbon, and provides a very concentrated form of energy.

Fuel buried less deep is less squashed. This less concentrated fuel is called brown coal or lignite.

Refraction

A straight rod dipped in a glass of water seems to bend in the middle, because the glass and water refract (bend) the light.

How is light bent?
Light rays are bent when they are refracted. This happens when they strike a transparent material like glass or water, at an angle. The different materials slow the light waves down so that they slew round, like car wheels driving on to sand.

How do fibre optic cables bend light?
Actually they don't bend light, but reflect it round corners. Inside a cable are lots of bundles of glass fibres. Light rays zig-zag along the inside of each fibre, reflecting first one side, then the other. In this way, light can be transmitted through the cable no matter what route it takes.

Why is the sun red?
The sun is only red at sunrise and sunset, when the sun is low in the sky and sunlight reaches us only after passing a long way through the dense lower layers of the atmosphere. Particles in the air absorb shorter, bluer wavelengths of light or reflect them away from us, leaving just the red.

How do your eyes see things?

LIGHT SOURCES SUCH AS THE SUN, STARS AND ELECTRIC LIGHT SHINE light rays straight into your eyes. Everything else you see only by reflected light – that is, by light rays that bounce off things. So you can see things only if there is a light source throwing light on to them. Otherwise, they look black, and you can't see them at all.

How do mirrors work?
Most mirrors are made of ordinary glass, but the back is silvered – coated with a shiny metal that perfectly reflects all the light that hits it – at exactly the same angle.

Does light travel in waves?
In the last century, most scientists believed light did travel in tiny waves rather than bullet-like particles. Now they agree it can be both, and it is probably best to think of light as vibrating packets of energy.

What are photons?
Photons are almost infinitesimally small particles of light. They have no mass and there are billions of them in a single beam of light.

Reflection

You can see an object such as a plant in a pot by the light reflected from it.

How do things absorb light?

When light rays hit a surface, some bounce off, but others are absorbed by atoms in the surface, warming it up very slightly. Each kind of atom absorbs particular wavelengths (colours) of light. The colour of the surface depends on which wavelengths of light are absorbed and which reflected. You see a leaf as green because the leaf has soaked up all colours but green, and you see only the reflected green light.

The image in a mirror is back-to-front or reversed. Left is on the right, and right is on the left – a mirror image! A photograph gives a true right-way-round image.

What happens at an interference fringe?

INTERFERENCE IS WHAT HAPPENS WHEN TWO LIGHT WAVES MEET EACH OTHER. If the waves are in step with each other, they reinforce each other. This is positive interference, and you see bright light. If they are out of step, they may cancel each other out. This is negative interference, and you see shadow. Interference fringes are bands of light and shade created by alternating positive and negative interference.

Why is the sky blue?

Sunlight is white – which means it contains all the colours of the rainbow. The sky is blue because air molecules scatter – reflect in all directions – more blue from sunlight towards our eyes than other colours.

The reflection of the plant forms an image that appears to be behind the mirror – as if you were looking at it through a window.

What is an incident ray?

When scientists talk about reflections, they distinguish between the light falling on the reflector (which may be a mirror) and the light reflected. Incident rays are the rays hitting the reflector.

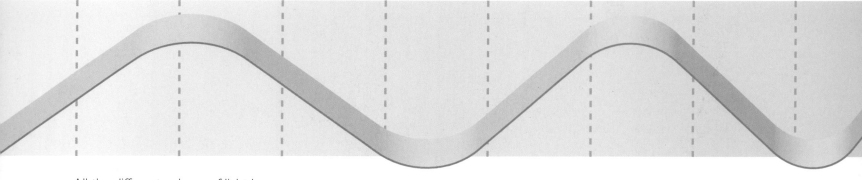

All the different colours of light have different wavelengths. The longest waves we can see are red.

Why can't you see ultraviolet?

Ultraviolet light is light with wavelengths too short for the human eye to register.

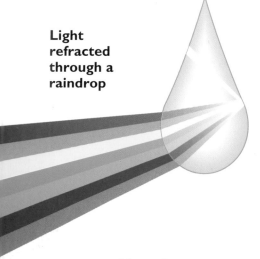

Light refracted through a raindrop

What is the electromagnetic spectrum?

LIGHT IS JUST A SMALL PART OF THE WIDE RANGE OF RADIATION EMITTED BY ATOMS – the only part we can see. This range of radiation is called the electromagnetic spectrum and ranges from long waves – such as radio waves and microwaves – to short waves – such as X-rays and gamma rays.

How does a prism split colours?

Prisms split white light into separate colours by refracting (bending) it. The longer the wavelength of the light, the more it is refracted. So long wavelength colours emerge from the prism at a different point from short wavelength colours.

What is infrared?

Infrared is light with wavelengths too long for the human eye to register. But you can often feel infrared light as warmth.

How do TV signals travel?

TV signals travel in one of three ways. Terrestrial broadcasts are beamed out from transmitters as radio waves to be picked up by TV aerials. Satellite broadcasts are sent up to satellites as microwaves, then picked up by satellite dishes. Cable broadcasts travel as electrical or light signals along underground cables, straight to the TV set.

How do X-rays see through you?

X-rays are stopped only by the bones and especially dense bits of the body. They pass through the soft bits to hit a photographic plate on the far side of the body, where they leave a silhouette of the skeleton.

How do CT scans work?

CT (computed tomography) scans run X-ray beams right round the body, and pick up how much is absorbed with special sensors. A computer analyses the data to create a complete 'slice' through the body.

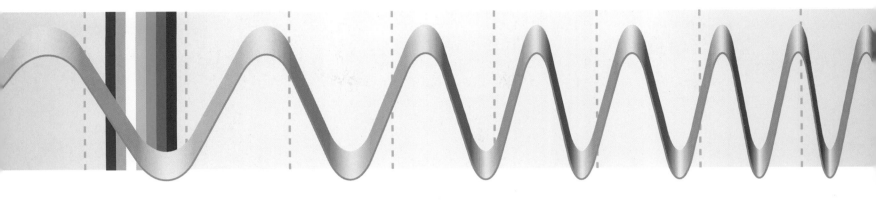

The shortest waves of light we can see are violet.

Electromagnetic spectrum

Who made the first radio broadcast?

Italian inventor Guglielmo Marconi first sent radio signals over 1.6 km (1 mile) in 1895. In 1898, he sent a message in Morse code across the English Channel. In 1901, he sent a radio message across the Atlantic.

Rainbows are formed by the reflection of the Sun off billions of drops of moisture in the air.

What are the colours of the rainbow?

THE COLOURS OF THE RAINBOW ARE ALL THE COLOURS CONTAINED IN WHITE LIGHT. When white light hits raindrops in the air, it is split up into a rainbow of colours, because each colour of light is refracted by the rainbow to a different extent. The colours of the rainbow appear in this order: red, orange, yellow, green, blue, indigo, violet.

What is an electric current?

A current is a continuous stream of electrical charge. It happens only when there is a complete, unbroken 'circuit' for the current to flow through – typically a loop of copper wire.

What is a silicon chip?

A silicon chip is an electronic circuit implanted in a small crystal of semi-conducting silicon, in such a way that it can be manufactured in huge numbers. This was the predecessor to the microprocessors that make computers work.

Silicon chip

How do electric currents flow?

The charge in an electric current is electrons that have broken free from their atoms. None of them moves very far, but the current is passed on as they bang into each other like rows of marbles.

Lightning flashes from a thundercloud when a massive negative electrical charge builds up in the base of the cloud.

Complex electrical circuits can be printed on to a tiny silicon chip.

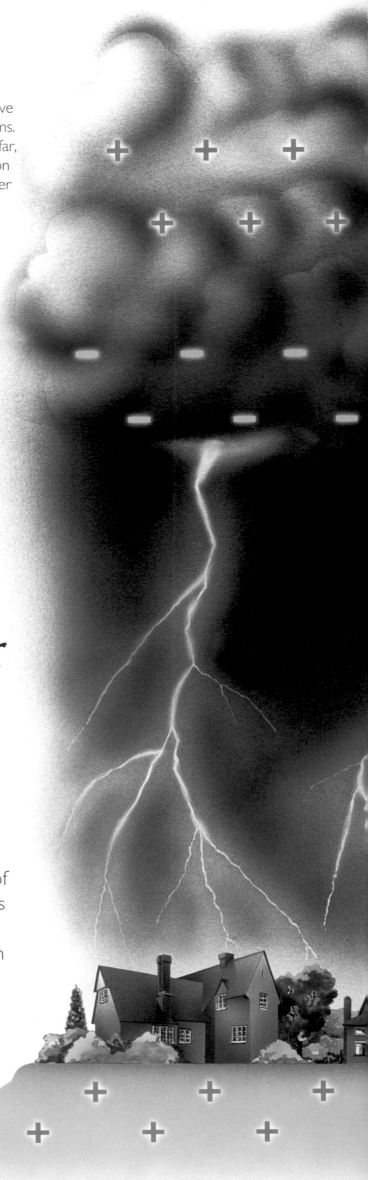

Why does your hair go frizzy?

WHEN YOU COMB DRY HAIR, TINY ELECTRONS ARE KNOCKED OFF the atoms in the comb as it rubs past. Your hair is coated with these tiny negative electrical charges and so is attracted to anything that has its normal quota of electrons, or more. An electric charge made like this is called 'static' because it does not move. Try rubbing a balloon on your jumper to create a static charge, then you can stick it on the wall.

What are the best conductors?

The best conductors are metals like copper and silver. Water is also a good conductor. Superconductors are materials like aluminium, which is cooled until it transmits electricity almost without resistance.

Lightning flashes to the ground to discharge because it always carries a slight positive electrical charge.

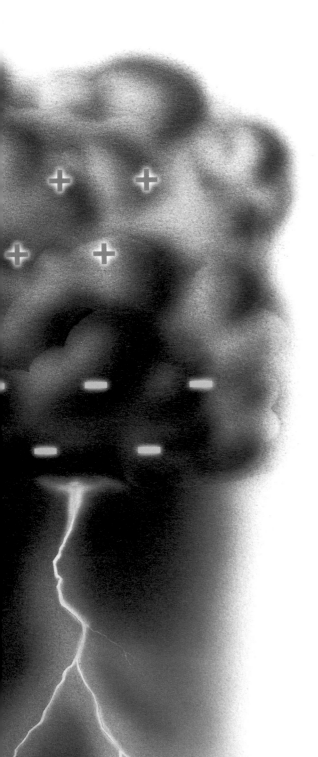

What makes lightning flash?

LIGHTNING FLASHES PRODUCE 100 MILLION VOLTS OF STATIC ELECTRICITY. Lightning is created when raindrops and ice crystals inside a thundercloud become electrically charged as they are flung together, losing or gaining electrons from each other. Negatively charged particles build up at the base of the cloud. When this charge has built up enough, it discharges as lightning, either flashing within the cloud or forking between the cloud and the ground.

What is a semi-conductor?
Semi-conductors are materials such as silicon or germanium, which are partly resistant to electric current and partly conducting. They can be set up so that the conductivity is switched on or off, creating a tiny electrical switch. They are used to make diodes, transistors and chips, and so are essential to electronics.

Who invented transistors?
Transistors were invented by three scientists working at the Bell Laboratories in the USA in 1948 – William Shockley, Walter Brattain and John Bardeen.

What is a volt?
Electrical current flows as long as there is a difference in charge between two points in the circuit. This difference is called a potential and is measured in terms of volts. The bigger the difference, the bigger the voltage.

What is resistance?
Not all substances conduct electric currents equally well. Resistance is a substance's ability to block a flow of electric current.

Light bulb

The pressure of the electric current through the bulb's thin wire filament makes it glow.

What is an alternating current?
A direct current (DC) flows in one direction only. Most hand-held torches use DC. Electricity in the house is alternating current (AC), which means it continually swaps direction as the generator's coil spins around past its electrodes.

How does electric light work?
An electric bulb has a very thin filament of tungsten wire inside a glass bulb filled with argon or nitrogen gas. When current flows through such a thin wire, the resistance is so great that the wire heats up and glows brightly. If it wasn't surrounded by non-reactive nitrogen or argon gas, it would quickly burn through.

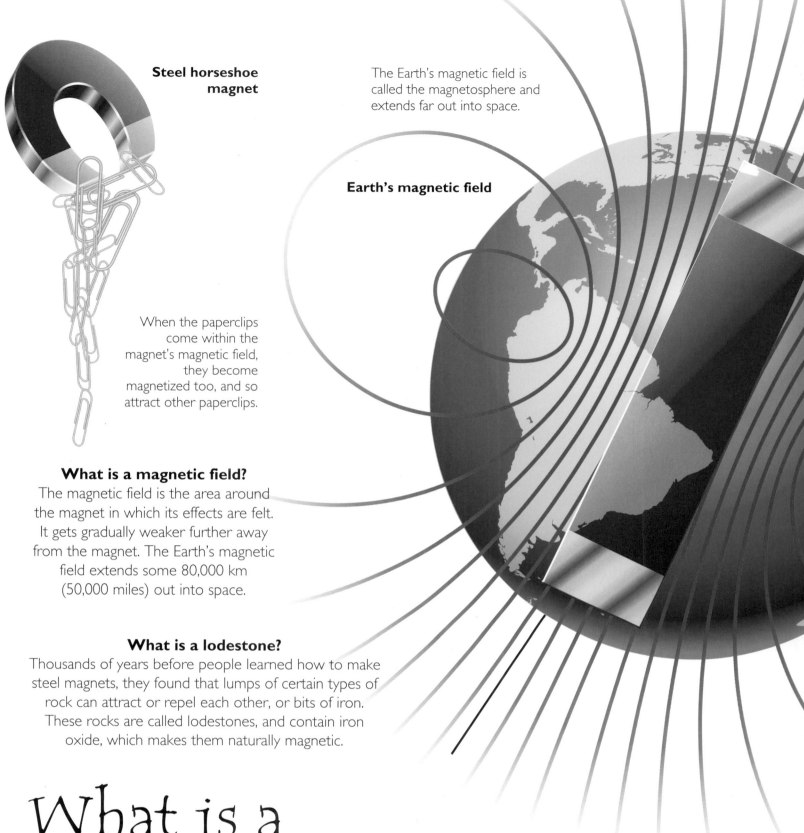

Steel horseshoe magnet

The Earth's magnetic field is called the magnetosphere and extends far out into space.

Earth's magnetic field

When the paperclips come within the magnet's magnetic field, they become magnetized too, and so attract other paperclips.

What is a magnetic field?

The magnetic field is the area around the magnet in which its effects are felt. It gets gradually weaker further away from the magnet. The Earth's magnetic field extends some 80,000 km (50,000 miles) out into space.

What is a lodestone?

Thousands of years before people learned how to make steel magnets, they found that lumps of certain types of rock can attract or repel each other, or bits of iron. These rocks are called lodestones, and contain iron oxide, which makes them naturally magnetic.

What is a magnetic pole?

MAGNETISM IS THE INVISIBLE FORCE THAT DRAWS TOGETHER SOME METALS, such as iron and steel – or pushes them apart. This force is especially strong at each end of the magnet. These two powerful ends are called poles. One is called the north (or north-seeking) pole, because if the magnet is suspended freely this pole swings round until it points north. The other is called the south pole. If the opposite poles of two magnets meet, they will be drawn together. If the same poles meet, the magnets will push each other apart.

Why is the Earth like a magnet?

As the Earth spins, the swirling of its iron core turns the core into a giant magnet. It is a little like the way a bicycle dynamo generates an electric current. Like smaller magnets, the Earth's magnet has two poles, a north and a south. It is because Earth is a magnet that small magnets always point in the same direction if allowed to swivel freely.

How does sound travel?

EVERY SOUND IS CREATED BY VIBRATION, BE IT AN ELASTIC BAND TWANGING or a loudspeaker cone shaking to and fro. But you can't hear any sounds in a vacuum. This is because the sound reaches your ears as a vibration – and there must be something to vibrate. Normally, this is the air. When a sound source vibrates to and fro, it pushes the air around it to and fro. The sound travels through the air as it is pushed to and fro in a knock-on effect – that is by being alternately stretched and squeezed. This moving stretch and squeeze of air is called a sound wave.

The lines in this picture show the pattern of Earth's magnetic force. Magnets and magnetic particles within the field line up along these lines.

What is resonance?

If allowed to vibrate freely, every object always tends to vibrate at the same rate. This is its natural frequency. You can make things vibrate faster or slower than this by jogging them at particular intervals. But if you can jog it at just the same rate as its natural frequency, it vibrates in sympathy and the vibrations become much stronger. This is resonance.

What is sound frequency?

Some sounds, like a car's squealing brakes, are very high-pitched. Others, like a booming bass drum, are very low-pitched. What makes them different is the frequency of the sound waves. If the sound waves follow very rapidly one after another, they are high-frequency and make a high sound. If there are long gaps between each wave, they are low-frequency and make a low sound. A low-frequency sound is about 20 Hz or waves per second. A high-frequency sound is 20,000 Hz or waves per second.

What is an echo?

An echo is when you shout in a large empty hall or in a tunnel, and you hear the noise ringing back out at you a moment or two later. The echo is simply the sound of your voice bouncing back from the walls. You don't normally hear echoes, because they only bounce back clearly off smooth, hard surfaces – and in confined spaces. Even in a confined space, the wall must be at least 17 metres (55 ft) away, because you will hear an echo only if it bounces back at least 0.1 second after you shouted.

Long, low-frequency sound waves give low-pitched sounds.

Short, high-frequency sound waves give high-pitched sounds.

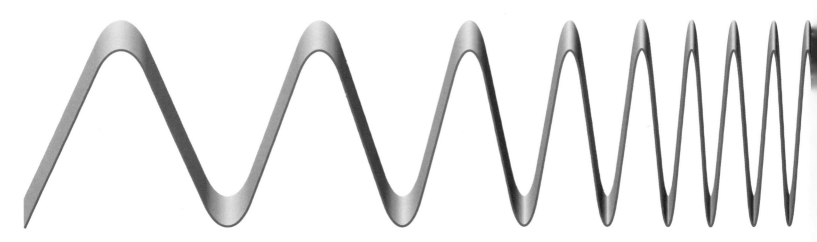

Animals

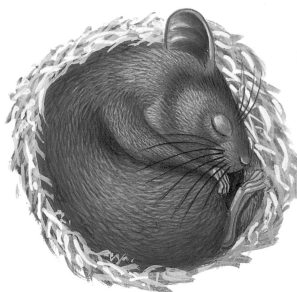

Dormouse

The dormouse normally weighs up to 25 g (1 oz), but it puts on extra fat before it hibernates.

Do dormice really sleep a lot?

Dormice do sleep through the winter. This hibernation may start in October and last until April, longer in cold climates. The dormouse sleeps in in a cosy nest on the ground or in a burrow.

Where do porcupines live?

There are two groups of porcupines. New World porcupines live in North and South America and live in trees. Old World porcupines live in Africa and parts of Asia. They are ground-dwelling animals. All porcupines are covered in long sharp spines, which look fearsome and help protect them from their enemies.

Porcupine

If attacked, the porcupine runs backwards toward its enemy, driving in its sharp spines.

Why do beavers build dams?

BEAVERS BUILD THEIR HOMES – OR LODGES – IN STREAMS OR RIVERS. But first they need to build a dam to make an area of still water, or the current would wash the lodge away. With their huge front teeth, the beavers cut down trees to build the dam. They plaster the sides with mud and fill gaps with stones and sticks. The lodge is built of sticks behind the dam and has an underwater entrance. The beavers sleep, store food and care for their young in the lodge. They have to keep repairing both the dam and the lodge with more sticks and mud. Beavers live in North America and in parts of Europe and Asia.

Which is the smallest rodent?

One of the smallest rodents is the pygmy mouse of North America. This is only about 10 cm (4 in) long, including its tail, and weighs 7 g (¼ oz). The harvest mouse of Europe and Asia is only slightly bigger.

What do beavers eat?

Beavers eat plant food. In spring and summer they feed on fresh green leaves and grasses. In autumn they gather woody stems to eat. Some of these are stored under water near the lodge to keep fresh for the winter months.

How many kinds of rodent are there?

There are more than 1,600 different species of rodent, including squirrels, hamsters and beavers as well as rats and mice. Rodents live all over the world in every kind of habitat from the icy Arctic to scorching deserts and humid rainforests.

Why do rodents get long in the tooth?

The two sharp teeth at the front of the rodent's jaw – called incisors – are the ones it uses for gnawing. A rodent's incisors get worn down as it gnaws tough food, but they keep on growing throughout its life.

Which is the biggest rodent?

The largest rodent in the world is the capybara, which lives in South America. It measures up to 1.3 metres (53 in) long and weighs up to 64 kg (140 lb). Capybaras live by water and feed on grasses.

How big is a beaver?

A fully grown beaver measures up to 1.7 metres (67 in) long, including its long flat tail. It weighs as much as 27 kg (60 lb) and is the second heaviest rodent in the world.

A beaver lodge

The beaver swims with the help of its webbed back feet and its large flattened tail.

The living chamber in the beaver's lodge is above the water level.

Can flying squirrels really fly?

No, but they can glide some distance from tree to tree. When the flying squirrel leaps into the air, it stretches out the skin flaps at the sides of its body. These act like a parachute, enabling it to glide gently down from one branch to another.

Is a guinea pig a rodent?

A guinea pig is a rodent. Wild guinea pigs, also known as cavies, live in South America, where they feed on leaves and grasses. Most cavies are about 22 cm (9 in) long, but one type, the long-legged, hare-like mara, is up to 75 cm (30 in) long.

When is a dog really a rat?

A PRAIRIE DOG IS ACTUALLY NOT A DOG AT ALL. IN FACT IT'S A TYPE OF RODENT, and lives in North America. Each prairie dog family, called a coterie, makes a burrow of connecting chambers and tunnels. A coterie contains one adult male and up to four females and their young. Groups of coteries live near each other in huge areas of burrows called towns. Prairie dogs feed mostly on grasses and other plants. While the family is feeding, one prairie dog keeps watch. It barks loudly to warn the others of any danger.

How many kinds of bear are there?

THERE ARE EIGHT SPECIES OF BEAR. THEY RANGE IN SIZE FROM THE SUN BEAR, which weighs only about 27 kg (60 lb), to huge polar bears and brown bears. The brown bear is the most widespread bear. It lives in northern North America and parts of Europe and Asia. In North America the brown bear is sometimes called the grizzly. Brown bears have a varied diet. They eat grasses, roots and berries, but they also catch insects, fish and other larger animals, as well as scavenging the carcasses of dead creatures such as deer and seals.

The panda's front paws have a special extra digit to help it grip bamboo stems.

Which is the biggest bear?
The polar bear, which lives in the Arctic. Fully grown males are up to 2.6 metres (8.5 ft) long. Polar bears have thick white fur to keep them warm in their icy home. They hunt seals and occasionally also young walrus and birds.

Is the giant panda a bear?
For many years experts argued about whether this animal should be grouped with bears or raccoons or classed in a separate family of its own. Genetic evidence now suggests that the panda is a member of the bear family.

What do giant pandas eat?
The main food of the giant panda is bamboo. An adult panda eats up to 15 kg (33 lb) of bamboo leaves and stems a day. Pandas also eat a small amount of other plants and even some little animals.

How many kinds of wild dog are there?
There are about 35 species in the dog family, including foxes, wolves, coyotes, and hunting dogs. Wild dogs live all over the world, except in New Zealand, New Guinea and a few other islands. All are good runners and hunt other animals to eat.

A red fox is up to 63 cm (25 in) long, with a bushy tail of up to 40 cm (16 in). Foxes live and hunt in an area called a territory, which they mark with their scent.

Where do giant pandas live?
Giant pandas live in bamboo forests in the mountains of central China. Most of these forests have now been made into special reserves to try and protect the rare pandas. Some pandas also live in captivity in zoos in China and other countries.

Red fox

What do foxes eat?
Foxes, such as the red fox, are hunting animals. They kill and eat small creatures, including rats, mice and rabbits. But foxes are very adaptable – they will eat more or less anything that comes their way, such as birds and birds' eggs, insects and even fruit and berries. And more and more foxes in cities are feasting on our discarded food from rubbish bins and compost heaps.

How big is a wolf pack?

In areas where there are plenty of large animals to catch, a pack may contain up to 20 wolves. Hunting in a pack means that the wolves can kill prey much larger than themselves, such as moose. A wolf pack has a home range, or territory, which it defends against other wolves.

How do wolf cubs learn how to hunt?

Wolf cubs learn how to hunt by watching their parents and other pack members and by playing. As the cubs run around and pounce on one another, they are also learning how to attack and ambush prey.

Can polar bears swim?

Polar bears can swim well and spend long periods in the freezing Arctic water. They are well equipped to survive the cold. A polar bear has a dense layer of underfur as well as a heavy, glossy outer coat. Under the skin is a thick layer of fat to give further protection.

Are there bears in the jungle?

Yes, there are two kinds of bear that live in jungle, or rainforest. Some spectacled bears live in South American rainforest, and the sun bear lives in rainforest in parts of Southeast Asia.

How big is a baby bear?

Although adult bears are so big they have tiny babies. A huge polar bear, weighing more than several people, gives birth to cubs of only about 800 g (28 oz), far smaller than most human babies. Baby pandas are tinier still. The mother weighs up to 100 kg (220 lb) but her newborn cubs are only 85–140 g (3–5 oz).

What is a dingo?

Dingoes are wild dogs that live in Australia. They are descended from dogs domesticated more than 3,500 years ago by the earliest aboriginal inhabitants. They live in family groups and hunt sheep and rabbits. A fence 5,322 km (3,307 miles) long has been built across southeastern Australia to try to keep dingoes out of important sheep-grazing lands.

Brown bear

A male brown bear stands up to 213 cm (84 in) tall and weighs up to 380 kg (838 lb). Bears like plant food and will reach up into trees to pick juicy fruit or berries.

Do bears sleep through the winter?

BROWN BEARS AND AMERICAN AND ASIAN BLACK BEARS THAT LIVE IN THE far north do sleep for much of the winter. Food supplies are poor and the bears hide themselves away in warm dens and live off their own fat reserves. Before their long sleep and fast, the bears eat as much food as they can to build up their body fat. They may not eat or drink again for as long as six months. A bear's body temperature drops only slightly during the winter sleep and it wakes easily if disturbed. Female bears may give birth to a litter of cubs during this time.

Meerkats on guard

Meerkats thrive in the hostile Kalahari desert by working as a team. A group of adults watch out for predators while others are out hunting.

What is a meerkat?

A meerkat is a type of mongoose, which lives in Africa. Meerkats form large groups of up to 30 or more animals, which share the guarding of young and finding of food. Sentry meerkats often stand up on their hind legs to watch out for danger.

Which cat runs the fastest?

The cheetah is the fastest running cat and one of the speediest of all animals over short distances. It has been timed running at 105 kph (60 mph) over 100 metres (110 yds). Olympic sprinters can reach only about 48 kph (30 mph).

What is a panther?

A panther is simply a leopard with a black coat instead of spots. It is not a separate species of cat. Leopards live in Africa and Asia.

What does a mongoose eat?

The mongoose is a fast-moving little hunter. It will kill small creatures such as rats, mice and frogs and will also take anything else it can find, including insects and birds' eggs. A mongoose will even tackle a large snake.

How many kinds of cat are there?

There are about 35 species of wild cat, ranging from the tiger to the African wild cat, which is the main ancestor of domestic cats. Cats live in most parts of the world in every sort of habitat from tropical rainforest and desert to the icy lands of Siberia. There are no wild cats in Antarctica, Australia or New Zealand.

The pattern of stripes on a tiger's skin is unique. No two tigers have quite the same pattern.

Tiger

Which big cat is the biggest?

TIGERS ARE THE BIGGEST OF THE BIG CATS. THEY MEASURE UP TO 3 METRES (10 FT) long, including the tail, and weigh 250 kg (550 lb) or more. Tigers are becoming very rare. They live in parts of Asia, from snowy Siberia in the north to the tropical rainforests of Sumatra. There is only one species of tiger, but those in the north tend to be larger and have thicker, lighter coloured fur than their relations further south. Tigers live alone, coming together only for mating. The female rears her cubs without the help of her mate. At first the cubs stay close to the den, but when they are about six months old they begin to go with their mother on hunts and learn how to find food for themselves.

What do lions do all day?

Like domestic cats, lions are actually asleep for a surprisingly large part of the day. As much as 22 hours a day are spent resting and grooming. The rest of the time is taken up with looking for prey, hunting and feeding. Lionesses do most of the hunting, but they share the catch with the rest of the pride.

Where do jaguars live?

Jaguars live in the forests of Central and South America. They are the largest South American cats and measure up to 1.8 metres (6 ft) long with a tail of up to 90 cm (36 in). Despite its size, the jaguar is a good climber and often clambers up a tree to watch for prey. It hunts other forest animals such as peccaries and capybaras as well as birds, turtles and fish.

Why are lions unlike other cats?

M OST CATS LIVE ALONE. LIONS LIVE AND HUNT IN A GROUP CALLED A PRIDE.
Tigers, cheetahs and other big cats live alone, unless rearing young. A lion pride includes several adult males and a number of females, young lions and cubs. Living in a group means that there are always some adults to look after the cubs while others are off hunting. And working together, lions can bring down animals much larger than themselves, such as wildebeest and zebra.

What is a snow leopard?

The snow leopard is a big cat that lives in the Himalaya Mountains. It has a beautiful pale coat with dark markings, which has made it the target of fur poachers. Killing snow leopards for their fur is now illegal, but poaching still goes on.

How different are our pet cats from wild cats?

Pet cats and wild cats have exactly the same body structure and skeleton. Both rely heavily on smell for information about the world and they mark their territories by spraying urine or by rubbing the body against trees or other objects. All cats are meat-eaters and cannot live on a diet of plant foods.

Is a civet a kind of cat?

No, civets belong to a separate family, which also includes mongooses, meerkats and genets. Most civets live in tropical forests in Southeast Asia or Africa. They have a long, slender body, short legs and a long tail. The African civet is about 95 cm (37 in) long with a tail of about 50 cm (20 in). It hunts small mammals, birds, reptiles and insects.

Why do tigers have stripes?

A tiger's stripes help it hide among grasses and leaves so it can surprise its prey. Tigers cannot run fast for long distances so they depend on being able to get close to their prey before making the final pounce. The stripes help to break up their outline and make them hard for prey to see.

How long are an elephant's tusks?
An elephant's tusks grow throughout its life, so the oldest elephants have the longest tusks. An old male elephant may have tusks that measure up to 3.5 metres (11 ft) and weigh 120 kg (264 lb).

African elephant

An elephant's tusks are actually very long upper teeth.

How much do elephants eat?
A fully grown elephant eats 100 to 200 kg (220 to 440 lb) of plant food a day, including grass, twigs, branches, leaves, flowers and fruits.

What do elephants do with their trunks?

THE ELEPHANT'S TRUNK IS VERY USEFUL. WITHOUT IT, AN ELEPHANT could not reach the ground to feed because its neck is so short. The trunk is also used for taking food from high in the trees and for breaking off branches. The elephant can smell with its trunk, pick up tiny objects and gently caress its young. It drinks by sucking up water into its trunk and squirting it into its mouth. It also sprays water or dust over itself to clean its skin.

The elephant flaps its huge ears to help keep itself cool.

How tall is a giraffe?
A male giraffe stands up to 5.5 metres (18 ft) tall to the tips of its horns. It has an extraordinarily long neck, and front legs that are longer than its back legs so the body slopes down toward the tail. The long neck allows it to feed on leaves high in trees that other animals cannot reach.

The giraffe's tongue can stretch out up to 46 cm (18 in) to help it gather leaves from tall trees.

How many bones are there in a giraffe's neck?
A giraffe has seven bones in its neck, just like other mammals, including humans. But the giraffe's neck bones are much longer than those of other animals, and have more flexible joints between them.

What is an okapi?
An okapi is a relative of the giraffe that lives in the African rainforest. It was discovered as recently as 1901 by a British explorer. It has small horns on its head and a long tongue like a giraffe's – but it does not have a long neck.

The elephant's grey skin is up to 4 cm (1½ in) thick and has a fine covering of hairs.

How can you tell an African elephant from an Asian elephant?

THE AFRICAN ELEPHANT IS BIGGER AND HAS LARGER EARS AND LONGER TUSKS. The head and body of the African elephant measures up to 7.5 metres (24.5 ft) long. The Asian elephant measures up to 6.5 metres (21 ft) and has a more humped back. There is another difference at the end of the long trunk. The African elephant's trunk has two flexible finger-like lips, while the Asian animal's trunk has only one.

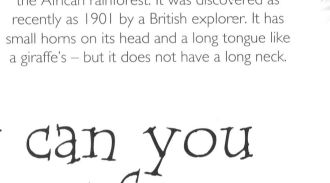

Are rhinoceroses fierce animals?
Despite their ferocious appearance and huge horns, rhinos are peaceful, plant-eating animals. But if threatened, a rhino will charge its enemy, galloping at high speed with its huge head held down ready to attack. Mothers defending their young can be particularly dangerous.

Can hippos swim?
The hippo spends most of its day in or near water and comes out on to land at night to feed on plants. It does not really swim, but it walks or runs along underwater or on the bottom of the river at surprising speeds.

How big is a baby elephant?
A newborn baby elephant weighs up to 120 kg (264 lb) and stands up to 1 metre (40 in) high. It feeds on its mother's milk for at least two years, by which time it may weigh more than 600 kg (1,322 lb), and it may continue suckling for up to six years.

Do all marsupials live in Australia?

Most of the 260 or so species of marsupial live in Australia and New Guinea, but there are about 80 species of marsupial opossum in South America. One of these also lives in North America.

Which is the smallest marsupial?

The smallest marsupials are the mouse-like ningauis, which live in Australia. These little creatures are only about 5 cm (2 in) long and weigh only a few grams. They feed on insects.

Do all marsupials have a pouch?

Most female marsupials have a pouch, but not all. Some very small marsupials such as the shrew opossums of South America do not have a pouch. Others, such as the American opossums, simply have flaps of skin around the nipples and not a full pouch. The tiny young cling on to the nipples.

Do any marsupials swim?

The water opossum, which lives in South America, is an excellent swimmer and has webbed back feet. Strong muscles keep its pouch closed when the opossum is in water.

Why does a kangaroo have a pouch?

AT BIRTH, KANGAROOS ARE VERY TINY AND EXTREMELY POORLY DEVELOPED. In fact, a kangaroo is only about 2 cm (³/₄ in) long when it is born. The female kangaroo has a pouch so that its young can complete their development in safety. The tiny newborn crawls up to the pouch by itself and starts to suckle on one of the nipples inside the pouch. A young kangaroo, or joey, stays in the pouch until it weighs about 9 kg (20 lb). Pouched animals like kangaroos are called marsupials.

How many kinds of kangaroo and wallaby are there?

There are about 60 different species of kangaroo and wallaby. All live in Australia or New Guinea. The red kangaroo, which weighs about 90 kg (198 lb), is the largest, and the tiny musky rat kangaroo, weighing only 0.5 kg (1.2 lb), is the smallest.

What do kangaroos eat?

Kangaroos eat grass and the leaves of low-growing plants, just like deer and antelopes do in the northern hemisphere.

Red kangaroo

Only the male red kangaroo has a reddish coat. Females are bluish-grey.

What is a Tasmanian devil?
The Tasmanian devil is the largest of the carnivores, or flesh-eating marsupials. It is about 90 cm (36 in) long, including its tail, and has sharp teeth and strong jaws. The devil feeds mostly on carrion – the flesh of animals that are already dead – but it does also kill prey such as sheep and birds.

How much does a koala eat every day?
A koala eats about 500 g (1 lb) of eucalyptus leaves every day, which it chews down to a fine pulp with its broad teeth. The leaves do not provide much energy, but koalas are slow-moving animals and sleep up to 18 hours a day.

Is a platypus a marsupial?
No, the platypus is not a marsupial, but it is an unusual animal and it does live in Australia. Unlike most mammals, which give birth to live young, the platypus lays eggs. The mother leaves her two or three eggs to incubate in a burrow for up to two weeks. When they hatch, the young feed on the milk that flows from openings in the mother's body.

What are bandicoots?
Bandicoots are a group of small marsupials that live in Australia and New Guinea. Most have short legs, a rounded body and a long pointed nose. They have strong claws, which they use to dig worms and other small creatures from the ground.

Koala bear

The koala has strong claws to help it hold on to branches as it climbs in search of food.

Is a koala really a kind of bear?

NO, IT'S A MARSUPIAL LIKE A KANGAROO AND NOT RELATED TO BEARS AT ALL. Koalas live in Australia in eucalyptus forests. They feed almost entirely on eucalyptus leaves, preferring those of only a few species. A baby koala spends its first six or seven months in the pouch and then rides on its mother's back until it is able to fend for itself. A baby weighs less than half a gram at birth, but when fully grown the average koala measures about 78 cm (30 in) long and weighs up to 11 kg (24 lb). Females are much smaller than males.

How fast do kangaroos move?
A kangaroo bounds along on its strong back legs at up to 65 kph (40 mph). It can cover 12 metres (39 ft) in one bound.

What is a wombat?
A wombat is a small bear-like marsupial with a heavy body and short strong legs. It digs burrows to shelter in and feeds mostly on grass. Its pouch opens to the rear so that it does not fill up with earth when the wombat is burrowing.

What do gorillas eat?

Gorillas eat plant food, such as leaves, buds, stems and fruit. Because their diet is juicy, gorillas rarely need to drink.

Which is the smallest monkey?

The smallest monkey is the pygmy marmoset, which lives in South American rainforest. It is about 40 cm (15 in) long, but half of this is tail, and it weighs only about 150 g (5 oz).

What is an ape?

Apes are the most advanced animals in the primate group, which also includes animals such as lemurs, bush babies and monkeys. There are three families of apes. One includes all the different kinds of gibbons. The second contains the gorilla, chimpanzee and orang-utan and the third has one species only – humans.

Where do orang-utans live?

Orang-utans live in Southeast Asia in the rainforests of Sumatra and Borneo. This ape has long reddish fur and spends most of its life in the trees. Fruit is its main food but the orang-utan also eats leaves, insects and even eggs and small animals. The orang-utan is active during the day. At night it sleeps on the ground or in a nest of branches in the trees.

Gorillas usually move on all fours, leaning on the knuckles of their front limbs.

Which is the biggest ape?

THE GORILLA – A FULLY GROWN MALE STANDS UP TO 1.7 METRES (5.5 FT) TALL and weighs as much as 180 kg (400 lb). Gorillas live in rainforest in West and Central Africa. A family group contains an adult male, several females and a number of young of different ages. The male, known as a silverback because of the white hair on his back, leads the group.

Gorilla family

Do chimpanzees hunt prey?

Yes they do. Although fruit is the main food of chimpanzees, they also eat insects and hunt young animals such as monkeys. Male chimpanzees usually do the hunting. They work together in a group, some cutting a couple of animals out of the herd and driving them towards other chimps, who will make the kill. The rest of the troop then joins in to share the meat.

Chimpanzee

An adult chimpanzee is up to 85 cm (33 in) long and does not have a tail.

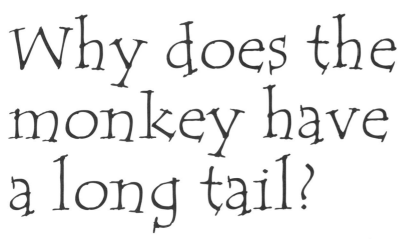

Why does the monkey have a long tail?

To help it balance and control its movements as it leaps from branch to branch in the rainforest. The tails of South American monkeys are even more useful than those of their African and Asian relatives, because they are prehensile. A prehensile tail has special muscles that the monkey can use to twine round branches and help it climb – it's almost like having a fifth leg. The naked skin on the underside of the tail is ridged to improve grip.

Chimpanzees climb well and find much of their food in trees.

Do any monkeys live in cold places?

Most monkeys are found in warm areas near to the equator, but some macaque monkeys live in cooler places. The rhesus macaque lives in the Himalayas as well as in parts of China and India, and the Japanese macaque survives freezing winters with the help of its thick coat.

Do chimpanzees use tools?

Yes. The chimpanzee can get food by poking a stick into an ants' nest. It pulls out the stick and licks off the ants. It also uses stones to crack nuts, and it makes sponges from chewed leaves to mop up water or wipe its body.

Which monkey makes the loudest noise?

Howler monkeys not only shout louder than other monkeys – they are among the noisiest of all animals. Troops of monkeys call to each other and their voices carry for more than 1 km (0.6 miles).

Where do chimpanzees live?

Chimpanzees live in forest and grasslands in West and Central Africa. There is another less familiar chimpanzee species called the pygmy chimpanzee, or bonobo, which lives in rainforests in Zaire/Congo in Africa. It is slimmer and lighter than the common chimpanzee and spends more of its time in trees.

How many kinds of monkey are there?

About 133 species in three main groups. One group lives in Africa and Asia. The other two groups live in Central and South America.

Do chimpanzees live in family groups?

Yes, in very large families that may include between 25 and 100 animals, led by a dominant male. Each group has its own home range.

Californian sea lion

The sea lion tucks its back flippers under itself when on land.

How can you tell a seal from a sea lion?

WITH PRACTICE! SEALS AND SEA LIONS BOTH HAVE STREAMLINED BODIES adapted to marine living, and flippers instead of limbs. But there are several differences between them. Sea lions have small ear flaps, but seals have only ear openings, no flaps. Sea lions can bring their back flippers under the body to help them move on land. Seals cannot do this – they simply drag themselves along. Sea lions swim by moving their front flippers. Seals swim by moving the back flippers and the rear of the body.

How do seals keep warm in cold sea?

A layer of fatty blubber under the skin helps to keep seals and sea lions warm. The blubber may be up to 10 cm (4 in) thick. These animals also have a covering of fur.

How fast do seals and sea lions swim?

A Californian sea lion has been timed swimming at 40 kph (25 mph). On land the crabeater seal can move at up to 19 kph (11 mph) as it toboggans over ice.

How deep do seals dive?

The Weddell seal, which lives in Antarctic waters, is one of the deepest-diving seals. It can go down to depths of more than 500 metres (1,640 ft) in search of food. When the seal dives, blood flow is cut off to all but essential organs such as the heart.

How big are sea lions?

The biggest, the huge steller sea lion, is about 230 cm (90 in) long and weighs as much as 1,000 kg (2,200 lb). Females are much smaller and weigh only about 270 kg (595 lb). The smallest is probably the Galapagos fur seal, which weighs only about 64 kg (140 lb).

Are baby seals and sea lions born in water?

No, they are born on land. Seals and sea lions spend most of their lives in water but they do come out on to land to give birth. They remain on land for a number of weeks, feeding their young on their rich milk.

Harp seal

Which is the smallest seal?

The ringed seal is one of the smallest seals. The male grows to about 1.4 metres (4.5 ft) long and weighs up to 90 kg (198 lb), although some are only 50 kg (110 lb). Females are slightly smaller than males. Ringed seals live in Arctic waters and eat fish and shellfish.

How big is a walrus?

The largest male walruses are more than 3 metres (10 ft) long and weigh 1,200 kg (2,645 lb). Females are smaller, averaging 2.7 metres (9 ft) long and weighing about 800 kg (1,760 lb). The walrus's skin is up to 4 cm (1½ in) thick and covered with coarse hairs. The thick skin helps protect the walrus from the tusks of others.

Do seals live in fresh water?

Yes, there is a species of freshwater seal in Lake Baikal in Russia. Baikal is the deepest freshwater lake in the world and holds more water than any other. Thousands of seals live there, feeding on freshwater fish and resting on the remote islands in the middle of the lake.

How long are a walrus's tusks?

The tusks of an adult male walrus can be up to 55 cm (22 in) long. Some people think that a walrus uses its tusks to dig shellfish from the sea bed, but other experts believe that the tusks are just for display and attracting mates.

Are any seals very rare?

Yes, monk seals, which live in the Caribbean, Mediterranean and Hawaiian seas, are extremely rare. The Caribbean seal is probably already extinct. These are the only seals that live in warm seas, closer to human activity than other seals, so they have suffered greater habitat disturbance.

Which is the biggest seal?

The male elephant seal is the biggest of all the seals. It is 5 metres (16 ft) long and weighs 2,400 kg (5,300 lb), nearly as much as an elephant.

How many kinds of seal and sea lion are there?

There are about 14 species of sea lion, 18 species of seal and one species of walrus. Most sea lions live along North Pacific coasts and on the southern coasts of Africa, Australia and South America. Most seals live in waters to the far north and south of the world, and the walrus lives in Arctic seas.

What do seals and sea lions eat?

FISH IS THEIR MAIN DIET, BUT SOME ALSO EAT SHELLFISH AND CATCH LARGER PREY. Some seals have a more varied diet. The crabeater seal feeds mostly on krill, small shrimp-like crustaceans. The bearded seal eats seabed creatures such as clams, and the leopard seal preys on the young of other seals as well as birds and fish.

Do seals and sea lions breathe air?

Seals and sea lions are mammals so they have to come to the surface regularly to breathe air. But they can stay underwater much longer than we can. Dives lasting 20 minutes or more are common and the Weddell seal has been timed making a dive of over 70 minutes.

Fur seals have extra-thick fur and look like true seals. But their small ear flaps show they are really types of sea lion.

Dolphins

How big is a baby blue whale?
A baby blue whale is about 7 metres (23 ft) long at birth and is the biggest baby in the animal kingdom. It weighs about 8 tonnes – that is more than a fully grown elephant.

Which is the biggest whale?

THE BLUE WHALE IS THE LARGEST WHALE, AND ALSO THE LARGEST MAMMAL THAT has ever lived. It measures more than 30 metres (100 ft) long. It weighs at least 90 tonnes and the biggest blue whales may weigh more than twice this amount. Although it is so huge, the blue whale is not a fierce hunter. It eats tiny shrimp-like creatures called krill. It may gobble up as many as four million of these in a day.

Dolphins leap out of the water as they swim and dive back in head first.

What is a porpoise?
A porpoise is a small whale with a rounded head, not a beaked snout like a dolphin. There are about six species of porpoise, which live in coastal waters in the Atlantic and Pacific. They feed on fish and squid.

Which whale dives deepest?
The sperm whale dives to at least 1,000 metres (3,300 ft) below the surface of the sea and may go down to even greater depths when chasing giant squid to eat.

Do whales ever come to land?
No, whales spend their whole lives in the sea. But they do breathe air and have to come to the surface regularly to take breaths.

Blue whales once lived in all oceans. Now most are found in Antarctic waters.

Blue whale

Is a dolphin a kind of whale?

A DOLPHIN IS A SMALL WHALE. MOST OF THE 37 OR SO SPECIES OF DOLPHIN live in the sea, but there are five that live in rivers. The biggest dolphin is usually known as the killer whale, or orca, and grows up to 9.4 metres (31 ft) long. Dolphins have a streamlined shape and a beaked snout containing lots of sharp teeth. They are fast swimmers and they catch sea creatures such as fish and squid to eat. A form of ultrasound helps dolphins find their prey. A dolphin gives off a series of high-frequency clicking sounds that bounce off anything in their path. The echoes tell the dolphin about the size and direction of the prey.

Do whales give birth in the water?

Yes, they do. The baby whale comes out of the mother's body tail first so that it does not drown during birth. As soon as the head emerges, the mother and the other females attending the birth help the baby whale swim to the surface to take its first breath.

What is a narwhal?

A narwhal is a whale with a single long tusk at the front of its head. The tusk is actually a tooth, which grows out from the upper jaw. It can be as much as 2.7 metres (9 ft) long. Only male narwhals have tusks and they may use them in battles with other males.

Do humpback whales really sing?

Yes, they do. They make a series of sounds, including high whistles and low rumbles, that may continue for hours. No one knows exactly why the humpback whale sings, but it may be to court a mate or to keep in touch with others in the group.

Why do some whales migrate?

Whales such as humpbacks migrate – travel from place to place – to find the best conditions for feeding and breeding. They spend much of the year feeding in the waters of the Arctic and Antarctic, where there is lots of krill to eat. When it is time to give birth, the humpbacks travel to warmer waters near the equator.

How fast do whales swim?

Blue whales normally swim at about 8 kph (5 mph) but can move at speeds of up to 30 kph (18 mph) when disturbed. Some small whales, such as pilot whales and dolphins, may swim at more than 50 kph (30 mph).

How does a blue whale feed?

A blue whale filters small shrimp-like creatures called krill from the water. Hanging from the whale's upper jaw are lots of plates of a fringed bristly material called baleen. The whale opens its mouth and water, and krill, flows in. The whale forces the water through the baleen with its tongue. The water flows out at the sides of the mouth, leaving the krill behind on the baleen for the whale to swallow.

Puffer fish

How fast do fish swim?
The sailfish is one of the fastest swimming fish. It has been timed moving at speeds of more than 100 kph (62 mph). Marlins and tunas are also fast swimmers. All these fish have sleek streamlined bodies.

This fish puffs up its body when in danger.

Does a stingray sting?
A stingray gets its name from the sharp spine near the base of its tail. This carries poison and causes a nasty wound if the fish drives it into the flesh of its enemy. It can even kill a human.

Are flatfishes born flat?
No, they are not. Young flatfishes have normal bodies with an eye on each side. As they grow, the body flattens and one eye moves, so that both are on the upper surface. The fish lies on the seabed with its eyed side uppermost so it can see.

Are there any poisonous fish?

YES, THERE ARE – AND THE PUFFER FISH IS ONE OF THE MOST POISONOUS OF ALL.
It has a powerful poison in some of its internal organs, such as the heart and liver, which can kill a human. Despite this, puffer fish is a delicacy in Japan, where chefs are specially trained to remove the poisonous parts and prepare the fish. A puffer fish also has another way of defending itself. It can puff its body up with water and air until it is at least twice its normal size. This makes it very hard for any predator to swallow. Some puffer fish are covered with spines that stick up when the body is inflated.

Which is the fiercest freshwater fish?
The piranha, which lives in rivers in tropical Central and South America, is the fiercest of all freshwater fish. Each fish is only about 30 cm (12 in) long, but a shoal of hundreds attacking together can kill and eat a much larger animal in seconds. The piranha's weapons are its extremely sharp triangular-shaped teeth, which it uses to chop flesh from its victim. But not all piranhas are dangerous killers. Some species feed only on plants.

How many kinds of shark are there?
There are about 370 different species of shark living all over the world. They range in size from tiny fish only 25 cm (10 in) long, to the giant whale shark, which can grow to 15 metres (50 ft).

Are electric eels really electric?
Yes, they are. The electric eel's body contains special muscles that can release electrical charges into the water. These are powerful enough to stun and kill its prey.

Why does a flying fish 'fly'?
A flying fish usually lifts itself above the water to escape from danger. It has extra large fins, which act as its 'wings'. After building up speed in the water, the fish lifts its fins and glides above the surface for a short distance.

How big is a great white shark?

Are all sharks killers?
No, two of the largest sharks, the whale shark and the basking shark, eat only tiny shrimp-like creatures. They filter these from the water through special sieve-like structures in the mouth.

GREAT WHITE SHARKS ARE MOSTLY ABOUT 7 METRES (23 FT) LONG, but some can grow up to 12 metres (40 ft). They live in warm seas all over the world. Great white sharks are fierce hunters and attack large fish and other creatures such as sea lions and porpoises. Their main weapons are their large, jagged-edged teeth, which they use to kill prey and to tear it apart. Behind these teeth are rows of new ones, ready to replace teeth at the front that get damaged or broken.

Great white shark

The shark's teeth may be up to 7.5 cm (3 in) long.

A shark may swim at speeds of up to 40 kph (25 mph) for short periods.

Poison-arrow frog

The poison-arrow frog is one of the most poisonous of all animals.

Do all frogs lay their eggs in water?

No, some frogs have very unusual breeding habits. The male marsupial frog, for example, carries his mate's eggs on his back. A layer of skin grows over them to protect them. The male Darwin's frog keeps his mate's eggs in his mouth until they have developed into tiny frogs.

What do frogs eat?

Adult frogs catch insects and spiders and other small creatures such as crayfish and even other frogs to eat. Tadpoles usually feed on small water plants.

What is an amphibian?

An amphibian is a creature that lives in water and on land. Amphibians evolved from fish and were the first vertebrates (creatures with backbones) to live on land. There are about 3,000 species of amphibian, including frogs, toads, newts and salamanders.

What is a tadpole?

A tadpole is the young, or larva, of an amphibian such as a frog or newt. The amphibian egg is usually laid in water and hatches out into a small, swimming creature with a long tail called a tadpole. The tadpole feeds on water plants and gradually develops into its adult form.

Why do frogs croak?

Male frogs make their croaking calls to attract females. The frog has a special sac of skin under its chin, which blows up and helps make the call louder.

Which is the smallest frog?

The smallest frog, and the smallest of all amphibians, is the Cuban frog, which measures only 12 mm long. The tiny gold frog, which lives in Brazilian rainforests, is only slightly bigger at about 2 cm (¾ in) long.

Are frogs and toads poisonous?

SOME ARE – THE CANE TOAD CAN SQUIRT POISON AT AN ENEMY FROM GLANDS near its eyes, and the fire-bellied toad has poison in its skin. But most deadly of all are the poison-arrow frogs that live in South American rainforests. Their skin contains one of the most powerful poisons known and a tiny drop can kill a person. Local people tip their hunting arrows with this deadly substance by simply rubbing the arrow over the skin of a frog. Poison-arrow frogs live in trees and are usually very brightly coloured. Their bold markings warn predators that they are poisonous and should be left alone. But there is a frog-eating snake in the rainforest that seems to be able to eat the frogs without coming to any harm.

How can treefrogs climb trees?

Treefrogs are excellent climbers. On each of their long toes is a round sticky pad, which allows them to cling to the undersides of leaves and to run up the smoothest surfaces. Treefrogs spend most of their lives in trees, catching insects to eat, and only come down to the ground to lay their eggs in water.

How did the spadefoot toad get its name?

The spadefoot toad got its name from the hard spade-like projection on each back foot, which it uses for digging its burrow. The toad backs into the ground, pushing soil away with its 'spades'. It usually spends the day deep in its burrow and comes out at night to find food.

Can the flying frog really fly?

NO, BUT IT CAN GLIDE 12 METRES (40 FT) THROUGH THE AIR BETWEEN TREES. When the frog jumps into the air it stretches out its legs and toes so that its webbed feet act like little parachutes. Small flaps of skin on the legs also help the frog to glide. The flying frog lives in rainforests in Southeast Asia and spends most of its life in trees. Being able to 'fly' in this way means that it does not have to go down to the ground and climb back up again to move from tree to tree.

How many types of frog and toad are there?

There are about 2,500 species of frog and toad. They live on all continents except Antarctica. Most live in areas with plenty of rainfall, but some manage to live in drier lands by sheltering in burrows.

Flaps of skin help the frog glide through the air.

Flying frog

How big is a giant toad?

The giant toad, which lives in parts of the southern United States, is up to 24 cm (9½ in) long. It eats beetles. It has been introduced into many parts of the world by farmers, in an effort to control the beetles that eat crops such as sugarcane.

What is a salamander?

A salamander looks like a lizard with its long body and tail, but it is an amphibian like frogs and toads. There are about 350 different kinds. The biggest is the giant salamander, which can grow to 1.5 metres (5 ft) long.

How can you tell a crocodile from an alligator?

YOU CAN RECOGNIZE A CROCODILE BECAUSE ITS TEETH STICK OUT WHEN ITS MOUTH IS SHUT!

In many ways, crocodiles and alligators are very similar. They both have long bodies covered with thick scales. And they both have long jaws with lots of sharp teeth. But when they shut their mouths, there is one difference between them that is easily spotted. In alligators, the fourth pair of teeth on the lower jaw disappears into pits in the upper jaws, but in crocodiles, these teeth slide outside the mouth into notches in the upper jaw, and can be seen when the mouth is closed.

Which is the biggest crocodile?
The Nile crocodile grows up to 6 metres (19.5 ft) long, but the Indopacific crocodile is even larger. This crocodile, which lives in parts of Southeast Asia, grows to 7 metres (23 ft) or more.

Do crocodiles lay eggs?
Crocodiles do lay eggs and they look after them very carefully. The female crocodile digs a pit into which she lays 30 or more eggs. She covers them over with earth or sand. While the eggs incubate for about three months, the female crocodile stays nearby guarding the nest. When the young hatch, the mother hears their cries and lifts them out of the pit with her mouth.

What do crocodiles eat?
Baby crocodiles start by catching insects and spiders to eat. As they grow, fish and birds form a larger part of their diet. Fully grown crocodiles prey on anything that comes their way, even large animals such as giraffes. The crocodile lies in the water near where animals come to drink, then suddenly lurches forward to seize the prey.

How big is a giant tortoise?

Giant tortoises grow up to 1.4 metres (4.5 ft) long and weigh as much as 250 kg (550 lb). They live on the Galapagos Islands in the Pacific and on the island of Aldabra in the Indian Ocean. Seychelles giant tortoises were thought to be extinct in the wild – to have died out completely – but some living animals have recently been discovered. Efforts are being made to breed more tortoises in captivity and release them into the wild.

Which is the biggest turtle?

The leatherback is the largest of all the turtles. It grows up to 1.6 metres (64 in) long and weighs up to 360 kg (794 lb). Leatherbacks also dive deeper than other turtles. They plunge down to more than 1,000 metres (3,300 ft).

What do sea turtles eat?

Most sea turtles eat a range of underwater creatures, such as clams, shrimps and snails, but some concentrate on certain foods. The hawksbill is one of the few creatures that feeds mostly on sponges. The leatherback's main food is jellyfish, while the green turtle eats sea grass.

The green turtle's broad shell is up to 1.5 metres (5 ft) long. Turtles 'fly' through the water with the help of their paddle-shaped flippers.

Green turtle

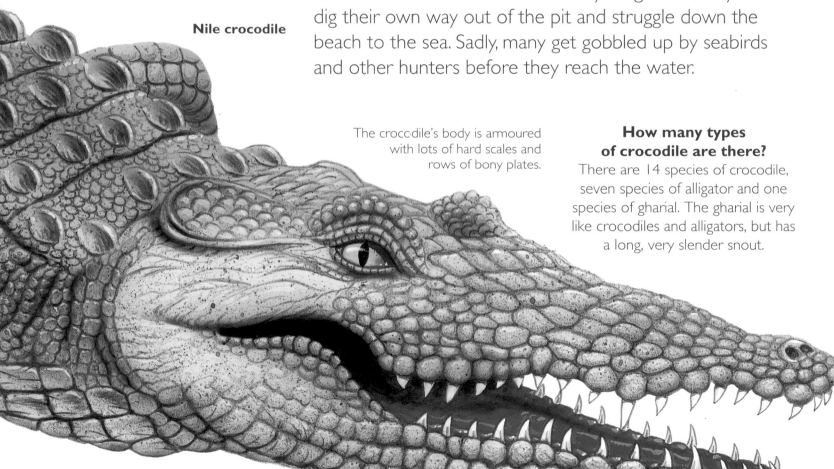

Nile crocodile

The crocodile's body is armoured with lots of hard scales and rows of bony plates.

Do turtles ever come to land?

SEA TURTLES SPEND NEARLY ALL THEIR LIVES IN THE WATER, BUT FEMALES do come to land to lay their eggs. The female green turtle drags herself up on to a sandy beach and digs a deep pit. She lays 100 or more eggs and covers them with sand. She then returns to the sea. When the young hatch, they must dig their own way out of the pit and struggle down the beach to the sea. Sadly, many get gobbled up by seabirds and other hunters before they reach the water.

How many types of crocodile are there?

There are 14 species of crocodile, seven species of alligator and one species of gharial. The gharial is very like crocodiles and alligators, but has a long, very slender snout.

Which is the most dangerous snake?
The saw-scaled carpet viper is probably the world's most dangerous snake. It is extremely aggressive and its poison can kill humans. Saw-scaled carpet vipers live in Africa and Asia.

How fast do snakes move?
The fastest-moving snake on land is thought to be the black mamba, which lives in Africa. It can wriggle along at up to 19 kph (12 mph).

Reticulated python

The python can coil its strong body around its prey and crush it to death.

Are there any snakes in the sea?
Yes, there are about 47 different species of snake that spend their whole lives in the sea. Most are completely helpless on land. They eat fish and other sea creatures, such as shrimp, and all are extremely poisonous. One, the beaked sea snake, has the deadliest poison of any snake.

Which is the biggest snake?

THE WORLD'S LONGEST SNAKE IS THE RETICULATED PYTHON, WHICH LIVES IN parts of Southeast Asia. It grows to an amazing 10 metres (33 ft). The anaconda, which lives in South American rainforests, is heavier than the python but not quite as long. Pythons and anacondas are not poisonous snakes. They kill with their teeth or by crushing prey to death. A python lies in wait for its prey, then creeps up and wraps the victim in the powerful coils of its body until it is suffocated.

Which is the largest lizard?
The komodo dragon, which lives on some Southeast Asian islands. It grows up to 3 metres (10 ft) long and hunts animals such as wild pigs and small deer.

Why does a rattlesnake rattle?
Rattlesnakes make their rattling noise to warn their enemies to stay well away. The rattle is made by a number of hard rings of skin at the end of the tail that make a noise when shaken. Each ring was once the tip of the tail. A new one is added every time the snake grows and sheds its skin.

How many kinds of snake are there?
There are about 2,700 species of snake in the world. They live on all continents except Antarctica, but there are no snakes in Ireland, Iceland or New Zealand. All snakes are carnivorous – that means that they feed on other animals.

Are all snakes poisonous?
Only about a third of all snakes are poisonous and fewer still have poison strong enough to harm humans. Non-poisonous snakes either crush their prey to death or simply swallow it whole.

Why do snakes shed their skin?
Snakes shed their skin, or moult, to allow for growth and because their skin gets worn and damaged. In its first year, when it is growing quickly, a young snake may shed its skin seven times or more. After this, it may only moult once a year or less.

Why does a chameleon change colour?

CHANGING COLOUR HELPS THE CHAMELEON GET NEAR TO ITS PREY without being seen and allows it to hide from its own enemies. The colour change is controlled by the chameleon's nervous system. Nerves cause areas of colour in the skin to be spread out or to become concentrated in tiny dots. Chameleons are also said to go darker in colour when angry and lighter when afraid.

Chameleon

Are there any poisonous lizards?
There are only two poisonous lizards in the world – the gila monster and the Mexican beaded lizard, both of which live in western North America. The poison is made in glands in the lower jaw. When the lizard seizes a prey and starts to chew, poison flows into the wound. Overpowered by the poison, the victim soon stops struggling.

How many kinds of lizard are there?
There are about 3,000 different species of lizard. These belong to different groups, or families, such as the geckos, iguanas, skinks and chameleons. There are lizards on all continents, except Antarctica, but most live in warm parts of the world.

Where do chameleons live?
There are about 85 different sorts of chameleon and most of these live in Africa and Madagascar. There are a few Asian species and one kind of chameleon lives in parts of southern Europe.

The python's jaws open extremely wide so it can swallow prey larger than itself.

Do all penguins live in Antarctica?

Most of the 18 species of penguin live in or near Antarctica, but some are found in warmer areas. There are several species around New Zealand, one in the tropical Galapagos Islands and one on South African coasts. There are no penguins in the northern hemisphere.

Which is the smallest penguin?

The little, or fairy, penguin is the smallest penguin – it is only about 40 cm (16 in) long. It lives in waters off the coasts of New Zealand and Tasmania.

Emperor penguins

Which is the biggest penguin?

THE EMPEROR LIVES IN ANTARCTICA, AND IS THE BIGGEST PENGUIN THE WORLD. It stands about 95 cm (37 in) tall. Like all penguins, the emperor cannot fly, but it is an expert swimmer and diver, using its wings as paddles. It spends most of its life in the water, where it catches fish and squid to eat. Emperor penguins do come to land to breed. The female lays one egg, which the male bird then keeps warm on his feet. The female goes back to the sea, but the male stays and incubates the egg for about 60 days. He cannot leave it, even to feed. The female returns when the egg hatches and cares for the chick while the starving male goes to find food.

What is a tropicbird?

A tropicbird is a seabird with two very long central tail feathers. There are three species, all of which fly over tropical oceans.

The emperor penguin has waterproof feathers and a thick layer of fat to keep out the cold of Antarctica.

152

Which bird makes the longest migration?

The Arctic tern makes the longest migration journey of any bird. Each year it makes a round trip of more than 40,000 km (25,000 miles). The birds nest in the Arctic in the northern summer and then travel south to spend the southern summer near Antarctica, where food is plentiful.

Why does a pelican have a pouch?

The pelican has a pouch to help it catch fish to eat. When the bird plunges its open beak into the water the pouch fills up with water and fish. As it brings its head up again, the water drains from the pouch, leaving any fish behind to be swallowed.

How many kinds of gull are there?

There are about 45 species of gull. They live in all parts of the world, but there are more species north of the equator. Gulls range in size from the little gull, which is only 28 cm (11 in) long, to the great black-backed gull, a huge 65 cm (26 in) long. Many gulls find food inland as well as at sea and some even scavenge in towns and cities.

How does a gannet catch its food?

The gannet catches fish and squid in spectacular dives into the sea. This graceful seabird flies over the water looking for prey. When it sees something, it plunges from as high as 30 metres (100 ft) above the ocean, dives into the water with its wings swept back and seizes the catch in its dagger-like beak.

Is a puffin a kind of penguin?

No, puffins belong to a different family of birds, called auks. They live in the northern hemisphere, particularly around the Arctic. Auks are good swimmers and divers, like penguins, but they can also fly.

Wandering albatross

The wandering albatross has a strong hooked beak that helps it catch its slippery prey.

Can all seabirds swim?

Not all seabirds can swim. Frigatebirds cannot swim and avoid going into the water. They seize food from the surface or rob other birds of their catches. Storm petrels, too, rarely land on the water, preferring to swoop close to the surface.

Which bird has the longest wings?

THE WANDERING ALBATROSS HAS THE LONGEST WINGS OF ANY LIVING BIRD. When fully spread they measure up to 3.3 metres (11 ft) from tip to tip. This majestic seabird spends much of its life soaring over the ocean far from land and it may travel several hundred kilometres a day. It lays its eggs and cares for its young on islands near Antarctica.

Can all cormorants fly?

There are about 30 different kinds of cormorant and all but one can fly. The flightless cormorant lives in the Galapagos Islands off the coast of South America. It has tiny wings and cannot fly, but it is an expert swimmer. It catches all of its fooc in the water.

How fast do penguins swim?

Penguins have been timed swimming at speeds of 10 kph (6 mph), but may move even faster for short periods. They can dive under water for two minutes or more. Emperors are believed to be able to stay under water for more than 18 minutes.

Harpy eagle

The harpy eagle has shorter wings than other eagles so that it can fly among the branches of rainforest trees.

Do eagles build nests?

Yes, and the nest made by the bald eagle is the biggest made by any bird. Some bald eagle nests are up to 5.5 metres (18 ft) deep. They are used again and again and the eagles add more nest material each year.

Which is the fastest flying bird?

As it dives to catch other birds in the air, the peregrine falcon may move at more than 160 kph (100 mph), faster than any other bird. The falcon circles above its victim before making its fast dive and killing the prey with a blow from its powerful talons.

What does an osprey eat?

The osprey feeds mostly on fish. When it sees something near the surface, it dives down towards the water and seizes the fish in its feet. The soles of its feet are covered with small spines to help it hold on to the slippery fish.

Which is the biggest eagle?

THE BIGGEST EAGLE IN THE WORLD IS THE HARPY EAGLE, WHICH LIVES IN RAINFORESTS in South America. It is up to 110 cm (43 in) long and has huge feet and sharp talons, which it uses to kill its prey. Unlike other eagles, the harpy does not soar high in the air looking for food. It hunts creatures such as monkeys and sloths in the trees, chasing its victims from branch to branch at high speed. Almost as big is the rare Philippine monkey-eating eagle, which lives in rainforests in the Philippines.

Bearded vultures gathering at a carcass

Which is the biggest bird of prey?

The Andean condor is the the biggest bird of prey in the world. It measures up to 110 cm (43 in) long and weighs up to 12 kg (25 lb). Its wingspan is over 3 metres (10 ft).

How do eagles kill their prey?

An eagle kills with the four long curved claws on each of its feet. It drops down on to the victim, seizes it in its long talons and crushes it to death. The eagle then tears the flesh apart with its strong hooked beak. The hook of a golden eagle's beak is as much as 10 cm (4 in) long.

Do eagles really catch snakes?

Yes, serpent eagles feed mostly on snakes and lizards. The rough surface of the serpent eagle's toes helps it hold on to slippery snakes.

How many kinds of owl are there?

There are about 142 different species of owl in two different families. The barn owl family contains about 12 species and the true owl family about 130 species. Owls live in most parts of the world, except a few islands. They usually hunt at night, catching small mammals, birds, frogs, lizards, insects and even fish.

The bearded vulture gets its name from the clump of black bristles that hangs under its beak.

Do vultures hunt and kill prey?

VULTURES DO NOT USUALLY KILL THEIR PREY. THEY ARE SCAVENGERS, FEEDING on animals that are already dead or have been killed by hunters such as lions. They have strong claws and beaks and the bald head allows them to plunge into carcasses without dirtying their feathers. The bearded vulture, or lammergeier, often picks up bones, which it drops on to rocks to smash them open. It can then feed on the marrow inside.

The bearded vulture soars on its long narrow wings high over remote mountains in parts of southern Europe, Asia and Africa .

Plants

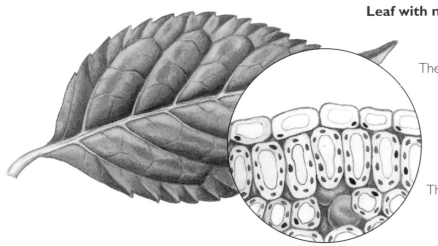

Leaf with magnified section

The leaf is made up of cells.

The dark green spots contain chlorophyll.

Why are most plants green?

Most plants are green because they contain the green pigment chlorophyll in their stems and leaves. Sometimes the green pigment is masked by other colours, such as red. This means that not all plants that contain chlorophyll look green.

How do green plants feed?

Green plants make their own food in a process called photosynthesis. Chlorophyll, the green pigment in plants, helps to trap energy from the Sun. Plants use this energy to convert water and carbon dioxide into sugars and starch. They get the water and carbon dioxide from the soil and the air.

How does a flower form so quickly?

WHEN A FLOWER OPENS OUT FROM A BUD, IT MAY APPEAR LIKE MAGIC in just a day or even a few hours. This is possible because the flower is already formed in miniature inside the bud, just waiting to open out. If you cut open a flower bud you will see that all the flower's parts are there inside the bud. The bud opens as its cells take in water and grow. Many flowers form their buds in the autumn, winter or early spring, ready to open quickly in the warmer, sunnier weather of spring or early summer.

What does a plant need to grow?

Plants need water, mineral salts, and foods such as carbohydrates. Green plants make their own foods, while other plants may take in food from decaying plants or animals, or direct from other living plants.

The bud turns up towards the Sun and the petals open further.

The development of a poppy flower

The bud begins to open in the warm sunshine.

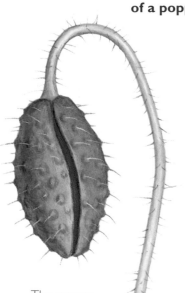

The poppy flower is ready to burst from its bud.

How does a parasitic plant feed?

Parasitic plants do not need to make their own food, and many are not green. Instead, they grow into the tissues of another plant, called the host, and tap into its food and water transport system, taking all the nourishment they need from its sap.

Why do shoots grow upwards?
Most shoots grow upwards, towards the sunlight. The growing tip of the shoot can detect the direction of the light, and chemicals are released that make it grow more on the lower or darker side, thus turning the shoot upwards.

Why do roots grow downwards?
Roots grow downwards because they can detect the pull of gravity. The root responds to gravity by releasing chemicals that cause more growth on the upper side, thus turning the root downwards.

What makes a seed grow?
To grow, a seed needs moisture, warmth and air. Some seeds can only germinate (begin to grow) if they have first been in the low temperatures of winter. The seeds of some plants can lie dormant (inactive) for years before germinating.

The fruit capsule, containing the ripened seeds, is fully developed. The seeds can be shaken by the wind through the holes at the top.

The petals have fallen off, leaving the seed capsule.

How does a Venus fly-trap catch its prey?
The fly-trap is a carnivorous (meat-eating) plant that catches insects and other small animals. The trap is a flattened, hinged pad at the end of each leaf, fringed with bristles. When an insect lands on the pad and touches one of the sensitive hairs growing there, the trap is sprung and closes over the insect, and the bristles interlock to prevent its escape.

The poppy is now fully open with its petals unfurled.

How fast does sap flow through a tree?
In warm conditions, with a plentiful supply of water to the roots, and on a breezy day, sap may flow through a tree as fast as 100cm (40 in) every hour.

How do plants take in water?
Plants use their extensive root systems to take in water from the ground. Each root branches into a network of rootlets, which in turn bear root hairs. Water passes into the root across the cell walls of millions of tiny root hairs.

How much sugar does photosynthesis make in a year?

PLANTS TURN THE SUGAR THEY MAKE BY THE PROCESS OF PHOTOSYNTHESIS into other chemical compounds that they need for growth and development. They also use sugar to provide energy to run the reactions that take place in their cells. Some scientists have estimated that the total mass of green plants alive in the entire world make more than 150,000 million tonnes of sugar every year by their photosynthesis.

Strawberries reproduce vegetatively by sending out runners. The plantlet develops at the end of the runner and eventually grows into a separate plant.

Can plants reproduce without seeds?

Some plants, such as mosses, liverworts and ferns, do not produce seeds. Instead, they spread by dispersing spores. But even amongst seeding plants, reproduction without seeds is possible. Many plants can reproduce vegetatively by sending out runners or splitting off from bulbs, or swollen stems.

How are flowers pollinated?

POLLINATION IS AN IMPORTANT PART OF SEXUAL REPRODUCTION IN PLANTS. The pollen, containing the male sex cells, fertilizes the ovules, which are the female sex cells. This can happen in several different ways. The flowers of many trees release masses of tiny pollen grains into the air, and the breeze takes some to their destination. Many water plants produce pollen that floats downstream. Many flowers have evolved their structure, colours and scent to attract animals to pollinate them. The animal lands on the flower to feed from its nectar, gets showered with pollen, then moves off, transporting the pollen to the next flower it visits. Insects such as bees, wasps and butterflies often pollinate flowers in this way, but some (mainly tropical) flowers are pollinated by birds, bats, and even small mammals.

What happens in a flower after pollination?

After pollination, the pollen that has landed on the stigma of another flower of the same species will begin to germinate, if conditions are right. It sends a tube down into the style and eventually into the ovary of the flower, which it enters to fertilize an ovule.

How much pollen do flowers make?

Flowers can produce enormous quantities of pollen. Some American ragweeds can produce 1,500 million pollen grains in an hour. Thus they can release 18,000 million grains of pollen in one day. The American ragweed is a major cause of hay-fever, which is bad news for sufferers: US estimates put ragweed pollen production at a staggering 8 tonnes a week over a single square mile!

Why are many seeds poisonous?

Many mammals and birds eat seeds. Some plants have seeds that are poisonous to mammals and birds, which prevents them being eaten. Poisonous seeds are often brightly coloured so the seed-eaters quickly learn to spot them and avoid them.

Which flowers are pollinated by mammals?

The flowers of the African baobab tree are pollinated by bushbabies and bats. Those of the saguaro, or giant cactus, in the southwestern USA and Mexico, are pollinated by birds in the day, and bats at night.

How many seeds can a plant produce?

In the tropical forests of Central and South America, a single trumpet tree produces 900,000 tiny seeds. These end up in the soil and germinate when there is a gap in the canopy (the roof of the forest).

Which plants have the smallest seeds?

Orchids produce the smallest seeds. They are microscopic and are released in large numbers, to drift invisibly through the air. In some orchids, just 1 gram contains over 990 million seeds.

Why do flowers open in spring/summer?

In temperate regions many flowers open in spring or summer because this is the best time of year to attract insect pollinators. Ideally, the flowers open as early as possible in the season so that they can use the warm summer to grow and develop their seeds.

Which flowers last for only one day?

The flowers of morning glory open each morning and shrivel and die towards evening. Day lilies also produce flowers that last one day.

Where do seeds develop?

Each ovule is destined to become a seed, and develops inside the ovary of the flower. An ovule consists of the zygote, or fertilized egg, surrounded by the endosperm, the seed's initial food store.

How are seeds dispersed?

MANY SEEDS ARE DISPERSED BY ANIMALS. BIRDS EAT BERRIES AND PASS OUT THE tougher seeds unharmed in their droppings. Some fruit capsules have hooks that catch in animal fur and are transported that way, eventually falling free in another spot. Orchids have microscopic seeds that are dispersed by air currents. Some heavier seeds can also travel by air. The sycamore has 'helicopter' wings, and dandelion seeds have feathery plumes. Many legumes have pods that split open as they ripen and dry, flinging out the seeds in the process.

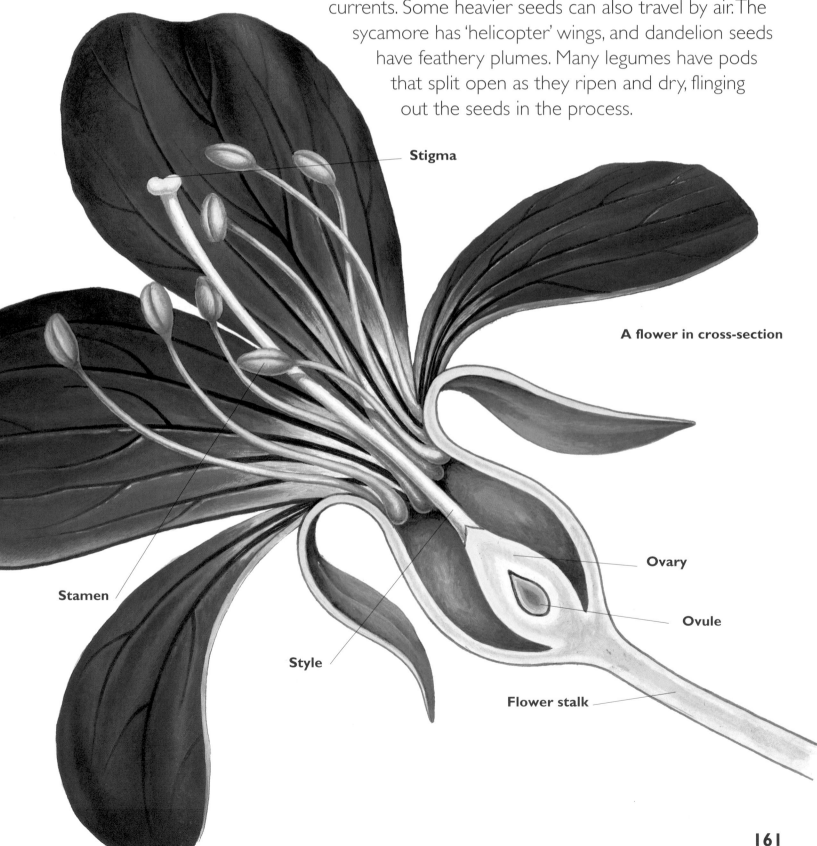

Stigma

A flower in cross-section

Ovary

Ovule

Stamen

Style

Flower stalk

How do forests help improve the air?

Forests help to preserve the quality of the air we breathe. They do this by releasing huge quantities of water vapour and oxygen into the atmosphere. Plants also absorb carbon dioxide, and help prevent this gas from building up to damaging levels.

How do plants colonize bare ground?

Some plants can quickly colonize bare soil. They do this by germinating rapidly from lightweight wind-blown seeds. Some colonizing plants spread by putting out shoots called runners, which split off, becoming new plants.

How do plants make the soil more fertile?

When plants die, they decompose, releasing the chemicals in their tissues into the surrounding soil. The mixture of rotting leaves and other plant material in the soil is called humus, and this makes the soil more fertile.

How are plants used to clean up sewage?

Sewage works use tiny algae and other microscopic organisms in their filter beds. The sewage beds contain layers of gravel and sand, which support the growth of millions of algae. These algae and other organisms feed on the pollutants in the water and help to make it clean.

What lives in a tree?

TREES PROVIDE HOMES FOR COUNTLESS ANIMALS, AND ALSO FOR OTHER PLANTS. The tree's leaves are eaten by the caterpillars of moths and butterflies and other insects, and many species of beetle lay their eggs in the tree's bark. Birds select a fork in a branch to build a nest, or use a natural hole in the trunk, and wild bees may also choose to nest inside a hollow tree. Many mammals are also tree dwellers, including squirrels, monkeys, sloths, bats and koalas. In moist climates, other plants – especially mosses and ferns, and in the tropics orchids and bromeliads – can grow directly on the tree, in hollows where leaf litter gathers; they are known as epiphytes.

Wildlife in an oak tree

How can plants be used to help stop erosion?

Erosion is when soil is loosened and removed by the action of natural forces such as wind and water. This can often be reduced or prevented by using plants. The roots of the plants trap the loose soil and stop it being blown away.

How do plants help us reclaim land?

SEVERAL TYPES OF GRASS, INCLUDING MARRAM, CAN BE PLANTED ON COASTAL dunes. Their roots anchor the sand and help to stop it blowing away. The plants also build up a layer of humus (decayed plant matter), enriching the developing soil. Plants can even begin to reclaim land contaminated by industrial poisons. Some species have evolved forms that can tolerate toxic substances. They gradually improve the fertility and build up the soil so that other plants can grow there too.

An oak tree is home to many birds, such as jays, owls and woodpeckers. Woodpeckers clamber up the branches to feed, and may also dig a nesting hole in the trunk. Tawny owls often roost close to the main trunk, and jays feed on the tree's acorns.

Many fungi, such as these bracket fungi, may grow from the tree's trunk.

How do plants recycle water?

Plants help to return water to the air through the process of transpiration. This is when water evaporates from the stems and leaves of plants. Water enters the plant through its roots. A column of water moves up through the plant, from the roots right through the trunk or stem, into the leaves.

What is the nitrogen cycle?

Bacteria in the soil use nitrogen from the air and turn it into a form that plants can use. Plants then use the nitrogen in their cells to make many complex compounds. When animals eat plants (or other animals that have eaten plants) they continue the cycle. The nitrogen returns to the soil in the droppings of animals or from the decaying bodies of plants and animals.

What happens to all the leaves that fall?

Huge quantities of leaves fall each season from forest trees, but they do not build up on the woodland floor from year to year. The dead leaves are attacked — for example by fungi and bacteria — and break down, gradually becoming part of the soil. The leaves are also eaten by many animals, including worms, insects, slugs, snails, millipedes and woodlice.

Cacti are protected by sharp spines. Many kinds also produce large colourful flowers.

A cactus in flower

What are living stones?
Living stones are special desert plants from southern Africa. They have swollen leaves and grow low down among the sand and gravel of the desert surface, looking themselves very much like small pebbles or rocks. It is only when they flower that they reveal their true nature.

Which is the coldest desert?
Antarctica is sometimes called a cold desert, and is in fact extremely dry, because all its water is locked up as ice. The deserts of central Asia – in Mongolia and western China – are chilled in winter by cold air from the Arctic. Even in summer, when the days are hot, the temperature can drop at night to below freezing.

What is the strangest desert plant?
Welwitschia is probably the strangest desert plant of all. It lives for centuries, growing very slowly and producing just two twisted leathery leaves. It lives in the coastal deserts of Southwest Africa and gets its water mainly from sea-fog.

Why are some deserts expanding?
Some deserts, such as the Sahara, are growing larger each year. This is partly because the climate is getting gradually warmer, but is mainly because the plant life on the edges of the desert has been destroyed by animals grazing there.

How deep do the roots of desert plants go?
Some desert plants have very long roots that can tap into deep underground water sources. Mesquite roots often grow as deep as 10 metres (33 ft), and there are reports of roots over 50 metres (164 ft) below the surface.

How do 'resurrection' plants survive the drought?
When conditions get very dry, the leaves of resurrection plants shrivel up and turn brown. This cuts down the loss of water. When it rains, the leaves take in water, expand and turn green again.

What is a desert?

DESERTS MAKE UP ABOUT A THIRD OF THE LAND SURFACE OF THE WORLD. They are found wherever there is not enough water available to support much plant growth. Examples of deserts are the Sahara, Namib and Kalahari deserts in Africa; the Atacama in Chile; and the Sonoran in North America. Central Asia and Australia also have large deserts. Antarctica is also sometimes called a desert – although it is frozen, it is also very dry.

How big is the largest cactus?
The largest of all cacti is the giant cactus or saguaro, of the southwestern USA and Mexico. Saguaros can reach 20 metres (66 ft) tall, and 60cm (2 ft) thick. They can weigh as much as 12 tonnes and may live to be 200 years old.

How do desert flowers survive droughts?
Many desert flowers live for only a short time and set seed rapidly during the rainy season. They live on as seeds in the desert soil, until the next rains trigger the seeds to germinate.

Some deserts become a sheet of flowers after a rainfall.

What lives in a large cactus?

Cacti are home to a variety of wildlife. Their flowers are visited by butterflies and moths, and also by hummingbirds. Holes in cactus stems provide nest sites for desert rodents, and also for birds like the tiny elf owl.

What is a Joshua tree?

The Joshua tree grows in the Mojave Desert, California, USA. It grows very slowly – only about 10 cm (4 in) a year – and its leaves can last for 20 years. The leaves have fibres inside, and they are sometimes used to make paper.

Which is the hottest desert?

Parts of the Sahara and the Mojave Desert in North America experience extremely high temperatures. The average summer temperature may be over 40°C (104°F). In Death Valley in the Mojave Desert, temperatures of 57°C (134°F) have been recorded.

What is an oasis?

An oasis is a place in the desert where water is in plentiful supply, such as at a pool permanently fed by a spring. Many plants can grow at an oasis, even in the heat of the desert. Date palms are commonly planted at oases, both for shade and to provide fruit.

How does a cactus survive in the desert?

CACTI ARE SPECIAL PLANTS THAT LIVE IN THE DESERTS of North and Central America. They have leafless, swollen stems that store water, and for this reason they are sometimes called succulents, as are similar fleshy plants of the African deserts. Since they lack leaves, they do not lose much water through transpiration. Most cacti are spiny, which probably protects them from being eaten by hungry (and thirsty) desert animals. Many cacti have furrowed stems. This allows them to expand with stored water after a rainstorm.

Which is the driest desert?

In parts of the Sahara the average yearly rainfall is less than 1 mm, making this one of the driest deserts. Parts of the Atacama Desert in Chile are also very dry – there, some years may pass before any rain falls.

American desert scene

The tallest plants in this American desert scene are the branched giant cacti or saguaros.

How do grassland fires start in nature?

Fires sometimes rage in grasslands, especially in the dry summer months. Fires can start quite naturally, for example when lightning strikes dead or dying grass. If a wind is blowing, the sparks can quickly turn into a fire that begins to spread.

Which garden flowers come from natural grasslands?

From the grasslands of Europe and Asia come flowers such as adonis, anemones, delphiniums and scabious. Flowers from the prairie grasslands of North America include the coneflower, sunflower and blazing star.

How do the plants survive fire?

Some grassland plants survive fires by persisting as thickened roots, and sprouting again after the fire has passed. Others may die, but germinate again later, from seeds left behind in the soil.

Why don't trees take over the grassland?

Trees cannot survive easily in natural grassland areas, mainly because the rainfall is too low to support their growth. But in areas where the rainfall is higher, trees will gradually invade grassland, unless they are chopped down or eaten by grazing animals.

What animals live in the grasslands of North America?

The original animals of the prairie were buffalo and deer, and smaller species such as ground squirrels and prairie dogs. The wild buffalo once numbered some 40 million, but was almost wiped out by settlers.

Where are the steppes?

The steppes – the grassland of Asia – cover a huge swathe of country from eastern Europe, through southern Russia, right across Asia, to Mongolia in the east.

What makes grassland?

IN TEMPERATE REGIONS WITH WARM OR HOT SUMMERS AND COLD WINTERS, natural grassland develops in areas that don't have enough rainfall for trees and woods to grow. Many types of grasses dominate in these habitats. Mixed in with the grasses are other, mostly low-growing plants, many of which have bright colourful flowers to attract insects during the spring and summer. Grasslands have rich fertile soils built up gradually as generations of grasses and herbs grow up and die down, returning their goodness to the soil.

A scene on the pampas of South America

Many parts of the pampas are dominated by tussock grasses, and very few trees break the monotony of the landscape.

What animals live in the grasslands of South America?

The animals of the pampas include such strange creatures as the mara (long-legged and hare-like) and the plains viscacha (related to the chinchilla), as well as wild guinea pigs, giant anteaters, the maned wolf, and the rhea, a large, flightless bird.

Where is the pampas?

The pampas stretches across Argentina, Uruguay and southeastern Brazil, on the lowlands around the River Plate. The pampas is the largest area of temperate grassland in the southern hemisphere.

Where are the prairies?

The prairies extend from central southern Canada, through the mid-west of the USA, right down into northern Mexico, to the east of the Rocky Mountains. The area is known as the Great Plains, reflecting the open, largely treeless expanse of natural grassland.

What animals live in the grasslands of Asia?

Wild horses once grazed on the Asian steppe, along with antelopes and deer, but they are rare today. Many rodents live in the steppe, such as hamsters, voles, mice and sousliks (a kind of ground squirrel).

What are grasslands used for?

Grasslands have long been used for grazing herds of domestic animals, especially cattle. But because the soils are so fertile, much of the original prairie land has now been ploughed up and planted with crops, such as wheat and corn (maize).

Where are grasslands found?

THERE ARE GRASSLANDS IN THE CENTRAL PARTS OF ASIA, IN THE PLAINS OF NORTH America, and also in Argentina and in southern Africa. The Asian grasslands are called the steppes and the North American grasslands are called the prairies. In Argentina they are called the pampas, and in southern Africa the veld. Smaller areas of natural grassland are also found in parts of New Zealand and in Australia. The steppes are the largest area, stretching from Hungary to Manchuria.

Cattle ranching is a common form of farming in many parts of the pampas.

Gentian

Many alpine plants, like this gentian, have large showy flowers.

Why is it colder in the mountains?

The Sun heats the ground and this heat is trapped close to the ground by the Earth's atmosphere. As you go up a mountain, and rise above the zone in which the heat is held, the atmosphere gets thinner and the air gets colder. It falls about 1°C for every 150 metres (495 ft) in height.

How do plants survive the cold?

Plants have evolved many different ways of surviving mountain conditions. Many grow close to the ground, in cushion-like shapes, which keeps them out of the wind. Some have thick, waxy, or hairy leaves to help insulate them.

How does the plant life change as you go up a mountain?

CONDITIONS GENERALLY GET HARSHER, THE HIGHER YOU GO UP A MOUNTAIN, and the plant life reflects this. So, there may be temperate woodland in the lowlands, but as you climb, this changes, typically to coniferous woodland, then to mountain scrub, then to grassland, then again, with increasing height, to a tundra-like vegetation, and to rocky screes and snow-patches.

Why do different plants grow on different sides of a mountain?

Different sides of a mountain have different climates. On the south side (or north side in the southern hemisphere), there is more sun and conditions are warmer, while on the other side the snow and ice stay on the ground much longer.

How do mountain herbivores find their food?

Many mountain mammals burrow under the snow and continue to feed on mountain plants even at high altitudes. Others, such as marmots, store fat in their bodies and hibernate during the winter.

Why are alpine flowers so popular in gardens?

Many mountain plants, such as gentians and saxifrages, are known as alpines – because they come from the Alps. They are popular for their bright flowers, and also because they tend to grow well even in poor conditions, such as on a rock garden.

What is the tree-line?

Trees cannot grow all the way up a mountain, and the highest level for them is known as the tree-line. This varies according to the local climate of the region, but is around 2,800 metres (9,250 ft) in the Alps. Trees at this level grow slowly and are often stunted.

Alpine flowers

These alpine flowers are growing in a natural rock garden.

How do some mountain plants reproduce without flowers?

Many mountain plants have dispensed with flowers because of the lack of insects to pollinate them, and reproduce vegetatively instead. Thus some mountain grasses grow miniature plants where the flowers should be – these drop off and grow into new plants.

How can plants survive the snow and ice?

Few plants can survive being completely frozen, but many can thrive under the snow. Snow acts like a blanket to keep the freezing ice and wind at bay, and saves the plants from being killed. Alpine grasses stay alive and green under the snow, ready to grow again as soon as it melts.

How do mountain plants attract pollinators?

Many mountain plants have large, colourful flowers to attract the few insects that live there. Some, such as mountain avens, track the sun to warm their flowers, which attracts insects to sunbathe there.

What limits plant growth in the mountains?

THE CLIMATE CHANGES AS THE LAND RISES FROM VALLEY TO MOUNTAIN – it gets colder with increased height, and also windier. There is also usually much less level ground in the mountains, and the soils are thinner. Other factors that influence plant growth are the amount of sunshine, and the pattern of snow and ice accumulation. In very exposed sites, the wind chills the ground and prevents snow from gathering, creating conditions that defeat even the hardiest of plants.

Above the tree-line in the mountains, many plants, such as edelweiss and mountain avens, grow well in the poor rocky soils.

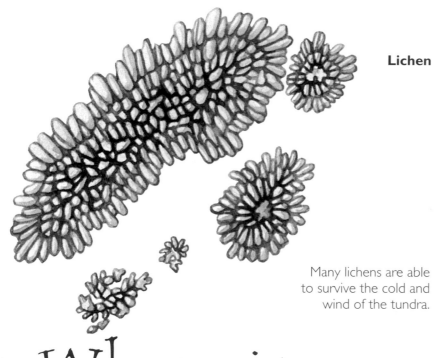

Lichen

Many lichens are able to survive the cold and wind of the tundra.

Where is the tundra?

THE TUNDRA LIES NORTH OF THE CONIFEROUS FOREST BELT, IN A BAND roughly following the Arctic Circle. It covers a huge area of land – about 25 million square km (10 million square miles), from Alaska, through Canada, Greenland, Iceland, across to North Norway and Sweden and on around the Arctic coast of Siberia. Only a small area of the Antarctic has similar conditions – the peninsula reaching north towards the tip of South America.

What plants do reindeer eat?
Reindeer (or caribou) survive the Arctic winter by foraging for food. They dig beneath the snow with their hooves and antlers to seek out tender lichens, mosses, sedges and grasses.

What is permafrost?
Even where the surface soil in the Arctic thaws in the summer, further down it is permanently frozen. This icy layer is known as the permafrost. Because the ice prevents rain water seeping further down, the surface can be wet.

Why are there so few plants in the Antarctic?
Most of Antarctica is covered with snow and ice all year. Only the Antarctic Peninsula has habitats where plants can survive, because it is warmed by the sea. Only two kinds of flowering plant – a hair-grass and a cushion plant – are native to Antarctica.

Why are there more plants in the Arctic?
The Arctic is surrounded by land masses – from Canada and Greenland to northern Europe and Siberia, with many islands. These offer many open habitats for plant growth, especially in the summer. About 900 species are native to the Arctic tundra.

Arctic scene

Why are many Arctic shrubs evergreen?

Many Arctic shrubs keep some or all of their leaves throughout the winter. Leaves formed in late summer stay on the plant, often protected by dead leaves formed earlier. Then as soon as the spring returns, the green leaves can begin to photosynthesize, so losing no time to make their food over the short summer months.

Why are many tundra flowers white or yellow?

Most tundra flowers are pollinated by insects. However, there are relatively few bees this far north, and the main pollinators are flies. Flies cannot distinguish colours like bees can, so the flowers do not need to be so colourful.

What is the tundra like?

THE MOST STRIKING FEATURE OF THE TUNDRA IS ITS TOTAL LACK OF TREES. Woody plants cannot survive here unless they are very small – there is simply not enough warmth in the summer for their growth. The dominant plants are grasses and sedges, mosses and lichens, with shrubs such as heathers, and dwarf willows and birches. There are also many flowers such as saxifrages, avens and Arctic poppies.

Why do many Arctic plants have swollen roots?

Many Arctic plants have swollen roots or underground stems. They contain food reserves in readiness for a quick spurt of growth in the following summer.

How do some polar plants melt the snow?

Several Arctic and mountain plants that survive under the snow have dark coloured leaves and stems. When the Sun begins to shine, they absorb the heat and melt the snow around them.

What is the most northerly flower?

A species of poppy has been found growing further north than any other flower – at 83°N, or on a level with the north of Greenland.

The plants of the Arctic include pretty flowers such as the Arctic poppy, low-growing cushion plants, and tiny trees such as dwarf birch and willow.

What is the temperate forest like in summer?

IN SUMMER THE TEMPERATE DECIDUOUS FORESTS ARE HUMMING WITH LIFE – birds and insects call from the trees, mice and voles rustle in the undergrowth, and plant growth is also at its height. The leaf canopy is fully developed, cutting out much of the sunlight from the forest floor. Nevertheless, most forests have well developed shrub and herb layers as well, with plants such as roses, honeysuckle, dogwoods and hazel, and flowers including anemones, sorrel and bluebells.

Why do most woodland flowers appear in spring?

By developing early they can benefit from the sunlight before it is shut out by the tree canopy. It is also possible that woodland insects find it easier to spot the flowers before the rest of the vegetation has grown up.

Which forest tree can be tracked down by its sound?

The leaves of the aspen tree move from side to side in the wind, and rustle against each other. Even the lightest breeze sets off their distinctive rustling, so the practised ear can easily track down an aspen.

How are temperate forests harvested for wood?

Many temperate forests are not natural, but have been managed for centuries to provide a crop of timber. Traditional management involves a rotation of timber extraction, with only a proportion of the tree being removed at one time. This allows the forest to regenerate. Sometimes poles are cut from trees, and the trees can then re-sprout from the base, to provide another crop of poles later. This is called coppicing.

What else do we get from temperate forests?

Temperate forests provide us with a range of products as well as wood. Charcoal is made by slowly burning certain kinds of wood. In the past, people depended upon woodland animals such as wild boar and deer for food and skins. Many edible fungi, including chanterelle, penny-bun and truffles grow in temperate woods. Some woodland plants, such as brambles and wild strawberries, have edible fruits, and cherries and currants were originally woodland plants.

What lives on the forest floor?

The forest floor is a mish-mash of dead leaves, twigs, fungi and the roots and stems of woodland plants. The invertebrate life here is richly varied, with beetles, woodlice, worms, slugs, snails, springtails, ants, mites, and millipedes, to name but a few of the groups. These help break down the organic material, as well as providing food for small mammals such as mice and voles.

Why do the trees lose their leaves in autumn?

Trees and other plants that lose their leaves all at once each year are known as deciduous. The majority of broadleaved trees of the temperate woodlands are winter-deciduous, losing their leaves in the autumn, and remaining bare through the winter. This way they shut down their main life processes, such as transpiration and photosynthesis, remaining largely dormant until the spring.

A year in a temperate forest

The trees in temperate woodlands lose their leaves in an annual cycle. Early flowers can benefit from the extra light filtering through in spring.

How old can forest trees get?

Many forest trees reach a great age, notably oaks, which have been dated at 400–500 years. Some woodland trees, like certain varieties of elm, which reproduce from suckers, are potentially immortal, as the original tree is constantly renewing itself, creating a whole grove of cloned individuals.

Which conifer is deciduous?

Larch is a coniferous tree – because it bears cones. But unlike most conifers, larch loses its leaves all at once, in the autumn, so it is also deciduous, like many broadleaved trees. In fact, there are also broadleaved trees that are evergreen, such as the oaks of the Mediterranean regions.

What is the temperate forest like in winter?

IN WINTER, THE TALL TREES FORMING THE WOODLAND CANOPY HAVE LOST ALL their leaves, the insects are quiet – they have either died or gone into hibernation – and there is not much bird song. Many of the loudest songbirds are summer visitors and have migrated south. Most of the flowers of the woodland floor have died back, many laying down underground stores of food for next spring's growth. Evergreen species such as holly, ivy and yew stand out at this time of year, and provide valuable cover for birds and other animals.

A rainforest tree teems with life

Where are the rainforests?

THE WORLD'S LARGEST RAINFOREST IS AROUND BRAZIL'S AMAZON RIVER, and also along the foothills of the Andes Mountains. The world's main areas of tropical rainforest are in South and Central America, in West and Central Africa, in Southeast Asia, and in northern Queensland, Australia.

What are lianes?
Lianes, or lianas, are plants that clamber over and dangle down from the trees in the rainforest. They may grow very long and they use the trees as supports. Animals such as monkeys and squirrels use lianes to help them move about in the branches.

How much rain falls in the rainforest?
The tropical rainforests are warm and wet. In many, the rainfall is more than 2,000 mm (80 in) per year. It may rain at any time, but there are often storms in the afternoon.

How tall are the biggest rainforest trees?
The main canopy of the rainforest develops at around 30 metres (95 ft), with occasional taller trees (known as emergents) topping out at 50 metres (165 ft) or more.

Many of the taller trees have flanged or buttressed roots to give them extra stability.

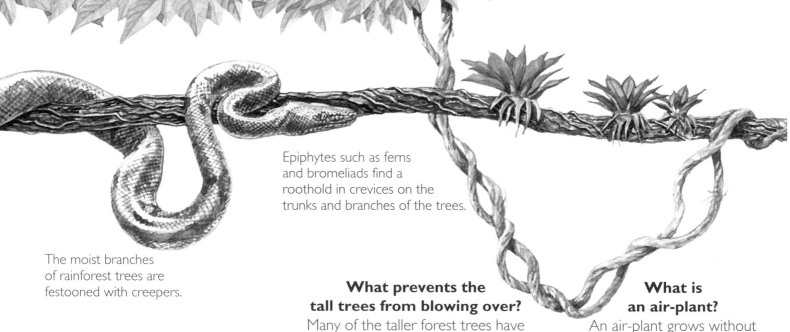

Epiphytes such as ferns and bromeliads find a roothold in crevices on the trunks and branches of the trees.

The moist branches of rainforest trees are festooned with creepers.

Which plants can trap their own rain water?

It rains very often in the tropical rainforest, and many plants trap the water before it reaches the ground. Bromeliads have special leaves that form a waterproof cup for this purpose.

Why are rainforests being cut down?

Many rainforests are destroyed so the land can be used for crops, or for grazing. Tropical forest soils are fertile, and many crops, such as cocoa and sugar cane, can be grown after the trees have been felled. However, the fertility of the soil is short-lived – see below.

How fast are the rainforests being destroyed?

Every year an area the size of Belgium is lost or badly damaged. Estimates in Brazil point to some 80,000 sq km (over 30,000 sq miles) of forest being lost each year, and similar destruction continues elsewhere. When the forest is cleared, the tropical rainstorms work directly on the soil, erosion sets in, and in a short time all the fertile topsoil is washed away, making the ground useless for crops.

What prevents the tall trees from blowing over?

Many of the taller forest trees have special supporting flanges near the base of their trunks, called stilts or buttresses. These make the tree less liable to be pushed over in a storm.

Why are the tropical rainforests so rich in species?

No one knows for certain, but it may be because they have been undisturbed for so long, and also perhaps because they have such a stable, warm climate.

What is an air-plant?

An air-plant grows without anchoring itself with roots. Air plants are common in some tropical forests. They get the moisture they need direct from the damp air.

What do we get from rainforests?

We get many things from rainforests, including timber, Brazil nuts, fruit, rubber, rattan (a kind of palm from which furniture is made), cosmetics and even medicines.

How rich are the rainforests?

THE WORLD'S RAINFORESTS ARE THE MOST COMPLEX OF ALL NATURAL ECOSYSTEMS, with an enormous wealth of plant and animal species – they contain some 40 per cent of the world's plants. They are the richest habitats on earth – for example just 1 hectare (2.5 acres) of Malaysian tropical rainforest can contain as many as 180 different species of trees. The forests also contain untold riches in the shape of timber and fruits and herbs that can be used as food and medicine. The rainforests are important not just for their rich wildlife, but also because they help to preserve climate and soil stability. Without the tropical forests, climate change would almost certainly accelerate – the forests help preserve the atmosphere, releasing huge quantities of water vapour and oxygen, and absorbing carbon dioxide. If the forests are to be conserved, efforts must be made to use their resources wisely, without destroying the forests themselves.

How are wetlands damaged?
When soil is drained, or too much water is pumped from the land nearby, wetlands suffer as the water-table is lowered. Wetlands are easily damaged by pollution as well. Sewage and chemicals released from factories easily find their way into streams and rivers, where they can upset the balance of nature and poison the wildlife.

Why do some lakes have very few plants?
Lakes vary in the chemical composition of the water that they contain. Some lakes, such as those draining from lime-rich soils, are very fertile and can support a lot of plants. Others, especially those whose water is acid (as in granite areas), are poor in nutrients and therefore poor in plant life.

How do water plants stay afloat?

SOME WATER PLANTS STAY AFLOAT BECAUSE THEIR TISSUES CONTAIN CHAMBERS OF AIR, making their stems and leaves buoyant. Others, such as water lilies, have flat, rounded leaves that sit boat-like on the water surface. They may also have waxy leaves, which repel the water and help to keep the leaves afloat, or up-curved rims to the leaves. Some combine wax with hairs so that the leaves are unwettable. Duckweeds are so small and light that the surface tension of the water is enough to keep them afloat, and the water hyacinth has inflated leaf-bases that act as floats.

Why is the water hyacinth sometimes a problem?
Water hyacinth is a floating plant with beautiful mauve flowers. However, it is also a fast-growing weed, and can spread rapidly to choke waterways, alter the ecology and impede boat traffic.

How does a lake turn into land?
Over time, a lake will gradually turn into dry land by a process called succession. Slowly, the remains of the plants growing in the shallows accumulate, making the water more and more shallow. Eventually, the edges of the lake dry out and land plants can establish themselves.

How does the bladderwort feed?
Bladderwort is a carnivorous plant found in boggy pools. The underwater stems develop small bladders, each with a trigger. When a small animal, such as a water flea, bumps into the trigger, the bladder springs open, sucking in the animal with the in-rushing water.

How do river plants cope with the current?

FEW PLANTS CAN GROW IN THE CURRENT OF FAST RIVERS, EXCEPT for tiny algae encrusting stones on the river bed. But in the eddies and slower currents of the river bank they can gain a roothold. River plants have to anchor themselves firmly with roots. They then tend to grow narrow ribbon- or strap-like leaves that offer little resistance to the water flow. Others, like water milfoil, have finely divided, feathery leaves, for the same reason. Water crowfoot sends up thin, flexible stems that bend and sway in the current.

How do water plants disperse their fruits?
The running water of streams and rivers carries floating fruits along, and there is usually some water movement even in ponds and lakes. Many floating fruits have tough coats that stop them from germinating too soon, so that they can travel a good distance.

Why do most water plants grow only in shallow water?
Most plants need to root themselves in the soil, even if they live mainly submerged in the water. In deep water there is not enough sunlight for plants to grow successfully.

What food plants come from wetlands?
The most important wetland crop is rice, which is grown in many parts of the world, notably India and China. Rice grows best in special flooded fields, called paddies. Another aquatic grass crop is Canadian wild rice, a traditional food of native Americans, and now a popular speciality.

How do water plants get their flowers pollinated?
Even though their growth is mainly below the surface, most water plants hold their flowers above the water, for pollination by the wind or by insects. Some, like the water starwort, have water-resistant floating pollen that drifts to the female flowers.

What is papyrus?
Papyrus is a tall sedge that grows along rivers and in swamps. It was used in ancient Egypt from about 3000 BC to make paper, but the plant is rare there today.

The fresh young leaves of the tea bush are gathered to make tea.

Tea leaves

Which trees give us a sweet, sugary syrup?

The sugar maple has a sweet sap, which is harvested to make maple syrup. Most maple syrup comes from the province of Quebec, in Canada.

Which plants are used to make sugar?

The main source of sugar is the sweet stems of the sugar cane, a tall grass that grows in tropical countries. In some temperate areas, including Europe, there are large crops of sugar beet. This plant stores sugar in its thickened roots. In some parts of the tropics, the sap of the sugar palm is made into sugar.

Where were potatoes first grown?

Potatoes grow wild in the Andes Mountains of South America and were first gathered as food by the native people of that region. All the many varieties grown today derive from that wild source.

How is tea made?

Tea comes from the leaves of a species of camellia. This is planted on hillsides, especially in India and Sri Lanka, and in Indonesia, Japan and China. The young leaf tips are harvested, dried and then crushed to make tea.

Which plants give us oil?

The seeds of many plants are rich in oil, which they store as a source of food and energy. We extract oil from several of these plants, including olive, sunflower, corn (maize), soya bean, peanuts, oil-seed rape, sesame and African oil palm.

Sunflower seeds and olives are crushed to produce oil.

A selection of food plants

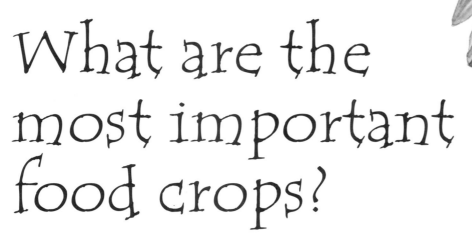

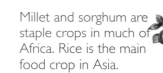

Millet and sorghum are staple crops in much of Africa. Rice is the main food crop in Asia.

What are the most important food crops?

SOME 12,000 SPECIES OF PLANT ARE KNOWN TO HAVE BEEN USED AS FOOD BY PEOPLE, and about 150 of these are in regular cultivation today. The most important crops are the cereals (grass-like crops) – wheat, rice and maize (corn), followed by barley, sorghum, oats, millet and rye. These form the basis of many people's diet throughout the world. Root crops are also widely grown. These include potatoes in temperate zones, and in tropical zones sweet potatoes, yams and cassava or manioc. All these foods provide carbohydrates, while seeds of the pea family (known as pulses) are rich in protein. As well as peas and beans, these include soya beans, chickpeas, lentils and peanuts.

Which fruits are grown for food?

FRUITS OF THE TEMPERATE REGIONS INCLUDE APPLES, PEARS, GRAPES, PLUMS, cherries, red and black currants, strawberries, raspberries, blackberries and gooseberries. In warmer regions, a different selection is available, including citrus fruits such as oranges, grapefruits, lemons and tangerines, and also pineapples, melons, dates, figs, bananas, coconuts, mangoes, papayas and guavas. Some fruits have a more savoury flavour, and are used as vegetables. Examples are tomatoes, avocados and peppers. Fruits are very good for us. They contain energy-giving stores of natural sugar, as well as protein and vital vitamins. They also provide roughage to aid digestion.

How is chocolate made?
The cocoa tree comes originally from the eastern Andes in South America. The fruits, called pods, develop on the sides of the trunk, and each pod contains about 20 to 30 seeds – the cocoa 'beans'. The beans must be fermented, roasted and ground before they become cocoa powder, the raw material for making chocolate. Cocoa is now grown mainly in West Africa, and also in the Caribbean.

Where did wheat come from?
Wheat is one of the oldest known crops. It was probably first cultivated over 6,000 years ago in Mesopotamia – present-day Iraq – between the rivers Tigris and Euphrates. Many useful crop plants have their origin in the Middle East. Other examples are barley, oats and rye, peas and lentils, onions, olives, figs, apples and pears.

What is breadfruit?
Breadfruit is a tree, native to Polynesia, which grows to about 20 metres (65 ft), and has large edible fruits. The fruits are up to 30 cm (1 ft) across and are cooked before being eaten as a vegetable. The related jackfruit, from India and Malaysia, also has edible fruits, and these are even larger – up to 90 cm (3 ft) long and weighing as much as 30 kg (66 lb).

Wheat, corn (maize) and barley are common in temperate regions.

Where does coffee come from?
The coffee plant is a large shrub, and its berries are used to make coffee. The ripe berries are harvested, then dried to remove the flesh from the hard stones inside. These are the coffee 'beans', which are then treated further, often being roasted.

What is the Amazon cow-tree?
The Amazon cow- or milk-tree is a tropical fig. It takes its name from the fact that it produces a milk-like sap, or latex, which can be drunk just like cow's milk.

Which countries use mainly herbal medicines?

IN MUCH OF THE WORLD, ESPECIALLY IN CHINA AND INDIA, HERBAL REMEDIES are used more than any other kind of medicine. Plants have been used as medicine for at least 100,000 years, and as long ago as 3000 BC, the Chinese had identified over 350 medicinal plants. Today the Chinese use around 5,000 plant remedies; more than 8,000 medicinal plants are in use in India and Southeast Asia.

Which plant helps combat malaria?

Quinine, from the bark of the quinine tree, which grows in the South American Andes, can cure or prevent malaria. Before the widespread use of quinine, malaria used to kill two million people each year.

What plants aid the digestion?

Many plants, including the herbs and spices used in cooking, are used to help digestion. In Europe, the very bitter extract of wild gentians provides a good remedy for digestive problems. Plantain is another herb used for this purpose.

Periwinkle

What links willow trees with aspirin?

Willow twigs were once chewed to give pain relief, and a compound similar to the drug aspirin was once extracted from willow bark, and also from the herb meadowsweet. Meadowsweet used to be known as spiraea – hence the name aspirin.

Feverfew

Valuable medicinal plants

What is ginseng?

Ginseng is a plant related to ivy, and has been used in herbal medicine for centuries. It is claimed to help many conditions, including fatigue and depression, kidney disease, heart problems and headaches.

Can plants help fight cancer?

Several plants are known to be effective against cancer tumours. One of the most famous is the rosy periwinkle. One of its chemical extracts, vincristine, is very effective against some types of leukaemia, a cancer of the blood.

Which herb is traditionally used to treat headaches?

Feverfew is a pungent plant belonging to the daisy family. It takes its name from its long use as a remedy for fevers, and it has also been proven to be effective against headaches.

What links yams with birth control?

Wild yams provided the medicines for the first contraceptive pills. Both the female and male sex hormones can be prepared using extracts of yam, and the first birth-control pills were made using this natural plant extract.

Foxglove

Opium poppy

White willow

What medicine comes from deadly nightshade?

Deadly nightshade has bright juicy berries, which are also very poisonous. However, they can be used to prepare the chemical atropine, which is used to dilate the pupil of the eye in medical examinations.

Which plants help with breathing problems?

Lungwort is a herb with purple flowers and spotted leaves. It is used to treat asthma and catarrh. Ephedrine, from the ephedra or joint-pine plant, is used to treat asthma and hay fever.

What are coca and cola?

A world-famous fizzy drink originally contained extracts of two South American plants called coca and cola. The seeds of cola are chewed as a pick-me-up, because they contain caffeine. Coca is the source of the powerful anaesthetic cocaine, which is used in dentistry. It is also a dangerous drug, if abused.

How can a deadly opium poppy save lives?

MANY USEFUL MEDICINAL PLANTS CAN ALSO YIELD DANGEROUS DRUGS, AND the beautiful pink-purple opium poppy is no exception. This poppy is a source of morphine – which is widely used as an anaesthetic, and codeine – which is used in cough mixtures and many other medicines. However, addictive and dangerous substances are also made from the opium poppy, including the deadly drug heroin.

Which plants are used to make paper?

Most paper is made from trees, the wood being first turned into pulp. Some conifers are planted specially for making paper, but much natural forest is also destroyed for the paper industry. About 215 million tonnes of paper and board are produced worldwide each year. The main trees used are species of spruce and pine, as well as aspen, poplar and eucalyptus. In India and Southeast Asia, bamboo is used to make paper. Straw and sugar cane are also used, as are reeds and other grasses, and also hemp.

What wood makes the best cricket bats?

The best cricket bats are made in northern India, from the timber of the cricket-bat willow, a form of white willow. The blade (the part the ball strikes) is made from willow, and the handle usually from a different wood or cane.

How many things can be made from bamboo?

Bamboo is one of the world's most useful natural plant products. As well as for making paper, bamboo is used for scaffolding, for building houses, furniture, pipes and tubes, walking sticks, and (when split) for mats, hats, umbrellas, baskets, blinds, fans and brushes. Some bamboos have young shoots that are edible.

How is cork produced?

Cork comes from a tree called the cork oak. This tree grows wild around the Mediterranean Sea, and has been cultivated in Portugal, Spain and North Africa. The cork is actually the thick spongy bark of the cork oak. The cork is harvested carefully to avoid killing the tree – it is stripped away from the lower trunk, then left to grow back for about 10 years before the next harvest. Cork is used to make many things – from bottle corks, to pinboards and floor tiles.

What is kapok?

Kapok is similar to cotton and also comes from a plant, this time from a tree, the kapok or silk cotton tree, which grows in tropical America and Africa and can get as tall as 70 metres (230 ft). The fluffy seed fibres are used to stuff mattresses, jackets, quilts and sleeping bags.

Can plants produce fuel to run cars?

WHEN TAPPED JUST LIKE A RUBBER TREE, THE COPAIBA TREE OF THE AMAZON rainforest yields an oil similar to diesel, at a rate of 18 litres (4 gallons) every 2 hours. This natural fuel can be used to run engines. The petroleum nut tree of Borneo and the Philippines produces a high-octane oil in its seeds, which is extracted by crushing. As the world's reserves of crude oil are used up, fuel from plants may become more important. Already cars run on sugar-cane alcohol, especially in Brazil.

What is balsa?

Balsa is the world's lightest timber and floats high n water. Balsa trees grow in tropical America. Balsa wood is used for making models such as airplanes, and also for rafts, life-belts and insulation.

What is jojoba?

Jojoba is a low-growing bush found in the Sonoron Desert of Mexico and the southwestern USA. The fruits have a high-grade oily wax. It is used as a lubricant, in printing inks, and in body lotions and shampoo.

How many things can you spot in this picture that have been made from plant materials?

What is raffia?

Raffia is a natural fibre made from the young leaves of the raphia palm, which grows in tropical Africa. Raffia is used in handicrafts such as basketry.

California redwood sprig and cones

What is the tallest tree?

The California redwood, which grows along the North American Pacific coast, is the tallest tree in the world, reaching 112 metres (365 ft). Some Australian eucalyptus trees may grow just as tall.

What is the oldest plant?

The oldest known plant is probably the creosote bush of the Mojave Desert in California, USA. Some of these bushes are thought to be 11,700 years old. The bristlecone pine, which grows mainly in the southwestern USA, notably in the White Mountains of California, is also very long-lived. The oldest is about 4,600 years old.

What is the largest seed?

The coco de mer of the Seychelles has the largest seeds, each measuring 50 cm (20 in) long. They are produced inside a large woody fruit that takes six years to develop.

Which plant has the longest leaf?

The raphia palm of tropical Africa produces the longest known leaves. The stalk can be nearly 4 metres (13 ft) and the leaf-blade almost 20 metres (60 ft) long.

How deep are the deepest roots?

Roots of a South African fig were found to have penetrated 120 metres (394 ft) below the surface.

What plant can spread across the widest area?

THE BANYAN OF INDIA AND PAKISTAN OFTEN STARTS LIFE AS AN EPIPHYTE, a small plant growing on another tree. As it grows, it sends down woody roots that come to resemble tree trunks. Eventually it can cover a large area and seem like a grove of separate trees, growing close together. One 200-year-old banyan covered 412 square metres (493 sq yd), had 100 separate 'trunks' and 1,775 prop-roots. The banyan is not the only tree with a peculiar spreading habit. The quaking aspen can spread from suckers and form a grove of trees that look separate, but which are connected underground. One aspen grove in the USA covered 43 hectares (106 acres), and was estimated to weigh 6,000 tonnes.

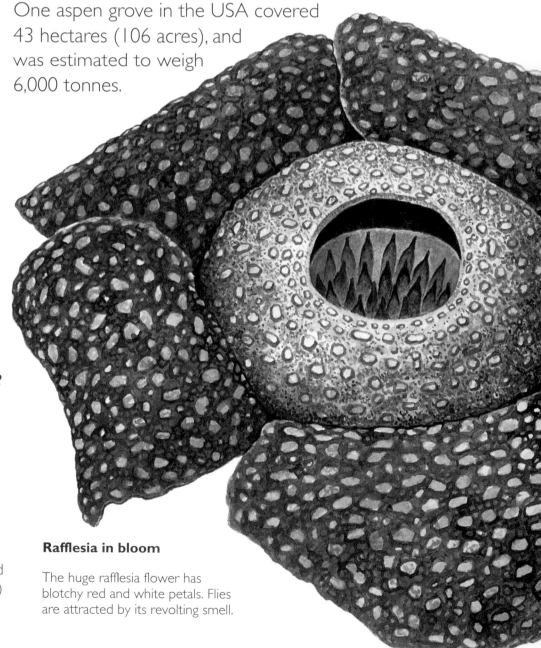

Rafflesia in bloom

The huge rafflesia flower has blotchy red and white petals. Flies are attracted by its revolting smell.

Which plant grows the fastest?

The giant bamboo of Myanmar (Burma) grows at up to 46 cm (18 in) a day, making it one of the fastest growing of all plants. However, another species from India, the spiny bamboo, holds the record for growth in a greenhouse – it achieved 91cm (36 in) in one day.

What is the world's longest seaweed?

Giant kelp is a huge seaweed that forms underwater forests in the coastal waters of California. Its fronds can reach 100 metres (323 ft), making it one of the tallest plants known.

What is the largest flower?

THE WORLD'S LARGEST FLOWER GROWS ON THE RAFFLESIA, A PLANT WITHOUT LEAVES THAT thrives in the tropical forests of Southeast Asia. It is a parasite, growing on the stems of lianes in the forest. Individual flowers can measure up to 1 metre (3 ft) across, making them the largest single flowers of any plant. Rafflesia's red and white flowers may look attractive, but they stink, mimicking the aroma of rotting flesh. The stench attracts flies, which then pollinate the flower. The largest flowerhead is that of a Bolivian plant, the puya. It is made up of more than 8,000 flowers and can measure 10.7 metres (35 ft) tall.

Which plant grows the slowest?

The record for the slowest growing plant probably goes to the dioon plant. The dioon grows in Mexico, and one specimen was recorded to have an average growth rate of 0.76 mm per year.

Giant kelp

The base of the giant kelp is anchored firmly by its holdfast, but the fronds may grow up hundreds of feet through the water.

What is the smallest flowering plant?

A tiny tropical floating duckweed is the world's smallest flowering plant. Some species measure less than 0.5 mm across, even when fully grown.

Which plant has the largest floating leaves?

The giant waterlily of the Amazon region has huge leaves. They grow up to 2 metres (6.5 ft) across, and can support the weight of a child.

Planet Earth

Archean 4,600–2,500 m.y.a.

Earth's formation

The geological time scale

The Earth was formed from a cloud of gas and dust around 4,600 million years ago.

What was the Earth like after it formed?

The Earth's surface was probably molten (hot and liquid) for many millions of years after its formation. The oldest known rocks are about 3,960 million years old.

When did living things first appear on Earth?

The oldest known fossils (of microscopic bacteria) are around 3,500 million years old. Primitive life forms may have first appeared on Earth about 3,850 million years ago.

Proterozoic 2,500–590 m.y.a.

The Archean and Proterozoic eons together occupied 87% of Earth history.

Why is the Cambrian period important?

During the Precambrian, most living creatures were soft-bodied and they left few fossils. During the Cambrian period, many creatures had hard parts, which were preserved as fossils in layers of rock.

What were the first animals with backbones?

Jawless fishes were the first animals with backbones. They appeared during the Ordovician period. Fishes with skeletons of cartilage, such as sharks, first appeared in the Devonian period.

Why did the dinosaurs become extinct?

THE DINOSAURS FIRST APPEARED ON EARTH DURING THE TRIASSIC PERIOD. They became the dominant animals during the Jurassic period, but at the end of the Cretaceous period, 65 million years ago, they became extinct. Scientists still argue about why they disappeared. But many experts now believe that around 65 million years ago an enormous asteroid struck the Earth. The impact threw up a huge cloud of dust, which blocked out the sunlight for a long time. Land plants died and so the dinosaurs starved to death.

When did plants start to grow on land?

The first land plants appeared in the Silurian period. Plants produced oxygen and provided food for the first land animals, amphibians. Amphibians first appeared in the Devonian period.

When did mammals first appear?

Mammals lived on Earth from at least the start of the Jurassic period. But they did not become common until after the extinction of the dinosaurs.

When did people first live on Earth?

Hominids (ape-like creatures that walked upright) first appeared on Earth more than four million years ago. But modern humans appeared only around 100,000 years ago.

How is Earth's history divided up?

The last 590 million years of Earth history are divided into eras and periods. 'M.y.a.' on the diagram means 'millions of years ago'.

SCIENTISTS DIVIDE THE LAST 590 MILLION YEARS OF EARTH'S HISTORY INTO THREE MAIN ERAS: the Paleozoic (a word meaning 'old life') era, the Mesozoic ('middle life') era, and the Cenozoic ('new life') era. The eras are then subdivided into periods – and some periods are further divided into epochs. The first period in the Paleozoic era is the Cambrian period. All of Earth's history before the Cambrian period is called the Precambrian. Scientists divide the Precambrian into two eons: the Archean and the Proterozoic. Scientists know little about life in the Precambrian, because fossils from that time are rare.

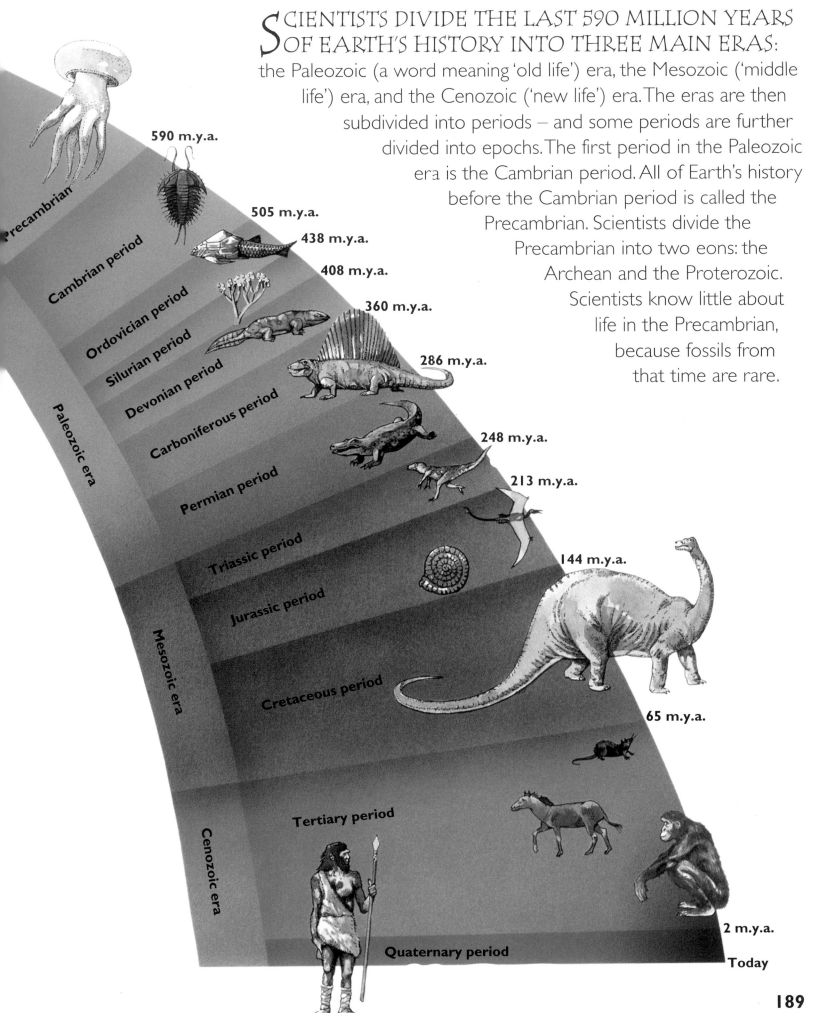

Precambrian

590 m.y.a.

Cambrian period

505 m.y.a.

438 m.y.a.

Ordovician period

408 m.y.a.

Silurian period

360 m.y.a.

Devonian period

Carboniferous period

286 m.y.a.

Paleozoic era

Permian period

248 m.y.a.

213 m.y.a.

Triassic period

144 m.y.a.

Jurassic period

Mesozoic era

Cretaceous period

65 m.y.a.

Tertiary period

Cenozoic era

Quaternary period

2 m.y.a.

Today

What are plates?

The Earth's hard outer layers are divided into large blocks called plates. Currents in the partly molten rocks inside the Earth slowly move the plates around.

How big are the plates?

The Earth's outer layers are split into seven large plates and about 20 small ones. The plates are about 70 to 100 km (43 to 62 miles) deep.

How the continents have drifted apart in the last 200 million years

Around 280 million years ago, the world's land areas moved together to form one supercontinent called Pangaea.

What happens when plates collide?

Along deep ocean trenches, one plate is pulled beneath another. There it is melted and destroyed. When continents collide, their edges are squeezed up into new mountain ranges.

How fast do plates move?

Plates move, on average, between 1 and 10 cm (0.4 and 4 in) a year. This may sound slow. But over millions of years, these small plate movements dramatically change the face of the Earth.

How do plates move apart?

PLATES CONSIST OF THE EARTH'S CRUST AND THE TOP PART OF THE MANTLE.
The plates float on a partly molten layer within the mantle. Huge underwater mountain ranges, called ocean ridges, rise from the ocean bed. Along the middle of these ridges are valleys, where plates are being pulled apart by currents in the partly molten rocks below. As plates move apart, liquid rock, called magma, rises and plugs the gaps. When the magma hardens, it forms new crustal rock.

Who first suggested the idea of continental drift?

In the early 1800s, an American, F.B. Taylor, and a German, Alfred Wegener, both suggested the idea of continental drift. But scientists could not explain how the plates moved until the 1960s, following studies of the ocean floor.

Have fossils helped to prove continental drift?

Fossils of animals that could not possibly have swum across oceans have been found in different continents. This suggests that the continents were once all joined together and the animals could walk from one continent to another.

How plates change the face of the Earth

The ocean floor has huge ridges, where plates are moving apart. The gaps are filled with rising magma.

Plates consist of the Earth's crust and the rigid upper layer of the mantle.

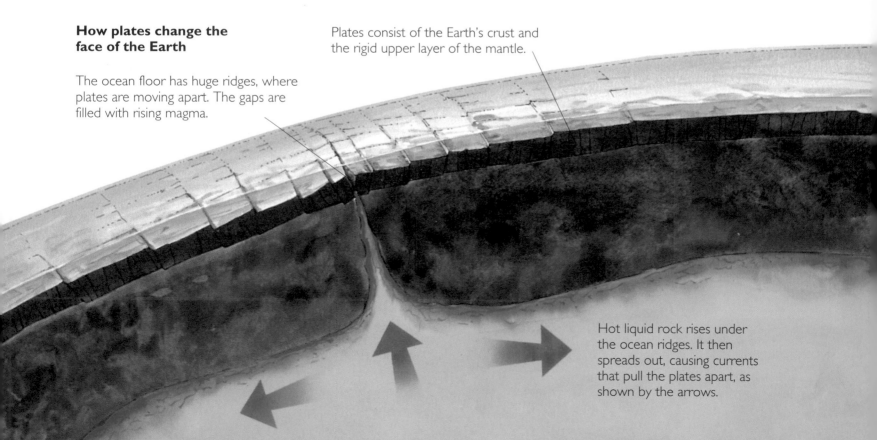

Hot liquid rock rises under the ocean ridges. It then spreads out, causing currents that pull the plates apart, as shown by the arrows.

How do volcanic islands form in the middle of oceans?

Volcanic islands form when magma rises from the mantle. Lava (the name for magma when it reaches the surface) piles up until it emerges above sea level.

Has the Earth always looked the same?

IF ALIENS HAD VISITED EARTH 200 MILLION YEARS AGO, THEY WOULD HAVE SEEN only one huge continent, called Pangaea, surrounded by one ocean. Around 180 million years ago, Pangaea began to break up. By 135 million years ago, a plate bearing South America was drifting away from Africa, creating the South Atlantic Ocean. By 100 million years ago, plates supporting India, Australia and Antarctica were also drifting away from Africa, and North America was moving away from Europe.

Pangaea began to break apart around 180 million years ago.

Can plates move sideways?

Plates not only move apart or push against each other, they can also move sideways along huge cracks in the ground called transform faults.

Around 65 million years ago, the Atlantic Ocean was opening up and India was moving towards Asia.

Along the deep ocean trenches, ocean plates are pushed beneath other plates. Here, the plate supports a continent.

The rocks on the edge of the continents are folded by the pressure of plate movements.

Magma from the melted plate rises. Some emerges through volcanoes.

The map shows our world today, but plate movements are still changing the face of our planet.

When plates move, the land is shaken by earthquakes.

The edge of the descending plate is melted, producing huge pockets of magma.

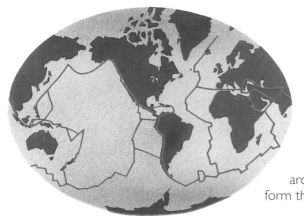

What earthquake in modern times caused the most damage?

In 1923, an earthquake struck Tokyo, capital of Japan. About 575,000 homes were destroyed in Tokyo and nearby Yokohama. About 142,800 people died.

Severe earthquakes occur around the edges of the plates that form the outer, rigid layers of the Earth.

Can scientists predict earthquakes?

In 1975, Chinese scientists correctly predicted an earthquake and saved the lives of many people. But scientists have not yet found any sure way of forecasting earthquakes.

Can animals sense when an earthquake is about to happen?

Scientists have noticed that animals often behave strangely before an earthquake. Horses rear up, dogs bark and snakes come out of their holes in the ground.

What is the San Andreas fault?

The San Andreas fault is a long transform fault in California. Movements along this plate edge have caused great earthquakes in San Francisco and Los Angeles.

Where are earthquakes likely to happen?

EARTHQUAKES CAN OCCUR ANYWHERE, WHENEVER ROCKS MOVE ALONG FAULTS (cracks) in the ground. But the most violent earthquakes occur most often around the edges of the plates that make up the Earth's hard outer layers. Plates do not move smoothly. For most of the time, their edges are jammed together. But gradually the currents under the plates build up increasing pressure. Finally the plates move in a sharp jerk. This sudden movement shakes all the rocks around it, setting off an earthquake.

Many earthquakes occur along transform faults

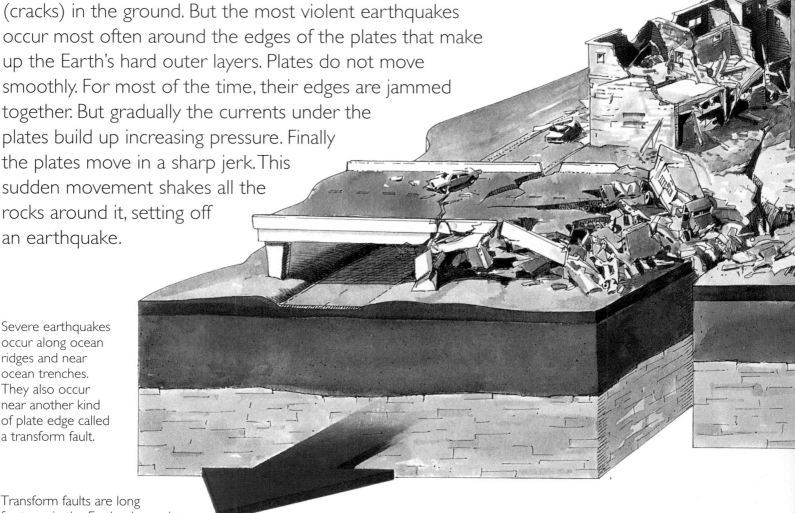

Severe earthquakes occur along ocean ridges and near ocean trenches. They also occur near another kind of plate edge called a transform fault.

Transform faults are long fractures in the Earth where plates move alongside each other.

What instruments record earthquakes?

Seismographs are sensitive instruments that record earthquakes. The shaking of the ground is recorded by a pen that marks the movements on a revolving drum.

Do earthquakes and volcanoes occur in the same places?

Most active volcanoes occur near the edges of plates that are moving apart and also where they are colliding. Earthquakes are common in these regions too.

How do earthquakes cause damage?

POWERFUL EARTHQUAKES SHAKE THE GROUND. THEY MAKE BUILDINGS SWAY and wobble until they collapse. The shaking sometimes breaks gas pipes or causes electrical short-circuits, starting fires. Earthquakes on high mountain slopes cause landslides that sometimes destroy towns in the valleys below. Earthquakes on the sea-bed trigger off waves called tsunamis. Tsunamis travel through the water at up to 800 kph (500 mph). As they approach land, the water piles up into waves many metres high. These waves cause great damage and loss of life.

Vibrations occur when the plates move, causing violent shaking of the ground. This destroys buildings and other structures, often with loss of life.

Pressure builds up until finally the rocks break and the plates move suddenly forwards.

Transform faults have ragged edges and, for most of the time, the plates are locked together.

When volcanoes erupt, they may hurl rocks and ash into the air, and lava may flow down slopes.

What makes volcanoes erupt?

VOLCANOES ERUPT WHEN HOT MOLTEN ROCK FROM DEEP DOWN IN EARTH'S mantle rises through the Earth's hard outer layers and reaches the surface. The molten rock is called magma, but when it reaches the surface, it is called lava. Most volcanoes occur near the edges of plates. Many rise along the ocean ridges where magma rushes up to fill the gaps formed as plates move apart. Other volcanoes get their magma from the plates that are melted as they are pulled beneath other plates.

Magma reaches the surface through vents, which are holes in the ground.

Lava may burst from a central vent or through side vents.

Lava flows burn everything in their paths.

Clouds of ash often block out the Sun. Ash falls on the land and it may bury towns. Mud flows occur when rain turns the ash into torrents of mud.

What are volcanoes made of?

Some volcanoes are cone-shaped and made of volcanic ash or cinders. Dome-shaped shield volcanoes are made of hardened lava. Intermediate volcanoes contain layers of both ash and lava.

Kinds of volcanoes
Shield volcano

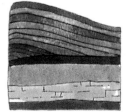

Some volcanoes, shaped like upturned shields, are formed by 'quiet eruptions', in which long streams of very fluid lava are emitted.

What is a dormant volcano?

Some volcanoes erupt continuously for long periods. But other active volcanoes erupt only now and then. When they are not erupting, they are said to be dormant, or sleeping.

What is an extinct volcano?

Volcanoes that have not erupted in historic times are said to be extinct. This means that they are not expected to erupt ever again.

Explosive volcano

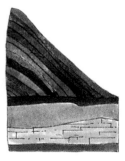

Explosive eruptions occur when the magma is thick and contains explosive gases. Explosive volcanoes are made of ash and cinders and are steep-sided.

Do volcanoes do any good?

Volcanic eruptions cause tremendous damage, but soil formed from volcanic ash is fertile. Volcanic rocks are also used in building and chemical industries.

What are 'hot spots'?

Some volcanoes lie far from plate edges. They form over 'hot spots' – areas of great heat in the Earth's mantle. Hawaii in the Pacific Ocean is over a hot spot.

Intermediate volcano

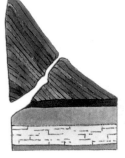

Intermediate volcanoes are cone-shaped. They are composed of alternating layers of ash and hardened lava.

Do all volcanoes erupt in the same way?

No, THEY DON'T. VOLCANOES CAN EXPLODE UPWARDS OR SIDEWAYS, OR erupt 'quietly'. Trapped inside the magma in explosive volcanoes are lots of gases and water vapour. These gases shatter the magma and hurl columns of volcanic ash and fine volcanic dust into the air. Fragments of shattered magma are called pyroclasts. Sometimes, clouds of ash and hot gases are shot sideways out of volcanoes. They pour downhill at great speeds destroying everything in their paths. In 'quietly' erupting volcanoes the magma emerges on the surface as runny lava and flows downhill.

What are hot springs and geysers?

Magma heats water in the ground. The hot water often bubbles up in hot springs. Sometimes, boiling water and steam are hurled into the air through geysers.

When lava and volcanic ash harden, they slowly break down to form soil.

What are the most valuable minerals?

Gemstones such as diamonds, rubies, sapphires and emeralds are valuable minerals. Gold and silver are also regarded as minerals, although they occur as native, or free, elements.

Ever since the Stone Age, people have used gemstones to make jewellery. Beautiful jewellery commands high prices.

Gemstones

What are the three main kinds of rock?

THERE ARE IGNEOUS, SEDIMENTARY AND METAMORPHIC ROCKS. IGNEOUS ROCKS are formed from cooled magma. Sometimes it cools on the surface to form such rocks as basalt. Other magma cools underground to create rocks called granites. Many sedimentary rocks are made from worn fragments of other rocks. For example, sandstone is formed from sand. Sand consists mainly of quartz, a mineral found in granite. And some limestones are made from the shells of sea creatures. Metamorphic rocks are rocks changed by heat and pressure. For example, great heat turns limestone into marble.

Can minerals make you invisible?

People once believed in many superstitions about minerals. In the Middle Ages, people thought that you would become invisible if you wore an opal wrapped in a bay leaf.

What is the hardest mineral?

Diamond, a pure but rare form of carbon, is formed under great pressure deep inside the Earth. It is the hardest natural substance.

What are the most common rocks?

Sedimentary rocks cover 75% of the Earth's land surface. But igneous and metamorphic rocks make up 95% of the rocks in the top 16 km (10 miles) of the Earth's crust.

What are birthstones?

Birthstones are minerals that symbolize the month of a person's birth. For example, garnet is the birthstone for January, while ruby is the stone for people born in July.

Fragments of sand, silt and mud are washed into lakes and seas. There they pile up in layers that harden into sedimentary rocks.

What are elements and minerals?

EARTH'S CRUST CONTAINS 92 ELEMENTS. THE TWO MOST COMMON ELEMENTS are oxygen and silicon. Also common are aluminium, iron, calcium, sodium, potassium and magnesium. These eight elements make up 98.59% of the weight of the Earth's crust. Some elements, such as gold, occur in a pure state. But most minerals are chemical combinations of elements. For example, minerals made of oxygen and silicon, often with small amounts of other elements, are called silicates. They include feldspar, quartz and mica – all found in granite.

What common rocks are used for buildings?

Two sedimentary rocks, limestone and sandstone, and the igneous rock granite are all good building stones. The metamorphic rock marble is often used to decorate buildings.

Earth movements and great heat turn igneous and sedimentary rocks into metamorphic rocks.

Igneous rocks are formed from magma, which may solidify beneath or on the Earth's surface. Surface rocks are constantly worn away by erosion.

Is coal a rock?

No. Rocks are inorganic (lifeless) substances. But coal, like oil and natural gas, was formed millions of years ago from the remains of once-living things. That is why coal, oil and gas are called fossil fuels.

Are some minerals more plentiful than others?

Many useful minerals are abundant. Other less common, but important minerals are in short supply and are therefore often recycled from scrap. Recycling saves energy, which has to be used to process metal ores.

How are fossils turned to stone?

When tree trunks or bones are buried, minerals deposited from water sometimes replace the original material. The wood or bone is then petrified, or turned to stone.

Fossils of ammonites are common in rocks of the Mesozoic era. Ammonites were molluscs, related to squid.

Ammonite fossil

What is carbonization?

Leaves usually rot quickly after plants die. But sometimes they float to the bottom of lakes and are buried under fine mud. Sediments above and below the leaf are gradually compressed and hardened into sedimentary rocks. Over time, bacteria gradually change the chemistry of the leaf until only the carbon it contains remains. The shape of the leaf is preserved in the rock as a thin carbon smear. This process is called carbonization.

Fossil teeth

What are fossils?

FOSSILS ARE THE IMPRESSIONS OF ANCIENT LIFE PRESERVED IN ROCKS. For example, when dead creatures are buried on the sea floor, the soft parts rot away, but the hard parts remain. Later, the mud and sand on the sea-bed harden into rock. Water seeping through the rock dissolves the hard parts, forming fossil moulds. Minerals fill the moulds to create casts, which preserve the shapes of the hard parts. Other fossils include outlines of leaves turned to stone, and insects in amber.

What are trace fossils?

Trace fossils give information about animals that lived in ancient times. Animal burrows are sometimes preserved, giving scientists clues about the creatures that made them. Other trace fossils include footprints preserved in hardened mud and quickly buried under more mud.

Fossil footprints

Fossil footprints are preserved in rocks. They are uncovered when overlying rocks are worn away.

What is amber?

Amber is a hard substance formed from the sticky resin of trees. Tiny animals were sometimes trapped in the resin. Their bodies were preserved when the resin hardened.

Fossil spider

Many tiny creatures have been fossilized in amber. They are unusual fossils because they consist of the actual bodies of ancient creatures.

Carbonized leaves

198

What was Piltdown man?

Some bones, thought to be fossils of an early human ancestor, were discovered at Piltdown, England, in 1913. But Piltdown man was a fake. The skull was human, but the jawbone came from an orang utan.

How do you date fossils?

Sometimes, dead creatures are found buried under volcanic ash. The ash sometimes contains radioactive substances that scientists can date. Hence, they can work out the time when the animals lived.

Trilobite fossils

What can scientists learn from fossils?

FROM THE STUDY OF FOSSILS – KNOWN AS PALAEONTOLOGY – SCIENTISTS CAN learn about how living things evolved on Earth. Fossils can also help palaeontologists to date rocks. This is because some species lived for only a short period on Earth. So, if the fossils of these creatures are found in rocks in different places, the rocks must have been formed at the same time. Such fossils are called index fossils. Important index fossils include species of trilobites, graptolites, brachiopods, crinoids, ammonites and belemnites.

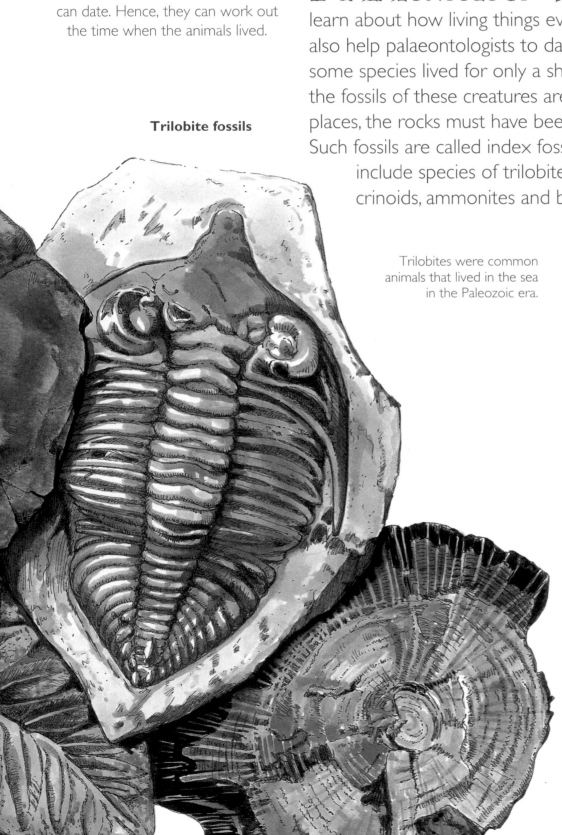

Trilobites were common animals that lived in the sea in the Paleozoic era.

Has flesh ever been preserved as a fossil?

In Siberia, woolly mammoths, which lived more than 40,000 years ago, sank in swampy ground. When the soil froze, their complete bodies were preserved in the icy subsoil.

What is eohippus?

Eohippus is the name of the dog-sized ancestor of the horse, which lived around 55 million years ago. Fossil studies of eohippus and its successors have shown how the modern horse evolved.

Petrified logs

Petrified logs were formed when water replaced the molecules in buried logs with minerals. Slowly, stone replicas of the logs were produced.

Limestone caves

Limestone caves are worn out by chemical weathering. They often contain stalactites and stalagmites.

What are stalactites?

Water containing a lot of calcium carbonate drips down from the ceilings of limestone caves. The water gradually deposits calcium carbonate to form hanging, icicle-like structures called stalactites.

How quickly is the land worn away?

Scientists have worked out that an average of 3.5 cm (1.4 in) is worn away from land areas every 1,000 years. This sounds slow but, over millions of years, mountains are worn down to make plains.

What are pot-holers?

Pot-holes, or swallow holes, are holes in the ground where people called pot-holers can climb down to explore limestone caves. Pot-holers may face danger when sudden rains raise the water level in caves.

What are stalagmites?

Stalagmites are the opposite of stalactites. They are columns of calcium carbonate deposited by dripping water. But stalagmites grow upwards from the floors of caves.

Does water react chemically with other rocks?

Water dissolves rock salt. It also reacts with some types of the hard rock granite, turning minerals in the rock into a clay called kaolin.

What is ground water?

Ground water is water that seeps slowly through rocks, such as sandstones and limestones. The top level of the water in the rocks is called the water table. Wells are dug down to the water table.

What are springs?

Springs occur when ground water flows on to the surface. Springs are the sources of many rivers. Hot springs occur in volcanic areas, where the ground water is heated by magma.

Weathering of the land

Weathering is rapid on sloping land, where worn rocks tumble downhill.

How does weathering help to shape the land?

WEATHERING IS THE BREAKDOWN AND DECAY OF ROCKS ON THE EARTH'S SURFACE. The wearing away of the rock limestone is an example of chemical weathering. Limestone consists mostly of the chemical calcium carbonate. This chemical reacts with rainwater containing carbon dioxide, which it has dissolved from the air. The rainwater is a weak acid that slowly dissolves the limestone. The rainwater opens up cracks in the surface, wearing out holes that eventually lead down to a maze of huge caves linked by tunnels.

Ground water flows out of limestone caves to form the source of a river.

Can the Sun's heat cause mechanical weathering?

In hot, dry regions, rocks are heated by the Sun, but they cool at night. These changes crack rock surfaces, which peel away like the layers of an onion.

Can plants change the land?

Plant roots can break up the rock. When the seed of a tree falls into a crack in a rock, it develops roots that push downwards. As the roots grow, they push against the sides of the crack until the rock splits apart.

What is biological weathering?

Biological weathering includes the splitting apart of rocks by tree roots, the breaking up of rocks by burrowing animals, and the work of bacteria, which also helps to weather rocks.

How does the action of frost break up rocks?

A T NIGHT IN THE MOUNTAINS, PEOPLE MAY HEAR SOUNDS LIKE GUNSHOTS. These sounds are made by rocks being split apart by frost action. Frost action, an example of mechanical weathering, occurs when water in cracks in rocks freezes and turns into ice. Ice takes up nearly one-tenth as much space again as water, and so it exerts pressure, widening the cracks until they split apart. On steep slopes, shattered rocks tumble downhill and pile up in heaps, called scree or talus.

Frost action affects high mountain slopes, where water freezes at night.

Surface water flows into layers of limestone and hollows out caves.

Worn rocks pile up in heaps called scree or talus.

The roots of trees can split rock apart.

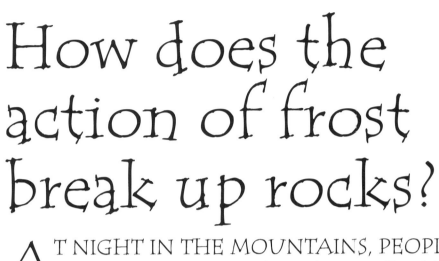

How do rivers shape the land?

R IVERS SWEEP AWAY WEATHERED ROCKS, AND THEY ALSO WEAR AWAY THE LAND. Young rivers push loose rocks down steep slopes. The rocks rub against river beds and deepen their valleys. The rocks rub against each other and break down into finer and finer pieces. Mature rivers flow down gentler slopes. They develop bends called meanders and they continue to wear away land. In old age, rivers move slowly across nearly flat plains, carrying huge loads of sand, silt and mud towards the sea.

Gorge

Oxbow lake

In their youthful stage, rivers flow swiftly. They sometimes wear out deep, steep-sided gorges.

Tributary river

Tributary river

In the mature stage, rivers contain much more water. They often develop vigorous meanders.

In old age, rivers flow more slowly. Sometimes they change course. Cut-off bends become oxbow lakes

Where do rivers start?
Some rivers start at springs, where ground water reaches the surface. Others start at the ends of melting glaciers or are the outlets of lakes.

Why do waterfalls occur?
Waterfalls occur when rivers cross hard rocks. When softer rocks downstream are worn away, the hard rocks form a ledge over which the river plunges in a waterfall.

When heavy rains swell old-age rivers, they may overflow their banks and cause floods.

What are tributary rivers?
Tributary rivers are rivers that flow into a main river. This swells the amount of water in the main river and increases its load of worn material.

What are deltas?
Deltas are areas of sediments – made up of sand, mud and silt – that pile up around the mouths of some rivers. In many rivers, currents sweep the sediments into the sea.

What are spits?

Waves and currents transport sediments along coasts. In places where the coasts change direction, the worn sand and pebbles pile up in narrow ridges called spits.

How can people slow down wave erosion?

Along the beaches at many coastal resorts, walls are built at right angles to the shore. These walls, called groynes, slow down the movement of sand on the beaches by waves and sea currents.

What is a baymouth bar?

Some spits join one headland to another. They are called baymouth bars, because they cut off bays from the sea, turning them into lagoons.

Does the sea wear away the land?

Waves wear away soft rocks to form bays, while harder rocks on either side form headlands. Parts of the coast of Northeast England have been worn back by up to 5 km (3 miles) since the days when the Romans ruled the area.

Caves, arches and stacks

Waves hollow out caves in rocky headlands. Blow-holes form above the caves.

When two caves in a headland meet, a natural arch occurs.

When a natural arch collapses, the tip of the headland becomes an isolated stack.

Can sea waves shape coasts?

LARGE STORM WAVES BATTER THE SHORE. THE WAVES PICK UP SAND AND PEBBLES, hurling them at cliffs. This hollows out the bottom layers of the cliff until the top collapses and the cliff retreats. Waves hollow out bays in soft rocks, leaving hard rocks jutting into the sea as headlands. Waves then attack the headlands from both sides, wearing out caves. When two caves meet, a natural arch is formed. When the arch collapses, all that remains is an isolated rock, called a stack.

Mud carried by a river is often dumped near the river's mouth to form large mud flats. At high tide the sea often covers these areas.

What are fiords?
Fiords are deep, steep-sided valleys that wind inland along coasts. They were once river valleys that were deepened by glaciers during the last ice age.

What are erratics?
Erratics are boulders made of a rock that is different from the rocks on which they rest. They were transported to their present positions by moving ice.

How much of the world is covered by ice?
Ice covers about 11% of the world's land area. But during the last ice age, it spread over much of northern North America and Europe. The same ice sheet reached what is now New York City in America, and covered London in England.

How does ice shape the land?

IN COLD MOUNTAIN AREAS, SNOW PILES UP IN HOLLOWS. GRADUALLY, THE SNOW becomes compacted into ice. Eventually, the ice spills out of the hollows and starts to move downhill to form a glacier. Glaciers are like conveyor belts. On the tops of glaciers are rocks shattered by frost action that have tumbled downhill. Other rocks are frozen into the sides and bottoms of glaciers. They give glaciers the power to wear away rocks and deepen the valleys through which they flow. Ice-worn valleys are U-shaped, with steep sides and flat bottoms. This distinguishes them from V-shaped river valleys.

A valley glacier

The ice spills downhill to form rivers of ice called glaciers. The glaciers carry much worn rock, called moraine.

At the end of the glacier, the ice melts, creating streams that sweep away the glacier's rocky load.

What are the world's largest bodies of ice?

The largest bodies of ice are the ice sheets of Antarctica and Greenland. Smaller ice caps occur in the Arctic, while mountain glaciers are found around the world.

The world map during the Ice Age

Ice covered much of northern North America, Europe and Asia during the Ice Age.

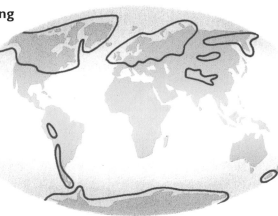

Snow falls on mountains. At the higher levels, the snow piles up year by year.

Snow in mountain basins, called cirques, becomes compressed into glacier ice.

What is an ice age?

During ice ages, average temperatures fall and ice sheets spread over large areas that were once ice-free. Several ice ages have occurred in Earth's history.

When did the last ice age take place?

The last ice age began about two million years ago and ended 10,000 years ago. The ice age included warm periods and long periods of bitter cold.

How can we tell that an area was once covered by ice?

CERTAIN FEATURES IN THE LANDSCAPE WERE MADE BY ICE DURING THE ICE AGES. Mountain areas contain deep, steep-sided valleys that were worn out by glaciers. Armchair-shaped basins where glacier ice once formed are called cirques. Knife-edged ridges between cirques are called arêtes, while peaks called horns were carved when three or more cirques formed back-to-back. Boulders and other material carried by ice is called moraine. Moraine ridges show that ice sheets once reached that area.

How does wind-blown sand shape scenery?

IN DESERTS, WIND-BLOWN SAND IS IMPORTANT IN SHAPING THE SCENERY. Winds lift grains of sand, which are then blown and bounced forward. Sand grains are heavy and seldom rise over 2 metres (6 ft) above ground level. But, at low levels, wind-blown sand acts like the sand-blasters used to clean dirty city buildings. It also polishes rocks, hollows out caves in cliffs and undercuts boulders. Boulders whose bases have been worn by wind-blown sand are top-heavy and mushroom-shaped, perched on a narrow stem.

Can water change desert scenery?

Thousands of years ago, many deserts were rainy areas and many land features were shaped by rivers. Flash floods sometimes occur in deserts. They sweep away much worn material.

What are dust storms?

Desert winds sweep fine dust high into the air during choking dust storms. Wind from the Sahara in North Africa is often blown over southern Europe, carrying the pinkish dust with it.

What are the main types of desert scenery?

Arabic words are used for desert scenery. Erg is the name for sandy desert, reg is land covered with gravel and pebbles, and hammada is the word for areas of bare rock.

Desert scenery

What are wadis?

Wadis are dry waterways in deserts. Travellers sometimes shelter in them at night. But a freak storm can soon fill them with water and people sleeping in the wadis are in danger of being drowned.

Why do people in deserts wear heavy clothes?

Deserts are often cold at night and heavy clothes keep people warm. Long cloaks and headdresses also help to keep out stinging wind-blown sand and dust and prevent sunburn.

Oases are places in deserts where water comes to the surface or where people can obtain water from wells.

Large areas of desert are covered with gravel and pebbles. These areas are called reg.

Wind-blown sand is responsible for carving top-heavy mushroom rocks that stand on thin stems.

Mushroom rocks

Wind-blown sand erodes the bottoms of rocks, wearing them to a narrow stem.

Barchans

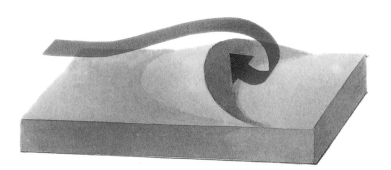

Crescent-shaped dunes form in sandy deserts where wind directions are constant.

How are sand dunes formed?

THE WIND BLOWING ACROSS DESERT SANDS PILES THE SAND UP IN HILLS CALLED DUNES. Where the wind directions keep changing, the dunes have no particular shape. But when they blow mainly from one direction, crescent-shaped dunes called barchans often form. Barchans may occur singly or in clusters. When winds drive sand dunes forward they form seif dunes, named after an Arabic word meaning sword. Sometimes, advancing dunes bury farmland. To stop their advance, people plant trees and grasses to anchor the sand.

What are oases?

Oases are places in deserts that have water supplies. Some oases have wells tapping ground water. Sometimes, the water bubbles up to the surface in a spring.

What is desertification?

Human misuse of the land near deserts, caused by cutting down trees and overgrazing grasslands, may turn fertile land into desert. This is called desertification. Natural climate changes may also create deserts. This happened in the Sahara around 7,000 years ago.

About one-fifth of the world's deserts are covered in sand (erg). There are also large areas of bare rock (hammada).

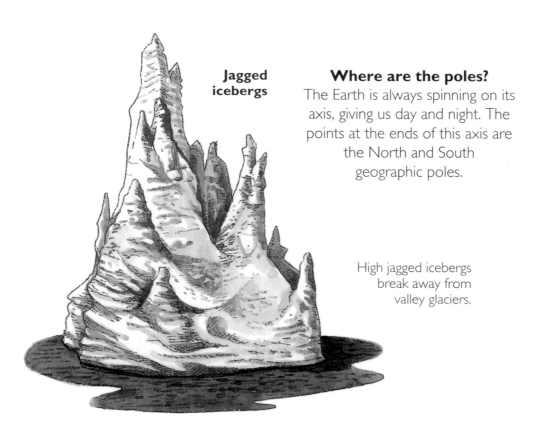

Jagged icebergs

Where are the poles?
The Earth is always spinning on its axis, giving us day and night. The points at the ends of this axis are the North and South geographic poles.

High jagged icebergs break away from valley glaciers.

Why are icebergs dangerous to shipping?
Icebergs are huge chunks of ice that break off from glaciers. They float in the sea with nine-tenths of their bulk submerged, which makes them extremely dangerous to shipping. Icebergs from Greenland have sunk ships off the coasts of North America.

What are magnetic poles?
The Earth is like a giant magnet, with two magnetic poles. They lie near the geographic poles, though their positions change from time to time.

Icebergs in the oceans

The bulk of the ice in icebergs is hidden beneath the waves.

What it is like around the North Pole?

IT IS BITTERLY COLD. THE NORTH POLE LIES IN THE MIDDLE OF THE ARCTIC OCEAN, which is surrounded by northern North America, Asia and Europe. Sea ice covers much of the ocean for most of the year. In spring, the sea ice is around 3 metres (9 ft) thick in mid-ocean and explorers can walk across it. The Arctic Ocean contains several islands, including Greenland, the world's largest. A huge ice sheet, the world's second largest, covers more than four-fifths of Greenland.

Is the ice around the poles melting?
In parts of Antarctica, the ice shelves began to melt in the 1990s. Some people think this shows that the world is getting warmer because of pollution.

Icebergs contain worn rocks that have been eroded from the land.

Icebergs melt as they float away from polar regions and the climate becomes warmer.

What animals live in polar regions?
Penguins are the best known animals of Antarctica. Polar bears, caribou, musk oxen and reindeer are large animals that live in the Arctic region.

As icebergs melt, the rocks in the ice sink down and settle on the ocean bed.

What are ice shelves?
Ice shelves are large blocks of ice joined to Antarctica's ice sheet but which jut out over the sea. When chunks break away, they form flat, table-topped icebergs. Some of them are huge. One covered an area about the size of Belgium.

How thick is the ice in Antarctica?

THE SOUTH POLE LIES IN THE COLD AND WINDY CONTINENT OF ANTARCTICA, which is larger than either Europe or Australia. Ice and snow cover 98% of Antarctica, although some coastal areas and high peaks are ice-free. The Antarctic ice sheet is the world's largest, and contains about seven-tenths of the world's fresh water. In places, the ice is up to 4.8 km (3 miles) thick. The world's record lowest temperature, −89.2°C (−128.6°F), was recorded at the Vostok research station in 1983.

Flat-topped icebergs form off the coast of Antarctica.

What is the Great Barrier Reef?

The Great Barrier Reef lies off the northeast coast of Australia. It is the world's longest group of coral reefs and islands. It is about 2,000 km (1,242 miles) long.

Where is the 'Great Pebble'?

The word Uluru is an Australian Aboriginal word meaning 'great pebble'. Also called Ayers Rock, it is the world's biggest monolith (single rock).

Grand Canyon

The Grand Canyon is regarded as one of the seven natural wonders of the world.

Uluru (Ayers Rock)

Uluru, or Ayers Rock, is a tourist attraction in central Australia.

Where can you find 'smoke that thunders'?

The local name of the beautiful Victoria Falls on the River Zambezi between Zambia and Zimbabwe is Mosi oa Tunya. This name means 'smoke that thunders'.

Victoria Falls

The Victoria Falls in Africa was named after Queen Victoria by the missionary David Livingstone.

What are natural wonders?

THE ANCIENT GREEKS AND ROMANS MADE LISTS OF THE SEVEN WONDERS of the World. They were all made by people, but the Earth also has many natural wonders, created by the forces that continuously shape our planet. Most lists of natural wonders include the Grand Canyon in the southwestern United States. It is the world's largest canyon and the most awe-inspiring. The canyon is 446 km (277 miles) long and about 1.6 km (1 mile) deep. It was worn out by the Colorado River over the last six million years.

Where is the Matterhorn?

The Matterhorn is a magnificent mountain on Switzerland's border with Italy. It was created by glaciers wearing away the mountain from opposite sides.

What mountains look like dragon's teeth?

Steep-sided hills made of limestone, found around the town of Guilin in southeastern China, resemble rows of giant dragon's teeth. Rainwater wore out these strange-looking hills.

What is the world's mightiest river?

The Amazon River in South America contains far more water than any other river. Its river basin (the region it drains) is also the world's largest.

What is Meteor Crater?

Meteor Crater in Arizona, America, is a circular depression. It resembles a volcanic crater, but was formed about 50,000 years ago when a meteor hit our planet. The crater is 1,275 metres (4,180 ft) wide and 175 metres (570 ft) deep.

Where is the world's highest mountain range?

The Himalayan range in Asia contains 96 of the world's 109 peaks that are more than 7,315 metres (24,000 ft) above sea level. One of these peaks is Mount Everest, the world's highest mountain.

Where do the world's natural wonders occur?

THE WORLD'S NATURAL WONDERS CAN BE FOUND IN EVERY CONTINENT AND some, such as Australia's Great Barrier Reef, occur in the oceans. Many people now work to protect natural wonders so that they can be enjoyed by people in the future. One important step in protecting them was made in 1872, when the world's first national park was founded at Yellowstone, site of the famous geyser called Old Faithful, in the northwestern United States. Since then, national parks have been founded around the world.

What Japanese wonder attracts pilgrims?

Mount Fuji in Japan is a beautiful volcanic cone. Many people regard it as a sacred mountain – a dwelling place for the gods – and they make long pilgrimages to the top.

Limestone peaks

Near Guilin, China, are strange limestone hills that have become a major tourist attraction.

How can people protect natural wonders?

People enjoy visiting natural wonders, but they can damage the land, cause traffic pollution and spread litter. Many natural wonders are now protected by governments in areas called national parks.

Matterhorn

The Matterhorn reaches a height of 4,478 metres (14,692 ft) above sea level.

The Amazon

The Amazon drains a huge region that contains the world's largest rainforest.

What is air pollution?

Air pollution occurs when gases such as carbon dioxide are emitted into the air by factories, homes and offices. Vehicles also cause air pollution, which produces city smogs, acid rain and global warming.

Will global warming affect any island nations?

Coral islands are low-lying. If global warming melts the world's ice, then sea levels will rise. Such countries as the Maldives and Kiribati will vanish under the waves.

What is coastal pollution?

Coral reefs and mangrove swamps are breeding places for many fishes. The destruction or pollution of these areas is threatening the numbers of fishes in the oceans.

Can the pollution of rivers harm people?

When factories pump poisonous wastes into rivers, creatures living near the rivers' mouths, such as shellfish, absorb poison into their bodies. When people eat such creatures, they, too, are poisoned.

Can deserts be farmed?

In Israel and other countries, barren deserts have been turned into farmland by irrigation. The land is watered from wells that tap ground water, or the water is piped from far-away areas.

What is soil erosion?

Natural erosion, caused by running water, winds and other forces, is a slow process. Soil erosion occurs when people cut down trees and farm the land. Soil erosion on land made bare by people is a much faster process than natural erosion.

What happens when people exploit the Earth?

What is happening to the world's rainforests?

The rainforests in the tropics are being destroyed. These forests contain more than half of the world's living species. Many of them are now threatened with extinction. Huge forest fires in 1997 and 1998 destroyed large areas of rainforest.

Rainforest destruction

IN MANY AREAS, PEOPLE ARE CHANGING THE EARTH AND CAUSING GREAT HARM through pollution. They are cutting down forests to produce farmland. But in some places, rain and winds wear away newly exposed soil, causing soil erosion and making the land infertile. Factories, vehicles and homes burn fuels that release gases into the air. These so-called greenhouse gases trap heat. They cause global warming and change world climates. Other kinds of pollution include the poisoning of rivers and seas by factory and household wastes.

Rainforests are cut down by loggers who want to sell valuable hardwoods.

Land stripped bare of trees is exposed to the wind and the rain, which cause serious soil erosion.

How have people turned sea into land?

IN CROWDED COUNTRIES, PEOPLE SOMETIMES TURN USELESS COASTAL LAND INTO FERTILE FARMLAND. The Netherlands is a flat country and about two-fifths of it is below sea level at high tide. The Dutch have created new land by building dykes (sea walls) around areas once under the sea, called polders. Rainwater washes out the salt from the soil and the polder land finally becomes fertile. Global warming could affect the Netherlands. Increasingly stormy weather and rises in the sea level could cause massive flooding.

What is the biggest continent?

ASIA COVERS AN AREA OF 44,009,000 SQ KM (16,992,000 SQ MILES).
The other continents, in order of size, are Africa (30,246,000 sq km/11,678,000 sq miles), North America (24,219,000 sq km/9,351,000 sq miles), South America (17,832,000 sq km/6,885,000 sq miles), Antarctica (14,000,000 sq km/5,400,400 sq miles), Europe (10,443,000 sq km/4,032,000 sq miles), and Australia (7,713,000 sq km/2,978,000 sq miles).

What is the world's largest island?
Greenland covers about 2,175,000 sq km (840,000 sq miles). Geographers regard Australia as a continent and not as an island.

How much of the world is covered by land?
Land covers about 148,460,000 sq km (57,300,000 sq miles), or 29 % of the world's surface. Water covers the remaining 71 %.

What is the world's largest bay?
Hudson Bay in Canada covers an area of about 1,233,000 sq km (476,000 sq miles). It is linked to the North Atlantic Ocean by the Hudson Strait.

What is the world's largest high plateau?
The wind-swept Tibetan Plateau in China covers about 1,850,000 sq km (715,000 sq miles).

Where is the world's lowest point on land?
The shoreline of the Dead Sea, between Israel and Jordan, is 400 metres (1,312 ft) below the sea level of the nearby Mediterranean Sea.

What is the world's highest peak?
Mount Everest on Nepal's border with China reaches 8,848 metres (29,029 ft) above sea level. Measured from its base on the sea floor, Mauna Kea, Hawaii, is 10,203 metres (33,474 ft) high. But only 4,205 metres (13,796 ft) appear above sea level.

Viewed from space, we can see how small Planet Earth is in the setting of the Universe. Pictures like this have made people aware of the necessity of protecting our planet home.

214

Which is the deepest lake?

Lake Baikal, in Siberia, eastern Russia, is the world's deepest lake. The deepest spot measured so far is 1,637 metres (5,371 ft).

What is the largest inland body of water, or lake?

The salty Caspian Sea, which lies partly in Europe and partly in Asia, has an area of about 371,380 sq km (143,390 sq miles). The largest freshwater lake is Lake Superior, one of the Great Lakes of North America. Lake Superior has an area of 82,350 sq km (31,796 sq miles).

Is there a lake under Antarctica?

Scientists have found a lake, about the size of Lake Ontario in North America, hidden under Antarctica. It may contain creatures that lived on Earth millions of years ago.

What is the world's largest river basin?

The Amazon river basin in South America covers about 7,045,000 sq km (2,720,000 sq miles). The Madeira River, which flows into the Amazon, is the world's longest tributary, at 3,380 km (2,100 miles).

What is the world's longest river?

The Nile in north-eastern Africa is 6,617 km (4,112 miles) long. The second longest river, the Amazon in South America, discharges 60 times more water than the Nile.

What is the deepest cave?

The Réseau Jean Bernard in France is the deepest cave system. It reaches a depth of 1,602 metres (5,256 ft).

What is the world's largest desert?

The Sahara in North Africa covers an area of about 9,269,000 sq km (3,579,000 sq miles). This is nearly as big as the United States.

Where do most people live?

THE CONTINENT WITH THE LARGEST POPULATION IS ASIA, WHICH HAS more than 3,000 million people. Europe ranks second in world population, followed by Africa, North America, South America and Australia. The continent of Antarctica has no permanent population at all.

The patterns of cloud show how weather changes. But pollution is changing the climate and this may have serious effects on all living things on Planet Earth.

215

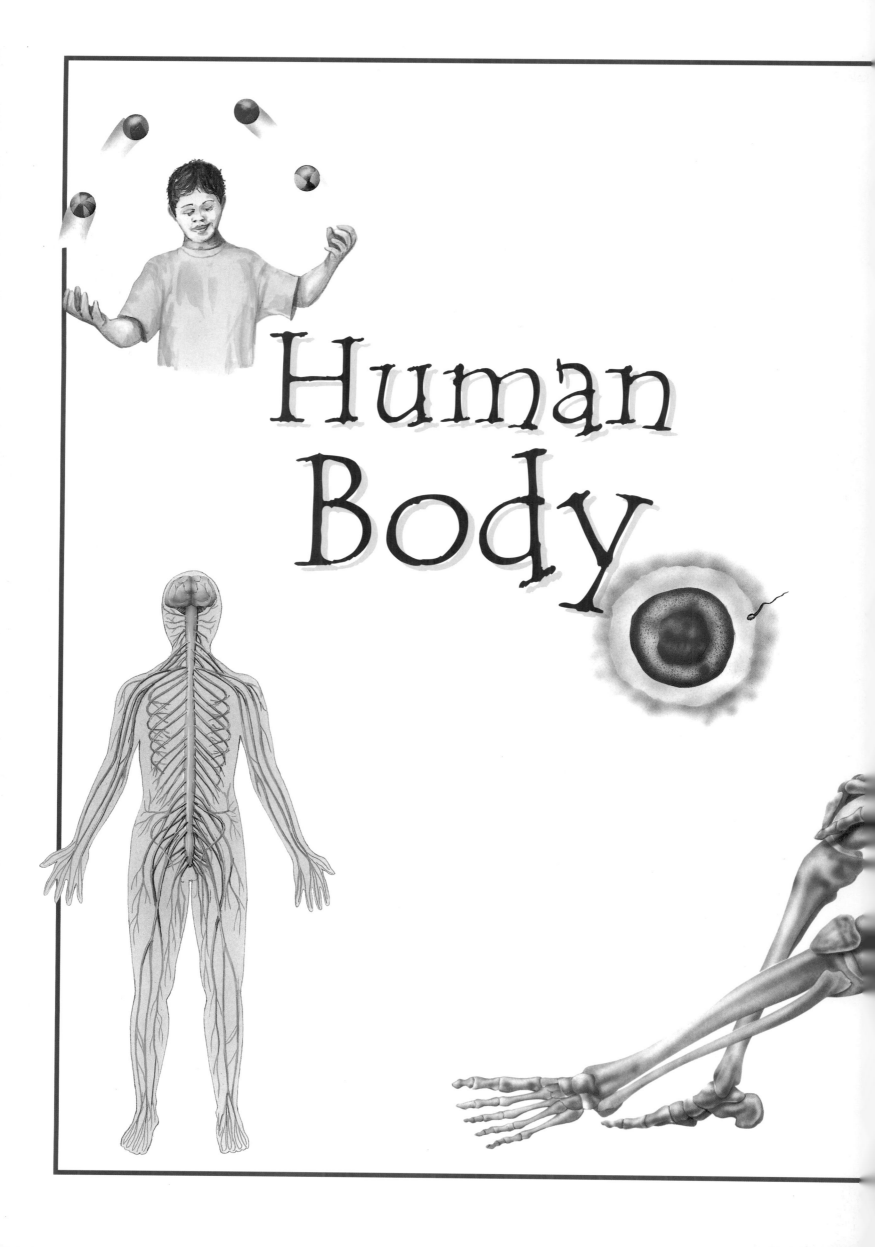

Human Body

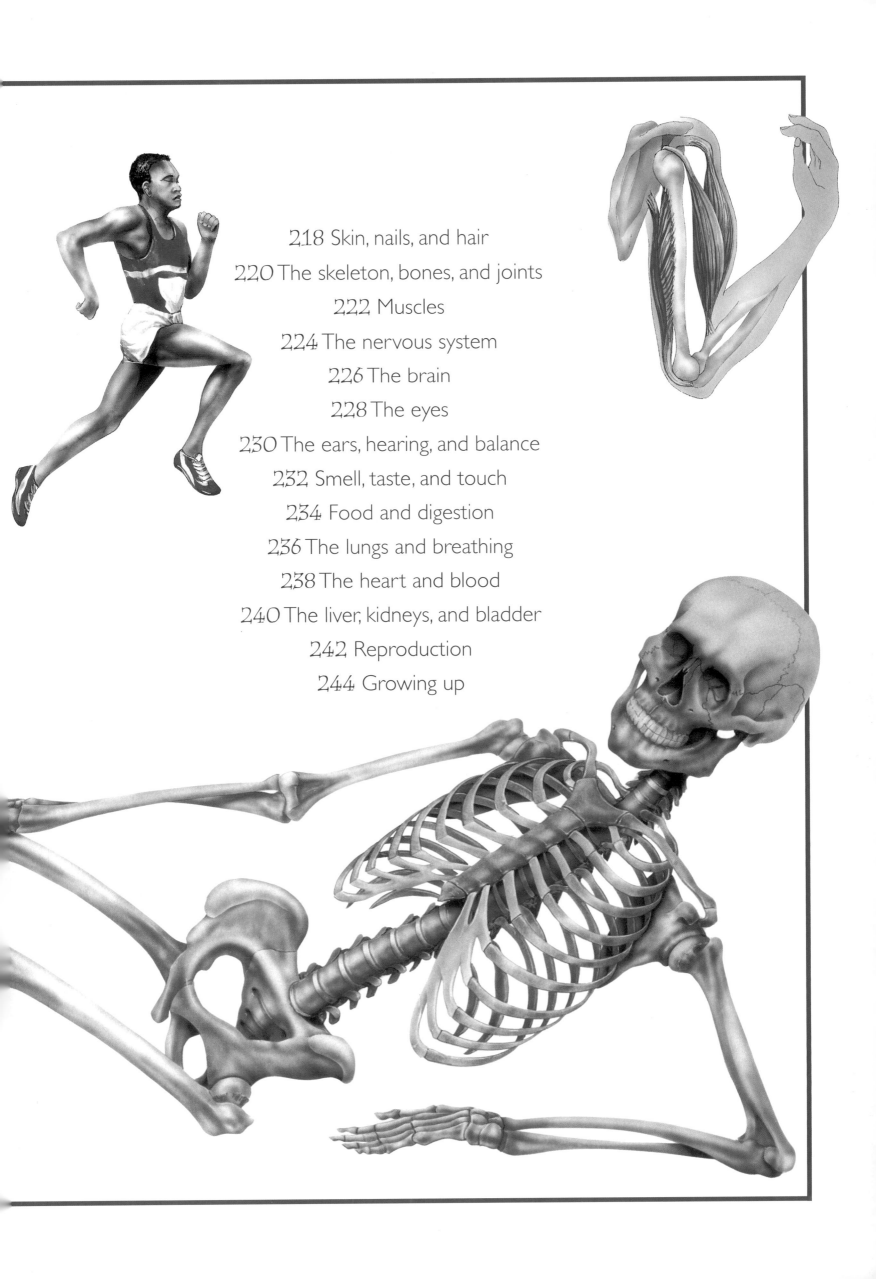

A strand of hair

What gives hair its colour?

The colour of your hair is determined mainly by the pigments (coloured substances) it contains. There are two kinds of pigment – melanin, which is very dark brown, and carotene, which is reddish-yellow – and all hair colour is formed by one or other or a mixture of both.

A section through the skin

Most people have about 100,000 hairs growing on their head.

Why do old people have grey hair?

Some people's hair stops making melanin as they grow older. Fair-haired people tend to go white, while dark-haired people usually go grey. Greyness is lack of melanin plus tiny air bubbles in the hair.

Why does skin have pores?

Skin has tiny holes in it called sweat pores to let out sweat and water vapour. When you are too hot, glands pump out sweat, which cools you as it dries.

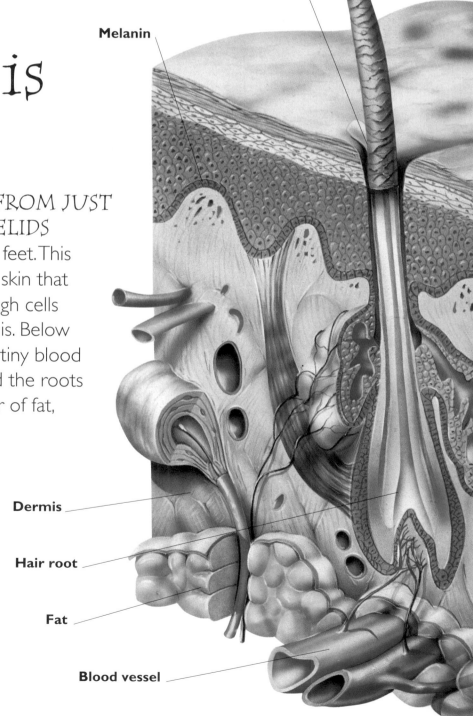

Hair follicle

Melanin

How thick is your skin?

SKIN VARIES IN THICKNESS FROM JUST UNDER 1 MM ON YOUR EYELIDS to 5 mm or more on the soles of your feet. This thin covering has two layers. The outer skin that you see and touch is made of hard, tough cells of dead skin and is part of the epidermis. Below the epidermis is the dermis. It contains tiny blood vessels, sweat glands, nerve endings and the roots of tiny hairs. Under the dermis is a layer of fat, which keeps you warm.

What are goose bumps?

Goose bumps are bumps on your skin formed by the tiny muscles that make the hairs on your skin stand up when you are cold.

Dermis

Hair root

What are freckles?

Freckles are small patches of darker skin made by extra melanin. Exposure to sunshine increases the amount of melanin in your skin and the darkness of freckles.

Fat

Blood vessel

What makes fingerprints unique?

A fingerprint is made by thin ridges of skin on the tip of each finger and thumb. The ridges form a pattern of lines, loops or whorls and no two people have the same pattern.

How do nails grow, and how fast do they grow?

Each nail grows about a millimetre every 10 days. As new nail forms behind the cuticle, under the skin, it pushes the older nail along.

Inside a fingertip

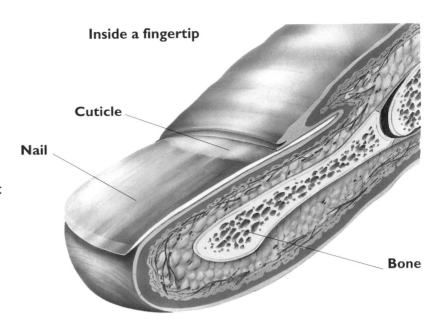

Cuticle

Nail

Bone

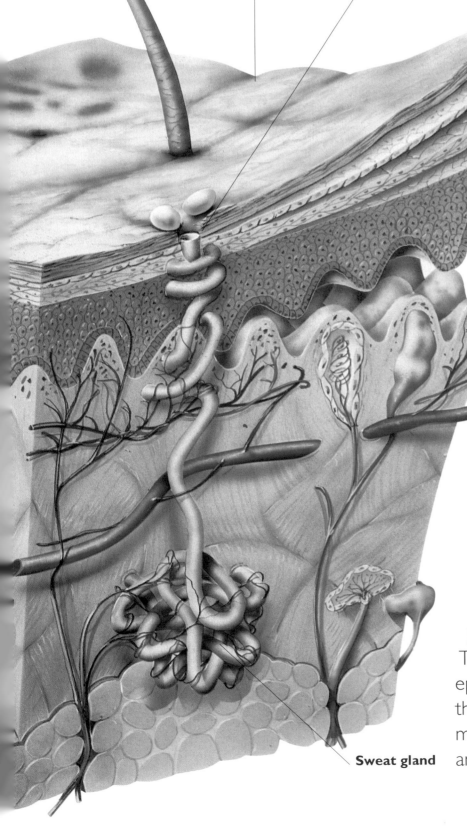

Epidermis

Sweat pore

Sweat gland

What makes hair naturally curly?

How curly your hair is depends on the shape of the follicle, the tiny pit from which it grows. Curly hair grows from flat hair follicles, wavy hair from oval follicles and straight hair from round follicles.

Why does hair fall out?

No hair lasts more than about six years. Every day you lose about 60 hairs, but since you have about 100,000 on your scalp you hardly notice. After a while new hairs grow from the hair follicles.

What does skin do?

SKIN IS A TOUGH, STRETCHY COVERING THAT ACTS AS a barrier between your body and the outside world. It stops the moisture inside the body from drying out and it prevents dirt and germs from getting in. Tiny particles of melanin inside the epidermis help to shield your body from the harmful rays of the Sun. The more melanin you have, the darker your skin and the better protected you are.

Which is the longest bone?

The thigh bone in the upper part of your leg is the longest bone in your body. It accounts for more than a quarter of an adult's height.

Which is the smallest bone?

The smallest bone is called the stirrup and is no bigger than a grain of rice. It is deep inside your ear and its job is to pass on sounds from the outer and middle ear to the inner ear.

Why do bodies need bones?

BONES PROVIDE A STRONG FRAMEWORK THAT SUPPORTS THE REST OF THE BODY. Without bones, you would flop on the floor like an octopus. Some of the bones form a suit of internal armour, which protects the brain, the lungs, the heart and other vital organs. All the bones together are called the skeleton. You can move and bend different parts of the body because the bones meet at joints.

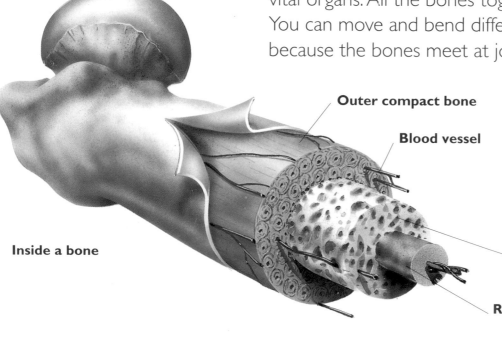

Outer compact bone

Blood vessel

Inside a bone

What's inside a bone?

Inside a bone is a criss-cross honeycomb of lighter bone. Blood vessels weave in and out of the bone, keeping the cells alive. At the centre of some bones is a core of bone marrow.

Softer spongy bone

Red marrow jelly

How many bones do you have?

As a baby you had over 300 bones, but, as you grow, some bones join together. When you are an adult, you will have about 206 bones in total.

Which joints move the least?

Your skull is made up of more than 20 bones fused together in joints that allow no movement at all. These are called suture joints.

What are ligaments?

Ligaments are strong, bendy straps that hold together the bones in a joint. Nearly all the body's joints have several ligaments.

What is a vertebra?

A vertebra is a knobbly bone in your spine. The 26 vertebrae fit together to make a strong pillar, the spine, which carries much of your weight. At the same time the vertebrae allow your back to bend and twist.

Which joint moves the most?

The shoulder joint is a ball and socket joint and it allows the greatest amount of movement in all directions.

The human skeleton

Finger bones

Patella (knee cap)

Tibia (shin)

Fibula

Femur (thigh)

Toe bones

Calcaneus (heel bone)

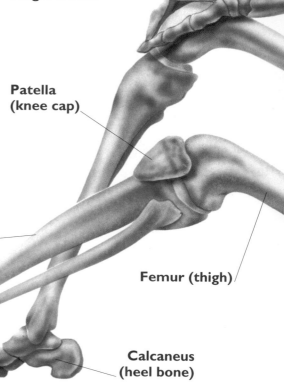

Ball and socket joint

The shoulder and hip have this joint.

Pivot joint

The pivot joint is found in the neck.

Saddle joint

This joint is found at the base of the thumb.

Hinge joint

A joint that works like a hinge is found at the knee and elbow, and in the fingers and toes.

What is a joint?

WHERE TWO BONES MEET, THEIR ENDS ARE SHAPED TO MAKE DIFFERENT

kinds of joint. Each kind of joint makes a strong connection and allows a particular kind of movement. For example, the knee is a hinge joint that lets the lower leg move only back and forward. The hip is a ball and socket joint that allows you to move your thigh around in a circle. The saddle joint at the base of the thumb also gives a good range of movement.

Why do joints not squeak?
Joints are cushioned by soft, squashy cartilage. Many joints also contain a fluid – called synovial fluid – that works like oil to keep them moving smoothly and painlessly.

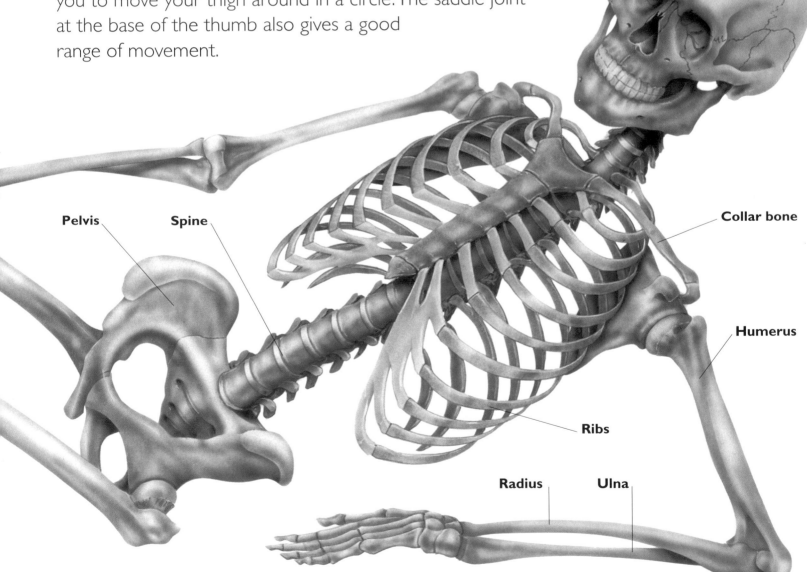

Skull

Collar bone

Pelvis   Spine

Humerus

Ribs

Radius   Ulna

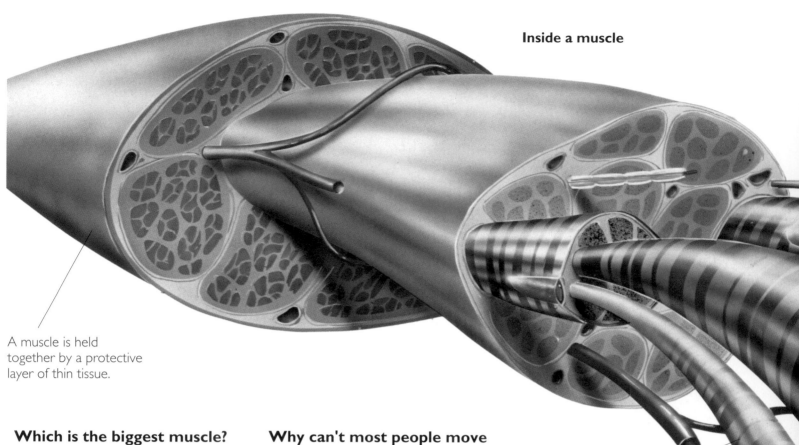

Inside a muscle

A muscle is held together by a protective layer of thin tissue.

A muscle is made up of many bundles of fibres.

Which is the biggest muscle?
The biggest muscle is the gluteus maximus in the buttock. You use it to straighten your leg when you stand up and it makes a comfortable cushion when you sit down.

Why can't most people move their ears?
Humans, like most other animals, have a muscle behind each ear. Animals can turn their ears to hear better, but most people never learn how to use their ear muscles.

Why does exercise make muscles stronger?
A muscle is made of bundles of fibres that contract when you use the muscle. The more you use the muscle, the thicker the fibres become. They contract more effectively, which means the muscle is stronger.

The body's muscles

How do muscles work?
Muscles work by contracting. This makes them shorter and thicker so that they pull on whatever bone or other part of the body they are attached to, thereby making it move.

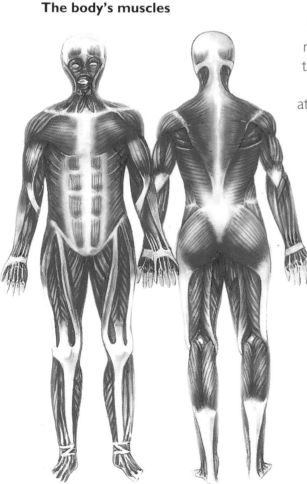

Here the skin is stripped away to show the muscles of the front and back of the body.

What do the muscles do?

MUSCLES MAKE PARTS OF YOUR BODY MOVE. THE SKELETON IS COVERED with muscles that move your bones and give your body its shape. Muscles in the face move your cheeks, eyebrows, nose, mouth, tongue and lower jaw. A different kind of muscle works in the oesophagus (food pipe), stomach and intestines to move food through your body. The heart is a third type of muscle – it never stops beating to move blood around your body.

Which is the strongest muscle?

The strongest muscle is the one that shuts your mouth! It is called the masseter and you use it for talking and chewing up food.

Why do muscles work in pairs?

MUSCLES CANNOT PUSH – THEY CAN ONLY PULL – AND SO YOU NEED TWO sets of muscles for many actions. For example, the biceps in your upper arm bends your elbow and you can feel it tighten when you clench your arm. To straighten the elbow again, you have to relax the biceps and tighten the triceps, which is the muscle at the back of your upper arm. In the same way, one set of muscles lifts the leg and another set of muscles straightens it.

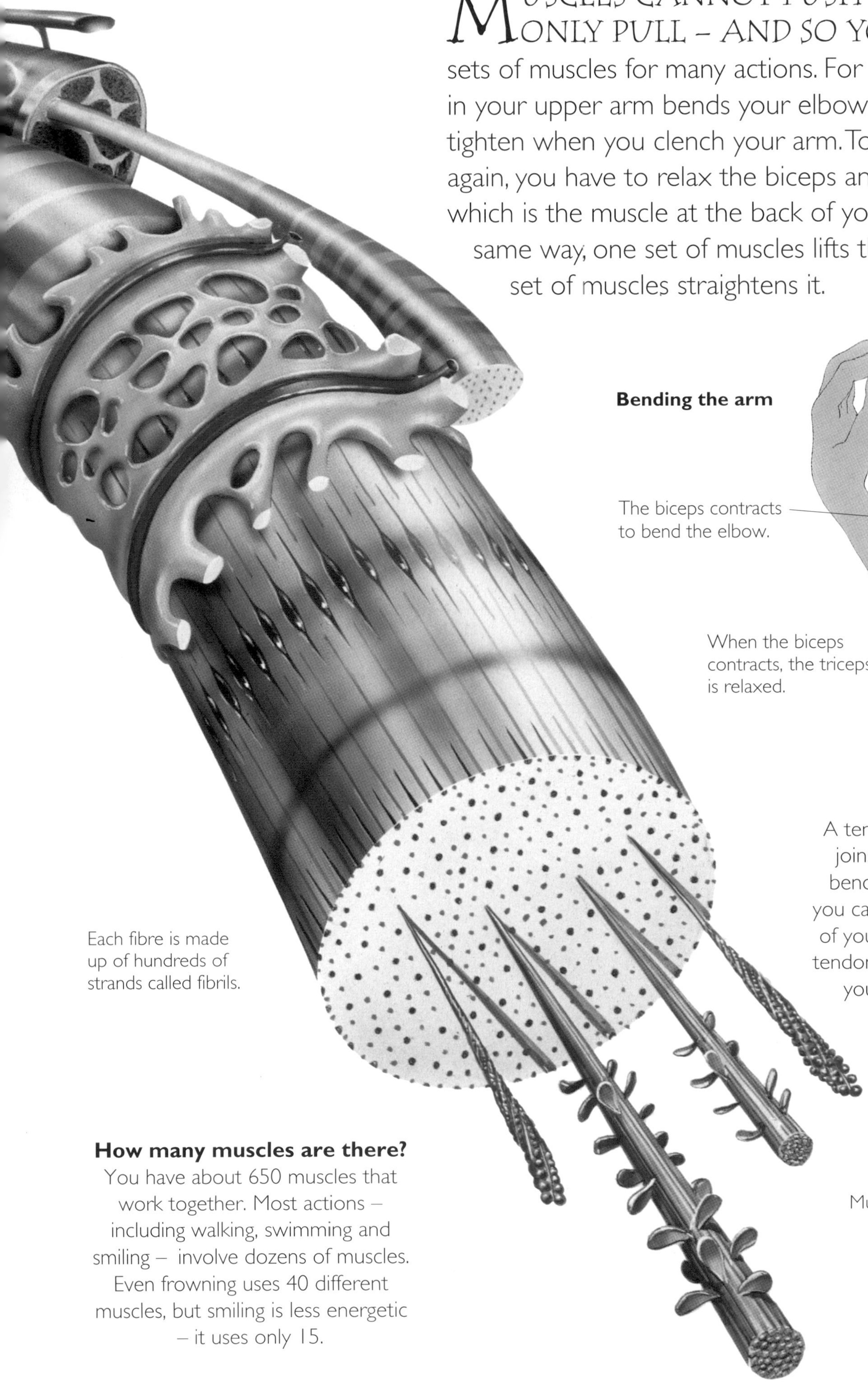

Bending the arm

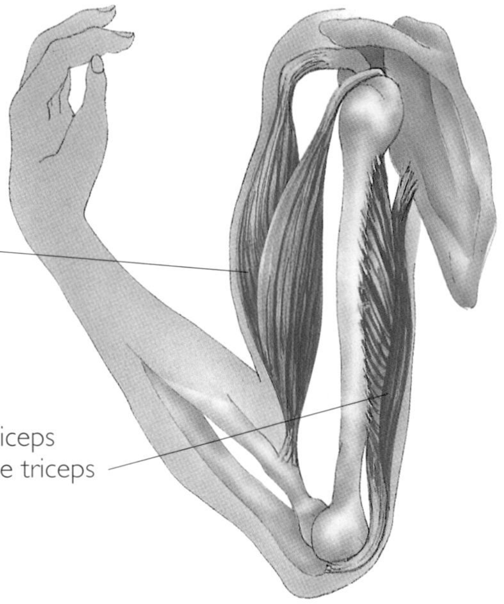

The biceps contracts to bend the elbow.

When the biceps contracts, the triceps is relaxed.

What is a tendon?

A tendon is like a tough rope that joins a muscle to a bone. If you bend and straighten your fingers, you can feel the tendons in the back of your hand. The body's strongest tendon is the Achilles tendon, which you can feel above your heel.

Each fibre is made up of hundreds of strands called fibrils.

How many muscles are there?

You have about 650 muscles that work together. Most actions – including walking, swimming and smiling – involve dozens of muscles. Even frowning uses 40 different muscles, but smiling is less energetic – it uses only 15.

Muscle fibres are so small that 1 sq cm ($\frac{1}{4}$ sq in) would contain a million of them.

What do the nerves do?

Juggling

Juggling takes great skill. As the juggler learns to co-ordinate throwing and catching, the actions become automatic.

NERVES CARRY INFORMATION AND INSTRUCTIONS TO AND FROM THE brain and from one part of the brain to the other. Sensory nerves bring information from the eyes, ears and other sense organs to the brain, and motor nerves control the muscles. For example, if you decide to bend your knee, electrical signals move from your brain to the muscles in your leg to make them contract.

What is a reflex action?

A reflex action is something you do automatically, without thinking about it. Swallowing, blinking and choking are reflex actions. So is snatching your hand away from a hot plate.

How fast do nerves act?

A nerve signal is a tiny pulse of electricity. It travels at about 1 metre (3 ft) per second in the slowest nerves to more than 100 metres (300 ft) per second in the fastest ones.

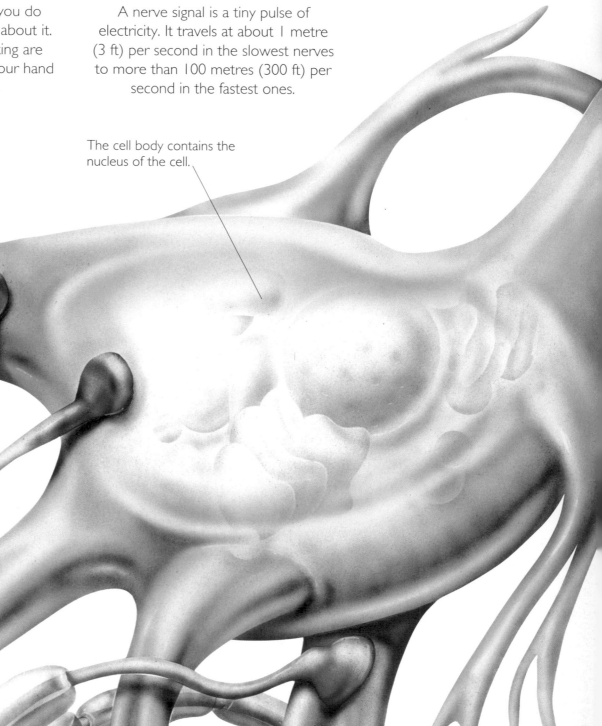

Dendrites (the arms of the nerve cell) collect signals from other cells.

The cell body contains the nucleus of the cell.

A single nerve cell

How does a nerve work?
A chain of nerve cells carries a signal
to or from the brain. The electrical
impulse is received by the nerve
endings and sent through the first
nerve cell and along its nerve fibre
to the nerve endings of the
next nerve cell.

What is the spinal cord?
The spinal cord is the largest nerve
in the body. It is 2 cm ($^3/_4$ in) wide
and runs through the centre of the
spine. It connects the nerves in the
body with the brain.

How do anaesthetics work?
An anaesthetic stops you feeling. A
local anaesthetic deadens the
sensory nerves so that part of your
body goes numb. A general
anaesthetic puts you into a deep
sleep so that none of your senses is
taking in information.

The axon is covered with a
fatty myelin sheath, which acts
as an insulator to stop the
signals leaking away.

The axon carries nerve signals
to the next nerve cell.

The nervous system

Nerves link the brain and spinal
cord to all parts of the body.

**How many nerves
do you have?**
Thousands of millions of nerves
reach out to all parts of the body.

Which is the longest nerve?
The longest nerve is the tibial nerve.
It runs alongside the tibia (the shin
bone), and in adults it is
50 cm (20 in) long.

**What causes
'pins and needles'?**
If a nerve gets squashed, it cannot
carry nerve signals. If you kneel for a
long time, your leg goes numb and
then, when you stretch it, it tingles
as the signals begin to flow again.

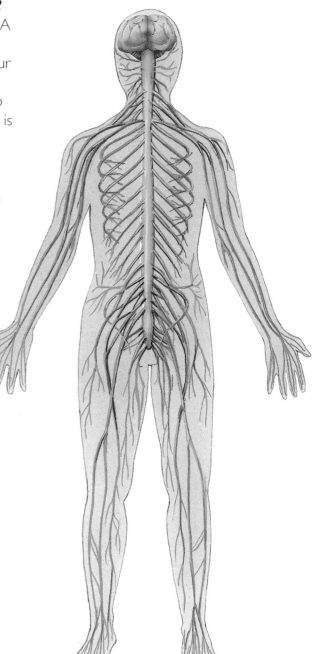

What are the body's five main senses?

THE FIVE MAIN SENSES ARE SEEING,
HEARING, SMELLING, TASTING AND
touching. Between them the five senses give you all the
information you have about the outside world. Each sense
has a special part of the body, called a sense organ, which
reacts to a particular kind of stimulus. For example, eyes
react to light and ears react to sound.

What does the brain do?

YOUR BRAIN CONTROLS YOUR BODY. IT KEEPS THE HEART, STOMACH, LUNGS, kidneys and other vital organs working. The information collected by the senses is processed by different parts of the brain. Some is discarded, some is stored and some is reacted to at once, with messages being sent from the brain to the muscles and glands. The brain also gives you your sense of who you are. Memories of the past are stored here and everything you think, feel and do is controlled by the brain.

What does the brain look like?
The brain looks soft and greyish pink. The top is wrinkled like a walnut and it is covered with many tiny tubes of blood. The spinal cord links the brain to the rest of the body.

What is the brain made of?
The brain consists of water and billions of nerve cells and nerve fibres. It is surrounded by protective coverings called the meninges.

Inside the brain

Why do you remember some things and forget others?
On the whole you remember things that are important to you in some way. Some things need to be remembered for only a very short while. For instance, you might look up a telephone number, keep it in your head while you dial it, and then forget it completely.

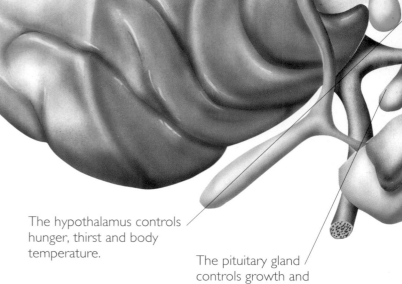

The front of the cortex is mainly involved with thinking and planning.

The hypothalamus controls hunger, thirst and body temperature.

The pituitary gland controls growth and many other body processes.

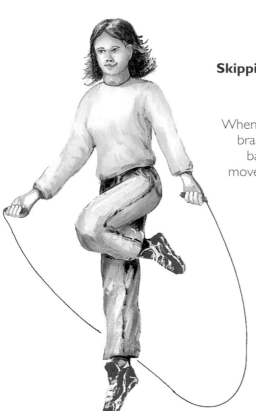

Skipping

When you skip, your brain co-ordinates balance with the movements of your arms and legs.

Why are some people more artistic than others?
One side of the brain deals more with music and artistic skills, and the other side deals more with logical skills. How artistic or mathematical you are depends on which side of your brain is dominant (stronger).

What does the skull do?
The skull is a hard covering of bone that protects the brain like a helmet. All the bones of the skull except the lower jaw are fused together to make them stronger.

Why are some people left-handed?

Most people are right-handed because the left side of their brain is dominant, but in left-handed people, the right side of the brain is dominant. The part of the brain that controls speech is usually on the dominant side.

The cerebral cortex covers most of the brain.

When you are asleep you are not aware of what is going on around you. The brain blocks incoming signals unless they are so strong they wake you up.

Sleeping

Why do you need to sleep?

A 10-year-old sleeps on average nine or 10 hours a night, but sleep time can vary a lot between four and 12 hours. If you sleep for eight hours a night, that's a third of your life! You need to sleep to rest your muscles and to allow your body time to repair and replace damaged cells.

How often do you dream?

You probably dream about five times every night, but you are only aware of dreaming if you wake up during a dream.

Why do some people sleep-walk?

People may walk in their sleep because they are worried or anxious. If someone is sleep-walking you should gently take them back to bed.

This part of the cortex deals with sight.

Does the brain ever rest?

Even while you are asleep the brain carries on controlling body activities such as breathing, heartbeat and digestion.

The cerebellum co-ordinates movement and balance.

What does the cerebral cortex do?

THE CORTEX IS THE WRINKLY TOP PART OF THE BRAIN. IT CONTROLS ALL THE brain activity that you are aware of – seeing, thinking, reading, feeling and moving. Only humans have such a large and well developed cerebral cortex. Different parts of the cortex deal with different activities. The left side controls the right side of the body, while the right side of the cortex controls the left side of the body.

How do the eyes see things?

Y OU SEE SOMETHING WHEN LIGHT BOUNCES OFF IT AND ENTERS YOUR EYES.
The black circle in the middle of the eye is a hole, called the pupil. Light passes through the pupil and is focused by the lens on to the retina at the back of the eye. Nerve endings in the retina send signals along the optic nerve to the brain. The picture formed on the retina is upside-down, but the brain turns it around so that you perceive things to be the right way up.

Why do people have different coloured eyes?
The iris is the coloured ring around the pupil. The colour is formed by a substance called melanin – brown-eyed people have a lot of melanin, while blue-eyed people have very little.

How big is your eyeball?
An adult eyeball is about the size of a golf ball, but most of the eyeball is hidden inside your head.

The cornea is a tough see-through layer that protects the eye.

The iris is a circular muscle that controls the size of the pupil to allow light into the eye.

The lens focuses light.

Why does the pupil change size?
The pupil becomes smaller in bright light to stop too much light from getting in and damaging the retina. In dim light the pupil opens to let in more light. The iris is a muscle that opens and closes the pupil automatically.

The eyes

Light hits the retina at the back of the eye.

Muscles hold and move the eyeball.

What is the blind spot?
The blind spot is a spot on the retina where the optic nerve leaves the eye. There are no light-sensitive cells here, making the spot 'blind'.

How light enters the eye

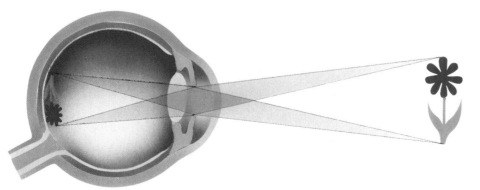

The image of the object projected on to the retina at the back of the eye is upside-down.

228

Can sunshine damage the eye?
Sunshine contains ultraviolet rays, which can damage your eyes as well as your skin. You should wear sunglasses in bright sunlight and never, never look directly at the Sun.

Why do you have two eyes?
Two eyes help you to judge how far away something is. Each eye gets a slightly different picture, which the brain combines into a single three-dimensional or 3D picture. A 3D picture is one that has depth as well as height and breadth.

What are eyelashes for?
Your eyelashes help to protect your eyes by stopping dust and dirt getting blown into them.

What keeps the eye in place?
The eyeball is held firmly in place by six muscles attached to the top, bottom and each side of the eye. These muscles work together to move your eyes so that you can look around.

The optic nerve takes signals from the retina to the brain.

The eyeball is filled with jelly, which keeps it in shape.

What makes you cry?
If dust or something gets into your eye, the tear gland above the eye releases extra tears to wash it away. Being upset can also make you cry.

The tear gland makes a constant supply of salty water.

The pupil is the black hole at the centre of the iris.

When too much water floods the eye, some spills over as tears and the rest drains into the nose.

The tear duct drains tears to the nose.

How do you see colour?
Different nerve cells in the retina react to the colours red, blue and green. Together they make up all the other colours.

Why can't you see colour when it starts to get dark?
The cells that react to coloured light – called cones – only work well in bright light. Most of the cells in the eye see in black, white and grey, and these – called rods – are the ones that work at night.

Why do you blink?

YOU BLINK TO CLEAN AND PROTECT YOUR EYES. EACH EYE IS COVERED WITH A THIN film of salty water, so every time you blink, the eyelid washes the eyeball and wipes away dust and germs. The water drains away through a narrow tube into your nose. You also blink to protect your eye when something comes too close to it. Blinking is so important, you do it automatically.

How do you hear?

SOUND REACHES YOUR EARS AS VIBRATIONS IN THE AIR. The vibrations travel down the ear canal to the eardrum, which then vibrates, making the bones in the middle ear vibrate too. These three small bones make the vibrations bigger and pass them through to the liquid in the inner ear. The cochlea in the inner ear is coiled like a snail shell. As nerve endings in the lining of the cochlea detect vibrations in the liquid inside it, they send electrical signals to the brain.

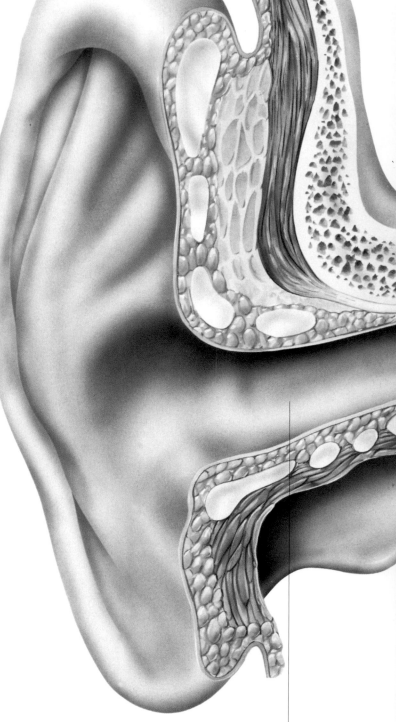

The ear

Outer ear (pinna)

The ear canal carries sound waves to the eardrum.

Why do you have two ears?
Two ears help you to detect which direction sounds are coming from.

How do you measure sound?
The loudness of a sound is measured in decibels. The sound of a pin dropping is less than 10 decibels, while the hum of a refrigerator is about 35 decibels. A loud personal stereo makes about 80 decibels while the noise of a jet aircraft just 30 metres (90 ft) away can reach 130 decibels.

A jet lifts off the runway

Why do your ears pop?
If you are flying in an aircraft and it changes height quickly, you may go a bit deaf, because the air inside and outside the eardrum are at different pressures. Your ears 'pop' when the pressures become equal again.

The noise of a jet aircraft just 30 metres (90 ft) away can reach 130 decibels.

Is loud noise dangerous?
Any noise over about 120 decibels can damage your hearing immediately, but, if you are constantly listening to sounds of 90 decibels or more, they can damage your hearing too.

What is earwax?
This yellow-brown wax is made by glands in the skin lining the ear canal. Wax traps dirt and germs and is slowly pushed out of the ear.

Where does the Eustachian tube go?
This tube joins the middle ear to the empty spaces behind your upper throat. If mucus from a cold fills the tube, it stops you hearing as well as usual.

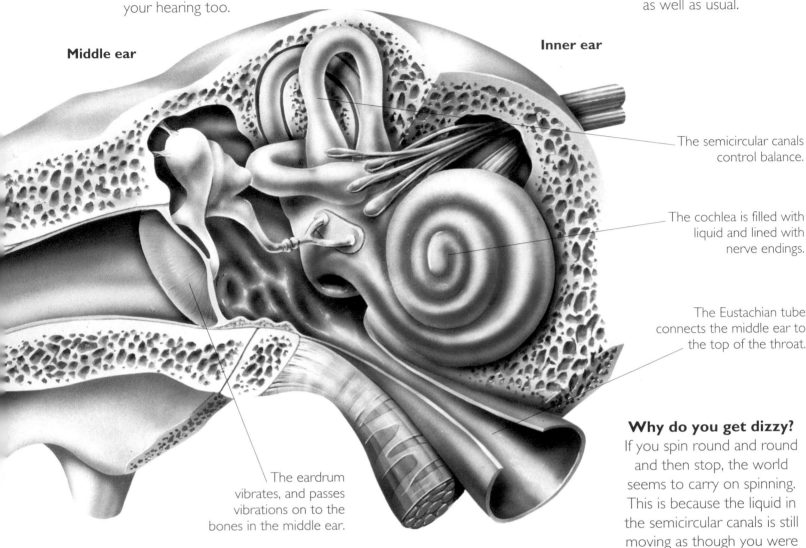

Middle ear

Inner ear

The semicircular canals control balance.

The cochlea is filled with liquid and lined with nerve endings.

The Eustachian tube connects the middle ear to the top of the throat.

The eardrum vibrates, and passes vibrations on to the bones in the middle ear.

Why do you get dizzy?
If you spin round and round and then stop, the world seems to carry on spinning. This is because the liquid in the semicircular canals is still moving as though you were still spinning.

How loud is a whisper?
A whisper is between 10 and 20 decibels. Some animals can detect much quieter sounds than we can.

What is sound?
Sound is waves of energy that are carried as vibrations through air, liquid and solid objects.

Ballet dancer

How do ears help you balance?

THREE CURVED TUBES IN THE INNER EAR HELP YOU TO BALANCE. THEY ARE filled with liquid and are called the semicircular canals. They are arranged at right angles to each other (like three sides of a box) so that as you move, the liquid inside them moves too. Nerves in the lining of the tubes detect changes in the liquid and send the information to the brain.

A spinning dancer stops herself getting dizzy by turning her head quickly and keeping her eyes on just one thing.

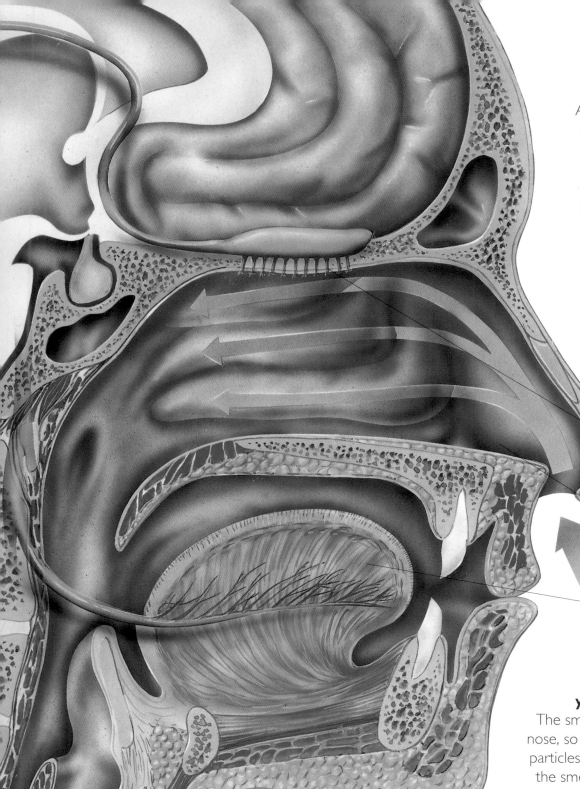

How do you smell?

A smell is made by tiny particles in the air. As you breathe in, some of these particles reach the smell receptors in your nose. Smell receptors react to chemicals dissolved in the mucus inside your nose and send a message to the brain.

Why do some things smell more than others?

Things that smell strongly, such as perfume or food cooking, give off more smell particles that float through the air.

Inside the nose and mouth

The smell receptors are situated at the top of the nose.

The inside of the nose is lined with mucus and fine hairs.

The tongue is a strong muscle covered with thousands of taste buds.

Why does sniffing help you detect smells better?

The smell receptors are at the top of your nose, so when you sniff you bring more smell particles up to them, which helps you detect the smell better. No one knows how your brain tells one smell from another.

Why does a blocked nose stop you tasting?

When you eat, you both taste and smell the food. If your nose is blocked with mucus from a cold, you can't smell properly and so food seems to have less taste too.

Why do some animals have keener smell?

Many animals rely on smell for finding food and smelling attackers. The inside of their nose is lined with many smell receptors, which are situated close to their nostrils.

How do you detect taste?

THE SURFACE OF THE TONGUE HAS ABOUT 10,000 MICROSCOPIC TASTE BUDS sunk in it. As you chew, tiny particles of food dissolve in saliva and trickle down to the taste buds. The taste receptors react and send messages about the taste to the brain. There are four basic tastes – sweet, salty, bitter and sour – and every taste is made up of one or a combination of these. The taste buds in different parts of the tongue react mainly to one of these basic tastes.

How does the sense of touch work?

A taste bud

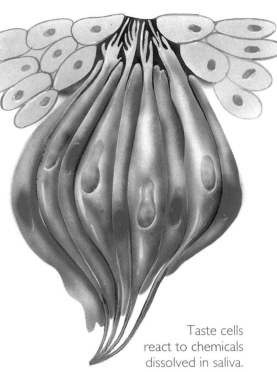

Taste cells react to chemicals dissolved in saliva.

THE SENSE OF TOUCH TELLS YOU WHETHER SOMETHING IS ROUGH, SHINY, WET, COLD and many other things. There are many different kinds of sense receptor in the skin, which between them react to touch, heat, cold and pain. Some touch receptors react to the slightest thing, while others need a lot of pressure to make them respond. The brain puts together all the different messages to tell you how something feels.

Which part of the body is least sensitive to touch?
The back is one of the least sensitive areas of the body.

Does taste matter?
Unpleasant tastes can warn you when food has gone bad or is poisonous. Your body needs healthy food, so enjoying the taste of it encourages you to eat.

How do blind people use touch to see?
Blind people can tell what something is like by feeling it. Outside, they may use a long cane to feel the way in front of them. Blind people read by touch: they run their fingertips over Braille – patterns of raised dots that represent different letters.

The tongue

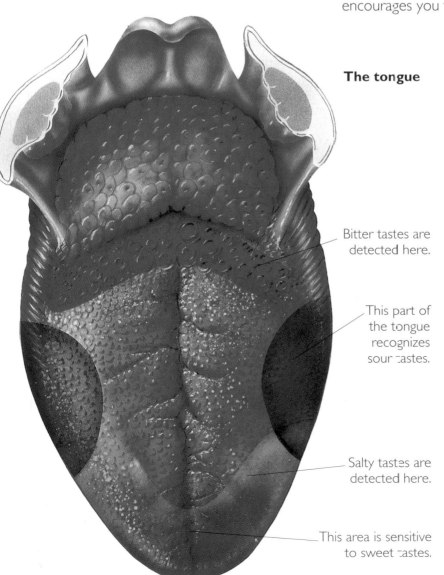

Bitter tastes are detected here.

This part of the tongue recognizes sour tastes.

Salty tastes are detected here.

This area is sensitive to sweet tastes.

Which parts of the body are most sensitive to touch?
Any part of the body that has lots of touch receptors is particularly sensitive to touch. These parts include the lips, tongue, fingertips and soles of the feet.

Which parts of the body are most sensitive to heat?
Your elbows and feet are more sensitive to heat than many other parts of the body. You may have noticed that bath water feels much hotter to your feet than it does to your hand. Your lips and mouth are very sensitive to heat too.

Why do you like some tastes better than others?
Most people prefer things that taste sweet or slightly salty, but your sense of taste can easily become used to too much sugar and salt. How you like food to taste is very much decided by your eating habits.

233

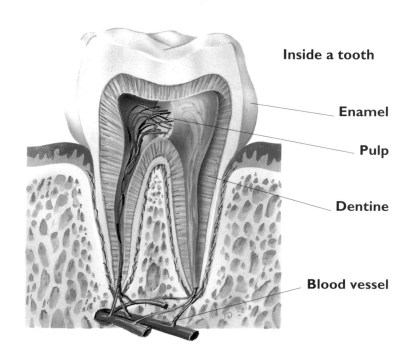

Inside a tooth

Enamel

Pulp

Dentine

Blood vessel

What are teeth made of?
The outside of a tooth is made of enamel and is the hardest substance in the body. Underneath is dentine, which is as hard as bone, and in the centre of each tooth is a tender pulpy mass of blood and nerves.

How many teeth do you have?
Each person has two sets of natural teeth during their life. The first set of 20 are called milk teeth and start to appear at about the age of six months. From about the age of six years, the milk teeth are gradually replaced by 32 adult teeth.

Why does vomit taste sour?
When you vomit you bring back partly digested food into your mouth. It tastes sour because it is mixed with acid made by the lining of the stomach. The acid kills germs and helps to break the food into smaller pieces.

Why are teeth different shapes?

DIFFERENT TEETH DO DIFFERENT JOBS TO HELP YOU CHEW UP FOOD. THE BROAD, flat teeth at the front slice through food when you take a bite. They are called incisors. The pointed canine teeth are like fangs, and grip and tear chewy food such as meat. The large flat-topped premolars and molars grind the food between them into small pieces, which mix with saliva to make a mushy ball, ready for swallowing.

Fruit, vegetables and wholemeal bread contain plenty of fibre. Fibre makes the muscles in the intestines work better.

Healthy food

Which foods give you energy?
Foods such as bread, rice, potatoes and pasta contain a lot of carbohydrates. Carbohydrates give you energy to move, work and grow. Fats and sugars also give you energy.

Which foods make you grow?
Foods such as milk, cheese, fish, meat and beans contain a lot of protein, a substance that the body needs to make new cells. A varied and balanced diet contains all the different substances that the body needs to grow.

Where does food go after it is swallowed?

WHEN YOU SWALLOW, THE MUSHY BALL OF FOOD GOES DOWN THE gullet or oesophagus into the stomach. Here it churns around for up to four hours, while it is broken down into chyme, a soupy liquid. It is then gradually squeezed out of the stomach and through a long, coiled tube called the small intestine. Here the nourishing parts of the food are absorbed into the blood and the remainder passes on into the large intestine. About 24 hours after swallowing, the remaining waste, called faeces, is pushed out of the body.

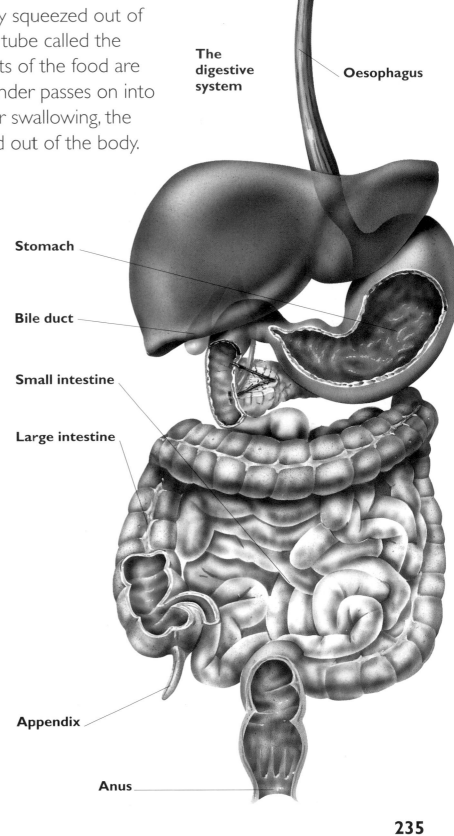

The digestive system

Mouth

Epiglottis

Oesophagus

Stomach

Bile duct

Small intestine

Large intestine

Appendix

Anus

What is the epiglottis?
The epiglottis is a kind of trap door that closes off your windpipe when you swallow. It stops food going down into the lungs.

How big is your stomach?
An adult's stomach holds about 1 litre (1 ¾ pints) of food, and a child's a bit less. Your stomach gets bigger the more you eat. A large adult can eat and drink up to 4 litres (7 pints) of food and liquid at one meal.

How long are the intestines?
The small intestine is more than three times as long as the whole body! In an adult this is about 6.5 metres (21 ft). The large intestine is a further 1.5 metres (5 ft) and the whole tube from mouth to anus measures about 9 metres (30 ft).

What is the appendix?
The appendix is a spare part of the large intestine that plays no part in digestion. Sometimes the appendix becomes infected and has to be removed.

Why do faeces smell?
Bacteria in the large intestine help to break down waste material, but they also make it smell.

A cluster of alveoli

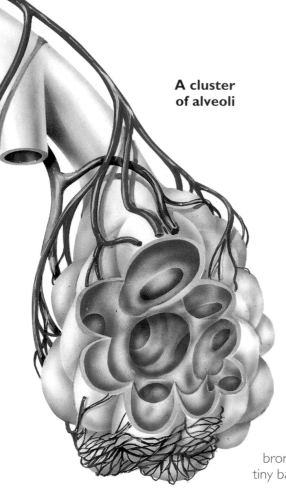

Why do the lungs have so many alveoli?

In order to provide a huge surface across which oxygen and carbon dioxide can move in and out of the blood. In fact the lungs have over 700 million alveoli. If an adult's alveoli were all laid out flat, they would cover seven car-parking spaces!

Why does your breath sometimes look misty?

The air you breathe out contains water vapour. On a cold day this condenses into a mist of tiny water droplets.

At the end of each bronchiole is a cluster of tiny balloons called alveoli.

The bronchial tubes divide into tiny tubes called bronchioles.

How long can you hold your breath?

You can probably hold your breath for about a minute. The longer you hold your breath the higher the carbon dioxide level in your blood rises, and the more you feel the need to breathe out.

The windpipe is attached to loops of cartilage to make sure the airways stay open.

The lungs

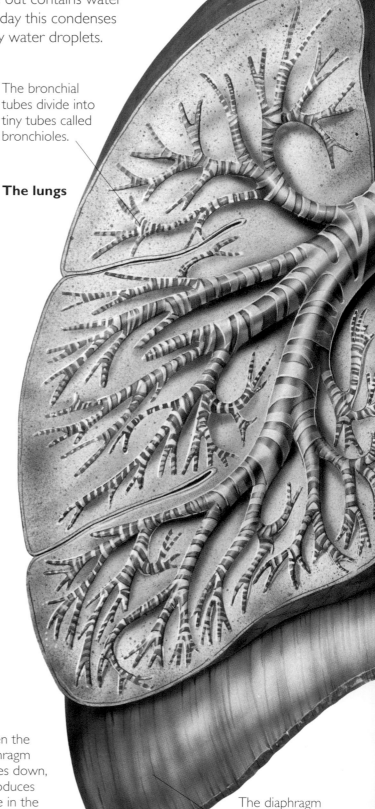

How do you breathe in and out?

The lungs do not have their own muscles to make you breathe in and out. The muscles between your ribs and the diaphragm – a sheet of muscle under the lungs – do the job instead. As your ribs move up and out, the diaphragm contracts and moves down. This pulls air into the lungs to fill the space. When the diaphragm and the muscles between the ribs relax, they squeeze air out of the lungs.

Breathing in and out

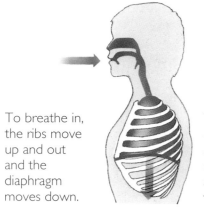

To breathe in, the ribs move up and out and the diaphragm moves down.

To breathe out, the ribs and diaphragm relax, pushing air out of the lungs.

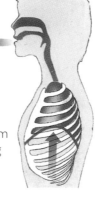

When the diaphragm moves down, it produces space in the lungs, which is filled by taking in air.

The diaphragm is attached to the lungs.

How much air do your lungs hold?

An adult's lungs hold about 6 litres (10 pints) of air, while a child's lungs hold less. You usually breathe about 16 to 20 times a minute, taking in less than 0.5 litre (1 pint) of air each time.

Why do you need to breathe in air?

THE AIR CONTAINS A GAS CALLED OXYGEN, WHICH THE BODY NEEDS TO STAY ALIVE. When you breathe in, you pull air through your mouth or nose into the windpipe and through narrower and narrower tubes in the lungs. At the end of each tiny tube, or bronchiole, are hundreds of minute balloons called alveoli. As these balloons fill with air, oxygen passes from them into the blood vessels that surround them. The blood then carries the oxygen to all parts of the body. At the same time, waste carbon dioxide passes out of the blood and into the lungs. It leaves the body in the air you breathe out.

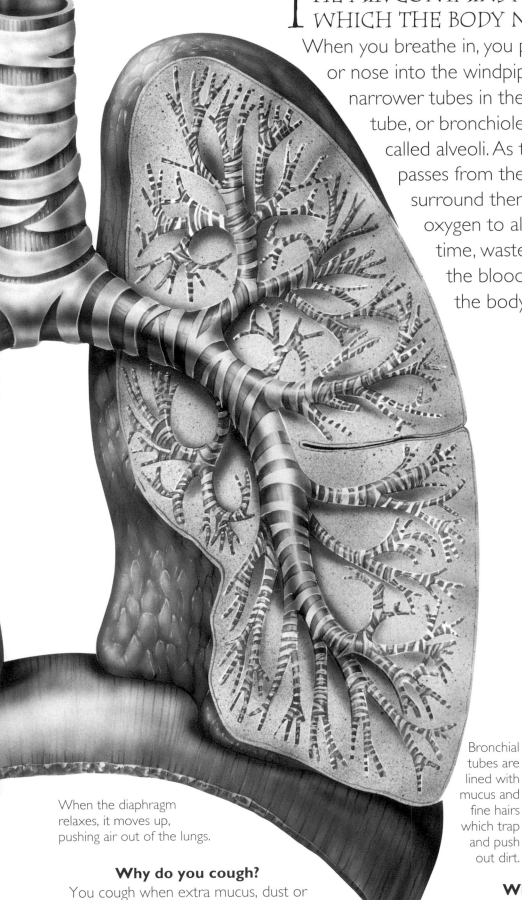

When the diaphragm relaxes, it moves up, pushing air out of the lungs.

Bronchial tubes are lined with mucus and fine hairs which trap and push out dirt.

How do you talk?

When you breathe out, the air passes over the vocal cords in the voice box or larynx in the neck. When the cords vibrate they make a sound. Changing the shape of your lips and tongue makes different sounds, which can be put together into words.

What happens when you sneeze?

When you sneeze, air rushes down your nose like a mini hurricane at 160 kph (100 mph) – up to 20 times faster than normal. Sneezing blasts away whatever dust, pollen or germs may be irritating your nose.

Why does running make you puff?

Muscles use up oxygen as they work. When you run, your muscles are working hard and need extra oxygen. Puffing makes you breathe in up to 20 times more air, to supply your muscles with the oxygen they need.

Why do you cough?

You cough when extra mucus, dust or other particles clog the air passages between your nose and lungs. The sudden blast of air helps to clear the tubes.

What happens when you hiccup?

Sometimes the diaphragm begins to contract in short, sharp spasms. These sudden movements make you 'hic' as the gulps of air pass over the vocal cords.

237

How often does the heart beat?

A child's heart usually beats about 80 times a minute, a bit faster than an adult's (70 times a minute). When you run or do something strenuous, your heart beats faster to send more blood to the muscles.

How big is the heart?

The heart is about the same size as your clenched fist. It lies nearly in the middle of your chest and the lower end tilts towards the left side of the body.

What is the heart made of?

The heart is made of a special kind of muscle, called cardiac (heart) muscle, which never gets tired.

What do white blood cells do?

White blood cells surround and destroy germs and other intruders that get into the blood.

What is plasma?

Just over half the blood is a yellowish liquid called plasma. It is mainly water with molecules of digested food and essential salts dissolved in it.

How much blood do you have?

An average man has between 5 and 6 litres (9 and 10 pints) of blood; an average woman has between 4 and 5 litres (about 8 pints). Children have less depending on how tall and heavy they are.

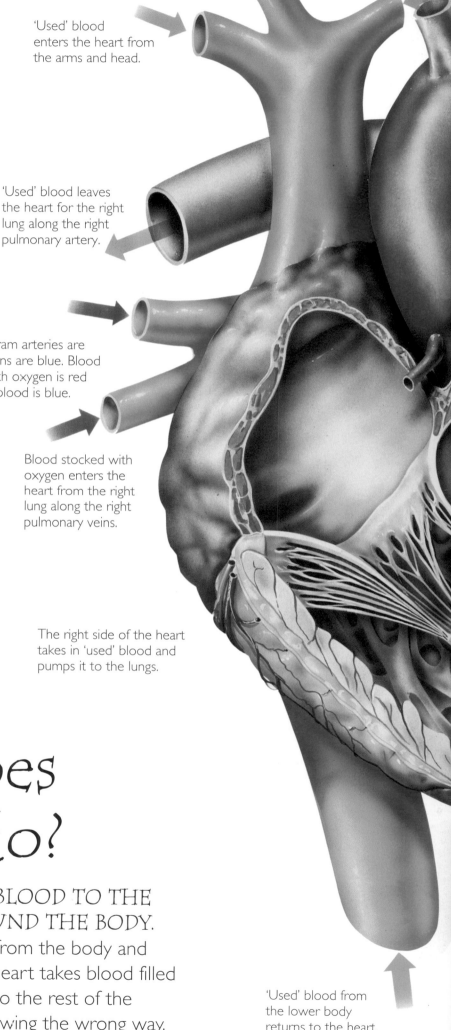

The heart

'Used' blood enters the heart from the arms and head.

'Used' blood leaves the heart for the right lung along the right pulmonary artery.

In this diagram arteries are red and veins are blue. Blood stocked with oxygen is red and 'used' blood is blue.

Blood stocked with oxygen enters the heart from the right lung along the right pulmonary veins.

The right side of the heart takes in 'used' blood and pumps it to the lungs.

'Used' blood from the lower body returns to the heart.

What job does your heart do?

THE HEART'S JOB IS TO PUMP BLOOD TO THE LUNGS AND THEN ALL AROUND THE BODY. The right side of the heart takes in blood from the body and pumps it to the lungs. The left side of the heart takes blood filled with oxygen from the lungs and pumps it to the rest of the body. Valves inside the heart stop blood flowing the wrong way. You can feel your heart beat if you put your hand on your chest.

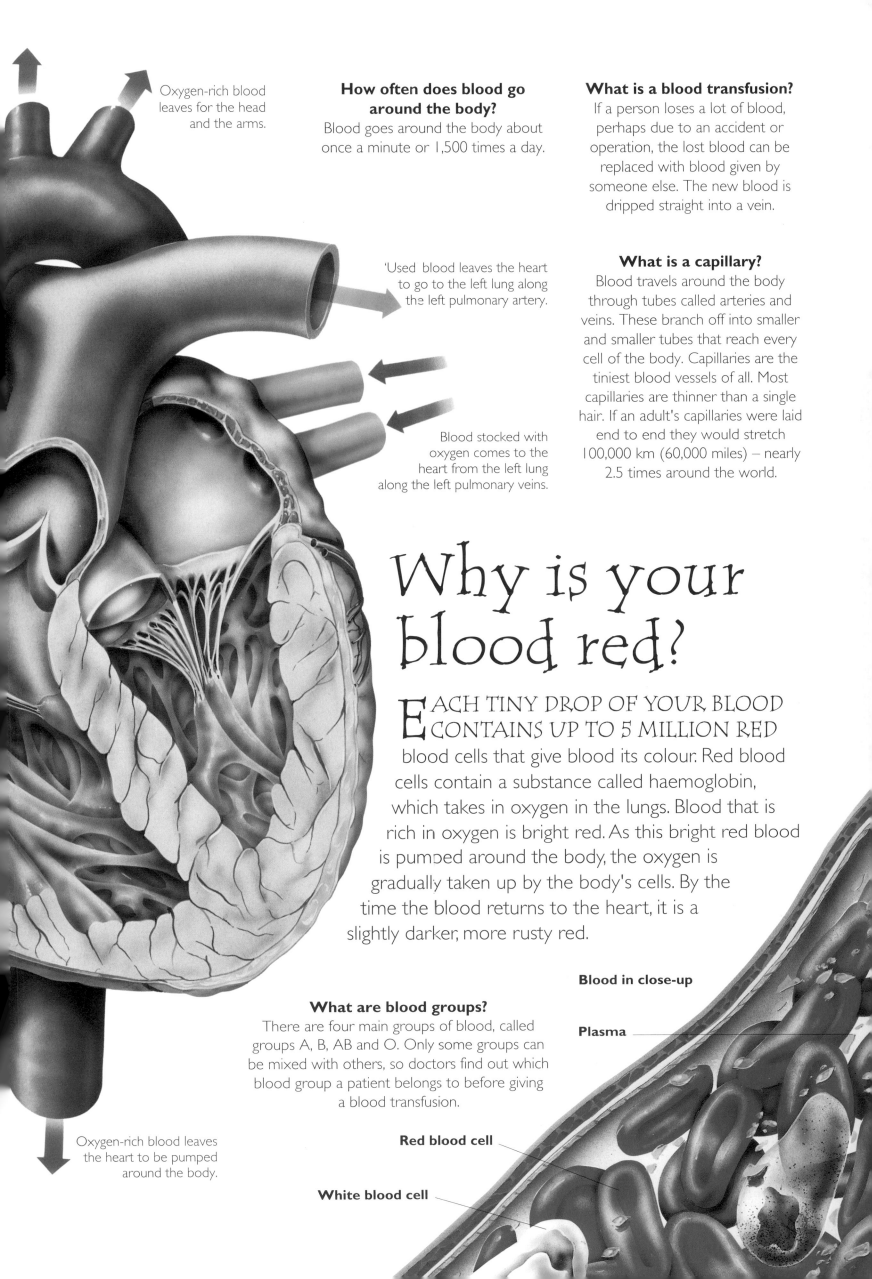

Oxygen-rich blood leaves for the head and the arms.

How often does blood go around the body?
Blood goes around the body about once a minute or 1,500 times a day.

What is a blood transfusion?
If a person loses a lot of blood, perhaps due to an accident or operation, the lost blood can be replaced with blood given by someone else. The new blood is dripped straight into a vein.

'Used' blood leaves the heart to go to the left lung along the left pulmonary artery.

What is a capillary?
Blood travels around the body through tubes called arteries and veins. These branch off into smaller and smaller tubes that reach every cell of the body. Capillaries are the tiniest blood vessels of all. Most capillaries are thinner than a single hair. If an adult's capillaries were laid end to end they would stretch 100,000 km (60,000 miles) – nearly 2.5 times around the world.

Blood stocked with oxygen comes to the heart from the left lung along the left pulmonary veins.

Why is your blood red?

EACH TINY DROP OF YOUR BLOOD CONTAINS UP TO 5 MILLION RED blood cells that give blood its colour. Red blood cells contain a substance called haemoglobin, which takes in oxygen in the lungs. Blood that is rich in oxygen is bright red. As this bright red blood is pumped around the body, the oxygen is gradually taken up by the body's cells. By the time the blood returns to the heart, it is a slightly darker, more rusty red.

Blood in close-up

Plasma

What are blood groups?
There are four main groups of blood, called groups A, B, AB and O. Only some groups can be mixed with others, so doctors find out which blood group a patient belongs to before giving a blood transfusion.

Red blood cell

White blood cell

Oxygen-rich blood leaves the heart to be pumped around the body.

What is bile?
Bile is a yellow-green liquid made by the liver and stored in the gall bladder. From there it passes into the small intestine, where it helps to break up fatty food.

Why is urine yellow?
Urine contains traces of waste bile and this makes it yellowish. If you drink a lot of water, your urine will be diluted and less yellow, but the first urine of the morning is usually stronger and darker. Some foods affect the colour of urine. Eating beetroot can turn it pinkish.

Kidneys and bladder

A large artery called the aorta brings blood from the heart to the kidneys.

Blood is filtered in the kidneys and the waste urine is funnelled into the ureters.

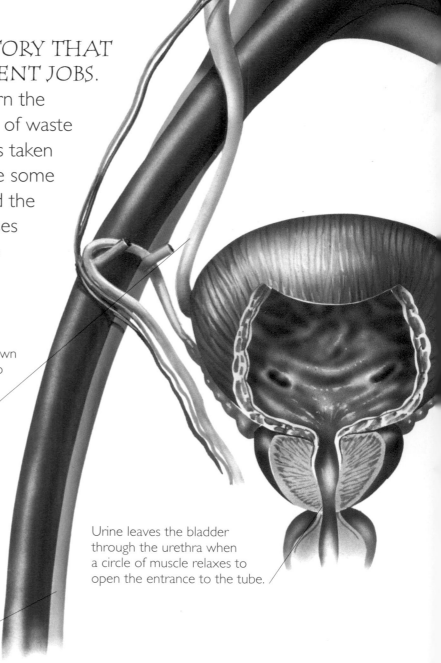

What does the liver do?

THE LIVER IS A CHEMICAL FACTORY THAT DOES MORE THAN 500 DIFFERENT JOBS. Some of its most important functions concern the processing of digested food and the removal of waste and poisons from the blood. Digested food is taken straight from the intestines to the liver, where some nutrients may be released into the blood and the rest stored to be used later. The liver processes poisons, and changes unwanted proteins into urea. The kidneys remove poisons and urea and make them into urine.

What makes you urinate?
The bladder stretches as it fills. When it has about 150 ml (¼ pint) in it, nerves in the walls of the bladder send signals to the brain and you feel the need to urinate.

As urine trickles down the ureters and into the bladder, the bladder stretches.

How much urine does the bladder hold?
An adult's bladder can hold up to about 600 ml (1 pint) of urine, and a child's holds less. But you usually need to go to the bathroom as soon as your bladder is about a quarter full.

Cleansed blood leaves the kidneys and returns to the heart.

Urine leaves the bladder through the urethra when a circle of muscle relaxes to open the entrance to the tube.

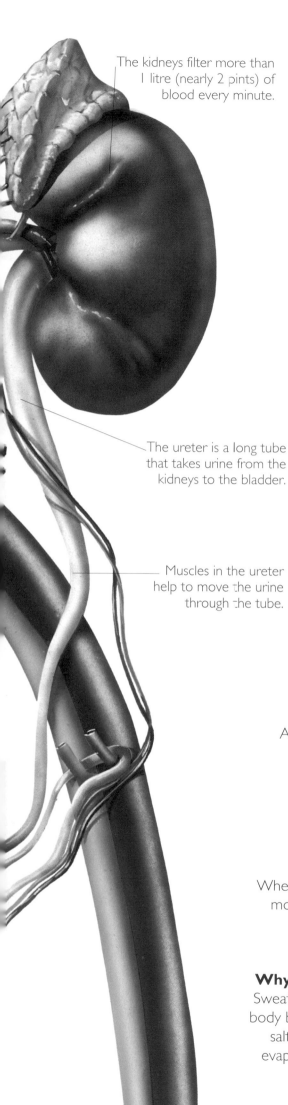

The kidneys filter more than 1 litre (nearly 2 pints) of blood every minute.

The ureter is a long tube that takes urine from the kidneys to the bladder.

Muscles in the ureter help to move the urine through the tube.

What do the kidneys do?

KIDNEYS FILTER THE BLOOD TO REMOVE WASTES AND EXTRA WATER AND SALTS. Each kidney has about a million tiny filters, which between them clean about a quarter of your blood every minute. The kidneys work by forcing many substances out of the blood and then taking back in only what the body needs. The unwanted substances combine with water to make urine, which trickles down to the bladder where it is stored.

How much liquid do you need to drink?
You need to drink about 1.2 to 1.5 litres (2 to 2 ½ pints) of watery drinks every day. The amount of water you take in balances the amount you lose. Most water is lost in urine and faeces. But sweat and the air you breathe out also contain water.

Why do you go red when you are hot?
As different parts of the body burn up energy they make heat. Blood carries the heat around the body. If the body becomes too hot, the tiny blood vessels near the surface of the skin expand to help the blood cool. Blood flowing near to the skin makes the skin look red.

How long can you live without water?
Although some people have lived for several weeks without food, you can survive only a few days without drinking water.

Athlete sprinting

Why do you need to drink more in hot weather?
When it is hot, you sweat more and so lose more water, which you then replace by drinking more.

Why do you sweat when you are hot?
Sweating helps to cool you down. When the body becomes hot, sweat glands pump lots of salty water on to the skin. As the sweat evaporates (changes into water vapour), it takes extra heat from the body.

When muscles work hard, they produce heat as well as movement.

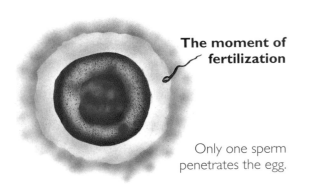

The moment of fertilization

Only one sperm penetrates the egg.

What is a condom?

A condom is a thin rubber sheath that fits over the man's penis. It stops sperm getting into the woman's vagina during sex, so that a baby cannot be conceived. Other contraceptives (things that prevent pregnancy) include the Pill, which is taken by women.

What is a period?

If the egg is not fertilized by a sperm, it passes out of the woman's body through the vagina. At the same time, the lining of the womb and some blood also pass out of the body. This slow flow of blood lasts about five days every month and is called a period.

What do babies do in the womb?

As the unborn baby gets bigger, it exercises its muscles by kicking, moving and punching. It also sucks its thumb sometimes, opens and shuts its eyes, and goes to sleep.

Where does a man's sperm come from?

Sperm are made in the testicles, two sacs that hang to either side of the penis. After puberty the testicles make millions of sperm every day. Any sperm that are not ejaculated are absorbed back into the blood.

Where does the egg come from?

When a girl is born she already has thousands of eggs stored in her two ovaries. After puberty, one of these eggs is released every month and travels down the Fallopian tube to the womb.

What is labour?

Labour is the process of giving birth. The neck of the womb stretches and opens, and then the womb, which is made of strong muscle, contracts to push the baby out. Labour can take several hours.

Male reproductive organs

Female reproductive organs

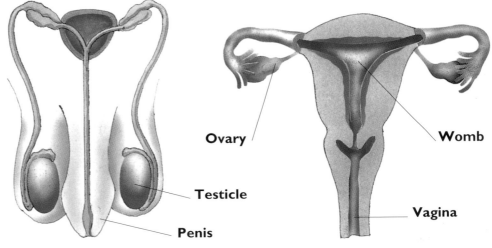

Ovary

Testicle

Penis

Womb

Vagina

Testicles hang outside the body to keep the sperm cool.

The vagina joins the womb to the outside of the body.

What are genes?

Genes are a combination of chemicals contained in each cell. They come from your mother and father and determine everything about you, including the colour of your hair, how tall you will be, and even what diseases you might get in later life.

Why do children look like their parents?

You inherit a mixture of genes from your parents, so in some ways you will look similar to your mother and in others to your father.

What is a foetus?

A foetus is an unborn baby from eight weeks after conception until birth. In the first seven weeks after conception it is called an embryo. By 14 weeks the foetus is fully formed, but it is too small and frail to survive outside the womb. Babies of 24 weeks can survive in an incubator if they are born early, but most stay in the womb for the full 36 weeks.

How does a new baby begin?

A NEW BABY BEGINS WHEN A SPERM FROM A MAN JOINS WITH AN EGG from a woman. This is called fertilization, and it happens after the man ejaculates sperm into the woman's vagina during sex. The cells of the fertilized egg begin to multiply into a cluster of cells, which embeds itself in the lining of the womb. There the cells continue to multiply and form the embryo of a new human being.

How fast does an unborn baby grow?

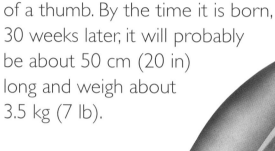

Y OU GROW FASTER BEFORE YOU ARE BORN
THAN AT ANY OTHER TIME IN YOUR LIFE.
Three weeks after the egg is fertilized, the embryo is no bigger
than a grain of rice. Five weeks later, almost every part of the new
baby has formed – the head, brain, eyes, heart, stomach and even
the fingers – yet it is only about the size
of a thumb. By the time it is born,
30 weeks later, it will probably
be about 50 cm (20 in)
long and weigh about
3.5 kg (7 lb).

How does an unborn baby feed?

Most of the cluster of cells
that embeds itself in the
womb grows into an organ
called the placenta. Food
and oxygen from the
mother's blood pass
through the placenta
into the blood of the
growing baby.

A baby in the womb

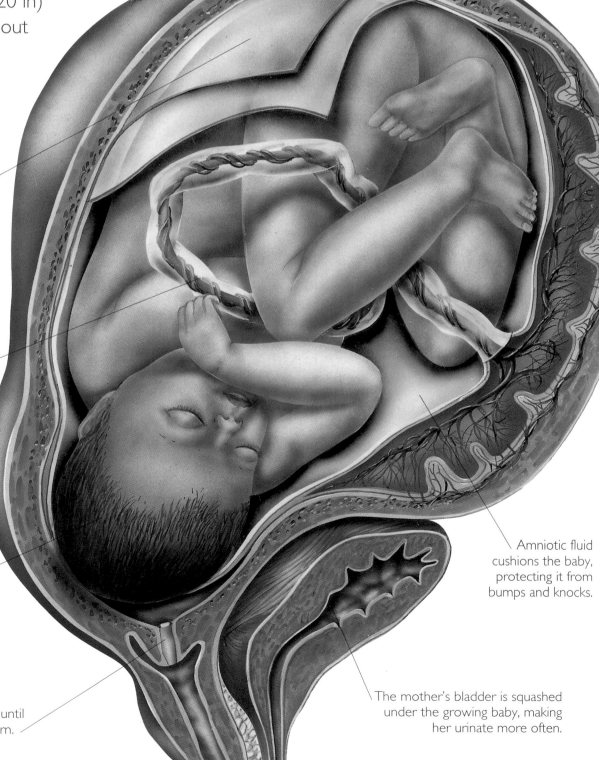

The placenta supplies
the unborn baby with
oxygen and food from
the mother's blood.

The umbilical cord
joins the baby to
the placenta.

This baby is ready
to be born head-first.

The cervix stays tight shut until
the baby is ready to be born.

Amniotic fluid
cushions the baby,
protecting it from
bumps and knocks.

The mother's bladder is squashed
under the growing baby, making
her urinate more often.

Why do babies cry?

A baby cries when it needs something – when it is hungry or lonely. It also cries when it has a stomach ache or other pain.

Are newborn babies completely helpless?

A baby can breathe, suck and swallow from the moment it is born, so it is not completely helpless.

When are you fully grown?

Boys and girls grow quickly during puberty, and then they grow more slowly until they reach their full height some time around age 20 years.

What do all new babies need ?

ALL NEWBORN BABIES NEED FOOD, WARMTH, LOVE AND PROTECTION. At first a baby can only drink liquids, so it sucks milk from its mother's breasts or from a bottle. Milk contains everything the new baby needs to grow and stay healthy. A baby also needs to be washed and have its nappy changed regularly. Babies sleep a lot of the time, but when they are awake they need plenty of smiles and cuddles. Babies and children rely on their parents for the things they need.

What happens when a boy's voice breaks?

A boy may be growing so fast during puberty that the muscles that control his vocal cords cannot keep up. His voice may suddenly change from high to low before finding the right pitch. The vocal cords also become thicker, making his voice deeper.

Stages of growth

At puberty the sexual organs begin to mature.

When do babies learn to walk and talk?

By its first birthday, a baby is usually already pulling itself up on to its feet and is nearly ready to walk. It may also be beginning to say a few words, though talking develops slowly over the next few years.

During childhood, the legs and arms grow longer and the child becomes more adept and confident.

Why do you have to support a young baby's head?

When a baby is born the muscles in its back and neck are very weak, too weak to hold up its own head. A baby's head is much bigger for the size of its body than a child's or an adult's.

A two-year-old is about half the height it will be when adult.

Why can't young babies sit up?

Young babies cannot sit up until their back muscles have grown strong enough to support them. This happens around 6 months.

Babies often learn to crawl before they take their first tottering steps.

What are hormones?

Hormones are chemicals released into the blood from various glands. Some glands make sex hormones that control the menstrual cycle.

Adults are fully grown and may decide to have children of their own.

What is puberty?

PUBERTY IS THE TIME IN WHICH YOU GROW FROM A CHILD INTO AN ADULT.

You grow taller and your body changes shape. A girl develops breasts and her hips become broader. Her waist looks thinner. A boy's chest becomes broader and his voice grows deeper. At the same time, the sex organs develop. A girl begins to have periods and a boy begins to produce sperm. Puberty lasts several years and affects moods, feelings and attitudes as well as bringing physical changes.

As people get older, they begin to slow down.

Very old people may become quite frail.

Why do people age?

The cells of the body are constantly being renewed, except for brain cells and other nerve cells. As people get older, the new cells do not perform as well as the cells of younger people.

How long do most people live?

Most people in the developed world live until they are over 70 and more and more people are living into their 80s and beyond.

What makes you grow?

A growth hormone tells your body to grow. This is produced in the pituitary gland in the brain and taken all round the body in the blood. Exactly how tall you grow is determined by genes inherited from your parents.

What is the menopause?

The menopause is when a woman's body changes so that she is no longer able to have children. As sex hormone levels drop, her ovaries stop producing eggs. The woman may experience uncomfortable hot flushes and unpredictable mood swings.

Who had the most children?

It is believed that a Russian woman who lived in the 1700s holds this record. She was called Madame Vassilyev and she gave birth to no fewer than 69 children.

Quiz questions

THE UNIVERSE

1. **When do eclipses of the Sun occur?**

2. **What is at the centre of our solar system?**

3. **Why do astronauts on the Moon need to take oxygen with them?**

4. **Which is the Red Planet?**

6. **Which was the first artificial satellite?**

7. **Which planet is named after the goddess of love?**

8. **What is a cosmonaut?**

9. **What is the name for an area in space which sucks everything into itself, even light?**

10. **What is a meteor?**

11. **Could you land on Jupiter?**

12. **When was the first space shuttle?**

SCIENCE

1. **Why do hot air balloons float in the air?**

2. **What is the force that pulls everything towards the Earth?**

3. **What does supersonic mean?**

4. **What is biology the science of?**

5. **What is produced in a blast furnace?**

6. **What is the word fax short for?**

7. **What does a television aerial do?**

8. **What is the study of acoustics?**

9. **Which scientist thought of gravity when he saw an apple fall?**

10. **What is an accurate seagoing clock called?**

LANDS AND PEOPLE

1. **Which is the longest and narrowest country?**

2. **What is the capital of Japan?**

3. **Who were the first people to grow potatoes maize, tomatoes, and tobacco?**

4. **Where is Fiji?**

5. **Where do people pay in Deutschmarks?**

6. **What is a gaucho?**

7. **Which is Islam's most holy city?**

8. **Where might you find the Abominable Snowman?**

9. **In which city could you ride in a gondola?**

10. **The Caribbean Sea is part of which ocean?**

Quiz Answers

HISTORY

1. Which French leader was defeated at the battle of Waterloo?

2. In which building in central Rome did the Romans hold contests between gladiators?

3. What was dropped on Hiroshima?

4. What is the name of the ancient Egyptian kings?

5. When did World War I begin?

6. Which German city was divided by a wall?

7. What did suffragettes fight for?

8. Howard Carter discovered which Egyptian pharaoh's tomb in 1922?

9. Who led the Russian Revolution in 1917 and became the first leader of communist Russia?

10. Which international organization was founded to care for soldiers wounded in war?

11. In which war was the Battle of Gettysburg fought?

Quiz questions

PLANET EARTH

1. What is an oasis?

2. What are cirrus, cumulus and cirrostratus examples of?

3. Which rock is formed from grains of sand?

4. What is an extinct volcano?

5. How long is a leap year?

6. Which are the three most important fuels?

7. What is the name for a large, slow-moving mass of ice on the surface of the land?

8. Which is colder, the North Pole or the South Pole?

9. Where is the world's largest rainforest?

10. Where would you find a delta?

11. What is the hardest natural substance?

12. The height of a mountain is measured from what base?

13. Which country produces the most gold?

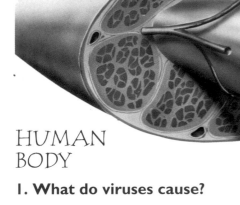

HUMAN BODY

1. What do viruses cause?

2. Pneumonia affects which part of the body?

3. What are your biceps?

4. What is the crown of a tooth?

5. Why is pain useful?

6. Which part of the body is affected by conjunctivitis?

7. For how long does a baby grow inside its mother?

8. What is another word for saliva?

9. What is the name of the tube which takes food from your mouth to your stomach?

10. Where would you find a ligament?

11. What are your canine teeth?

ANIMALS

1. Which animal lives on the seabed and has tentacles but looks like a flower?

2. How does a marsupial carry its young?

3. What is a young swan called?

4. Which elephants have larger ears: African or Indian?

5. Why do spiders build webs?

6. How many humps does a Bactrian camel have?

7. Which insect transmits malaria?

8. Which is the largest of the apes?

9. What does a bird have that no other animal has?

10. How does a dog cool itself down?

11. What are the horns of a stag called?

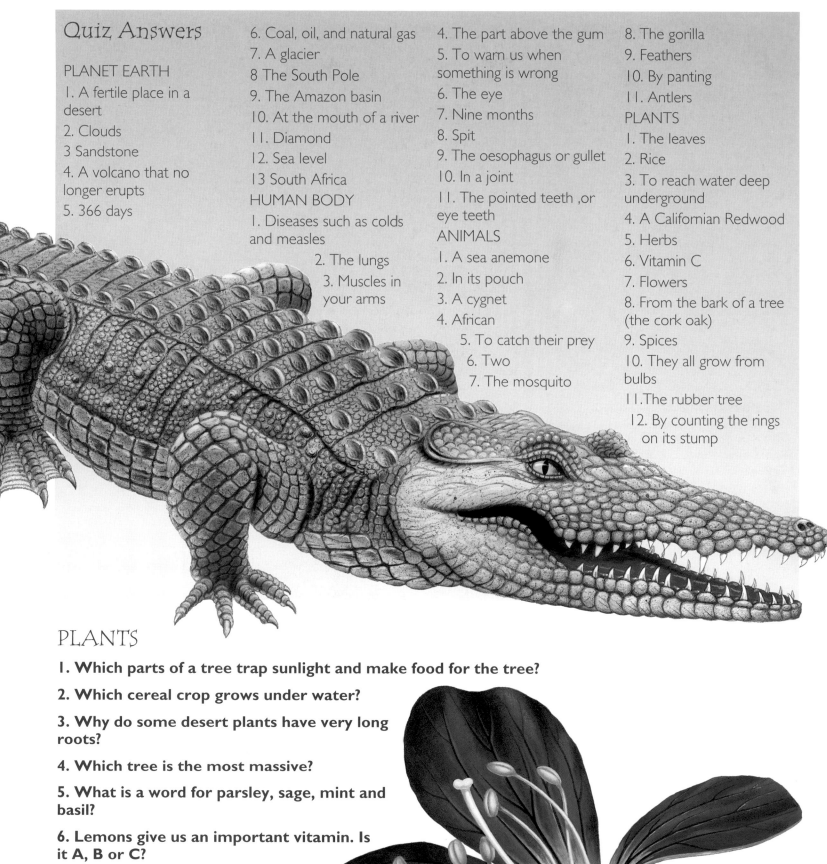

Quiz Answers

PLANET EARTH
1. A fertile place in a desert
2. Clouds
3 Sandstone
4. A volcano that no longer erupts
5. 366 days
6. Coal, oil, and natural gas
7. A glacier
8 The South Pole
9. The Amazon basin
10. At the mouth of a river
11. Diamond
12. Sea level
13 South Africa

HUMAN BODY
1. Diseases such as colds and measles
2. The lungs
3. Muscles in your arms
4. The part above the gum
5. To warn us when something is wrong
6. The eye
7. Nine months
8. Spit
9. The oesophagus or gullet
10. In a joint
11. The pointed teeth ,or eye teeth

ANIMALS
1. A sea anemone
2. In its pouch
3. A cygnet
4. African
5. To catch their prey
6. Two
7. The mosquito
8. The gorilla
9. Feathers
10. By panting
11. Antlers

PLANTS
1. The leaves
2. Rice
3. To reach water deep underground
4. A Californian Redwood
5. Herbs
6. Vitamin C
7. Flowers
8. From the bark of a tree (the cork oak)
9. Spices
10. They all grow from bulbs
11.The rubber tree
12. By counting the rings on its stump

PLANTS

1. **Which parts of a tree trap sunlight and make food for the tree?**

2. **Which cereal crop grows under water?**

3. **Why do some desert plants have very long roots?**

4. **Which tree is the most massive?**

5. **What is a word for parsley, sage, mint and basil?**

6. **Lemons give us an important vitamin. Is it A, B or C?**

7. **What are stigma, sepals and anthers part of?**

8. **Where does cork come from?**

9. **Ginger, cloves, pepper and nutmeg are all what?**

10. **What do daffodils, bluebells and crocuses have in common?**

11. **The sap of which tree is called latex?**

12. **How can you tell the age of a felled tree?**

Index